BRITAI
HERITAGE RAILWAYS

Published by Collins
An imprint of HarperCollins Publishers
Westerhill Road, Bishopbriggs, Glasgow G64 2QT
www.harpercollins.co.uk

HarperCollins Publishers
1st Floor, Watermarque Building, Ringsend Road, Dublin 4, Ireland

First Edition 2022

A catalogue record for this book is available from the British Library

ISBN 978-0-00-846798-2

10 9 8 7 6 5 4 3 2 1

Printed by GPS Group, Slovenia

All mapping in this publication is generated from Collins Bartholomew digital databases.
Collins Bartholomew, the UK's leading independent geographical information supplier, can provide a digital, custom, and premium mapping service to a variety of markets.
For further information, e-mail: collinsbartholomew@harpercollins.co.uk
or visit our website at www.collinsbartholomew.com

If you would like to comment on any aspect of this publication, please contact us at the above address or online.
www.collins.co.uk
e-mail: collinsmaps@harpercollins.co.uk

MIX
Paper from responsible sources
FSC™ C007454

This book is produced from independently certified FSC™ paper to ensure responsible forest management.

For more information visit: www.harpercollins.co.uk/green

BRITAIN'S HERITAGE RAILWAYS

JULIAN HOLLAND

Discover more than 100 historic lines

CONTENTS

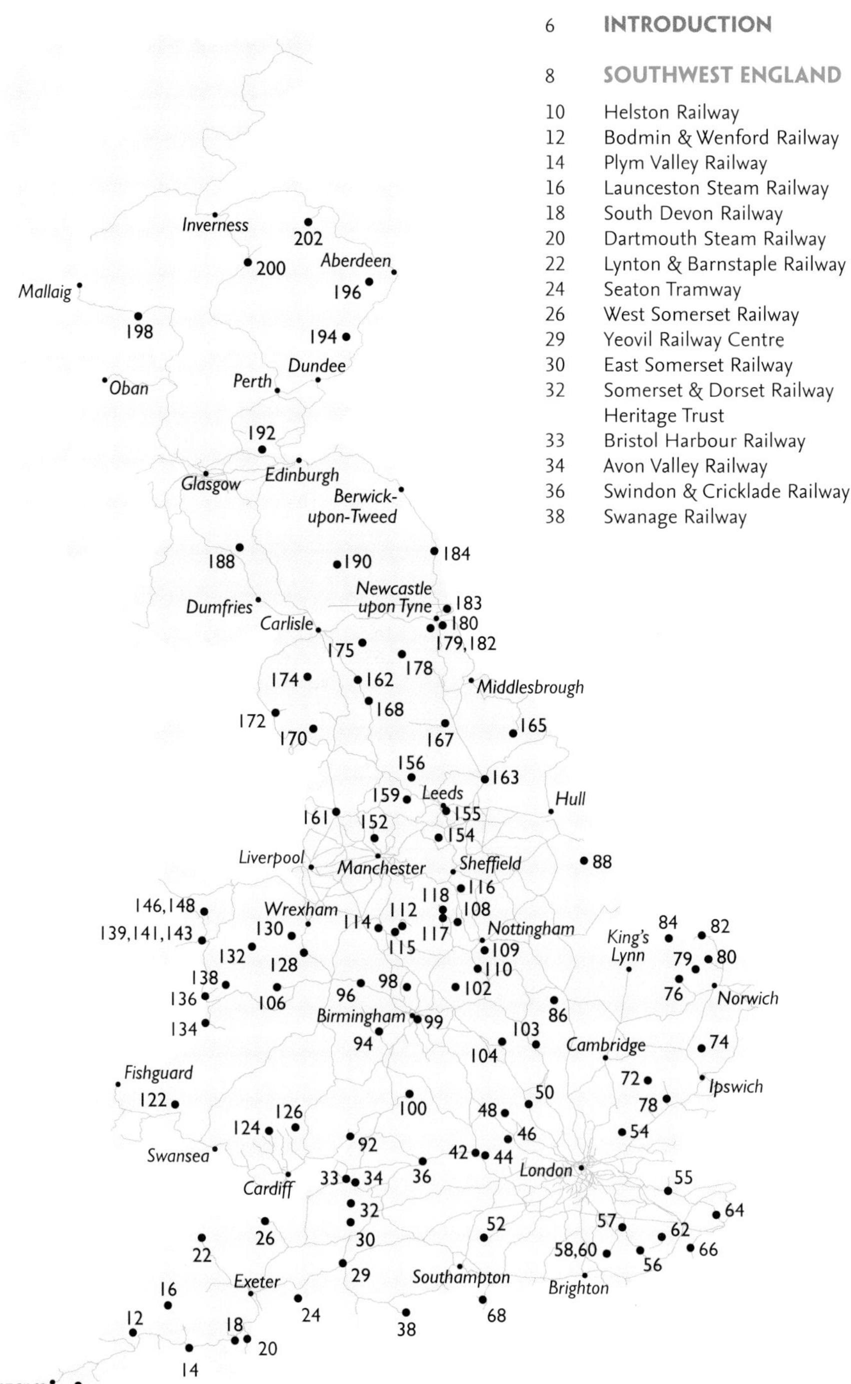
Inverness
202
200
Aberdeen
196
Mallaig
198
194
Dundee
Perth
Oban
192
Glasgow
Edinburgh
Berwick-upon-Tweed
184
188
190
Newcastle upon Tyne
183
Dumfries
Carlisle
180
179,182
175
178
174
162
Middlesbrough
168
172
170
167
165
156
163
159
Leeds
Hull
161
152
155
154
Liverpool
Manchester
Sheffield
88
116
118
146,148
Wrexham
112
108
114
139,141,143
130
117
Nottingham
115
King's Lynn
84
82
132
109
79
80
128
110
138
98
76
96
102
Norwich
136
106
86
Birmingham
99
103
134
94
104
Cambridge
74
Fishguard
72
Ipswich
122
50
100
78
126
48
124
46
54
92
Swansea
42
44
London
33
34
36
55
Cardiff
32
64
52
57
62
26
30
22
58,60
56
66
29
Southampton
Exeter
Brighton
16
24
12
18
38
68
20
14
Penzance
10

Despite the post-'Beeching Report' closure of thousands of miles of railways and thousands of stations in Britain during the 1960s and early '70s and the end of steam haulage on British Railways in 1968, the country's love affair with our railway heritage continues undimmed.

It all started in 1951 when a group of Birmingham-based railway enthusiasts got together and saved the narrow-gauge Talyllyn Railway in West Wales from closure. Then came the Middleton Railway in Leeds – the oldest continuously working railway in the world – which, in June 1960, became the first standard-gauge line to be run by volunteers (mainly Leeds University undergraduates). Following closely on their heels came the Bluebell Railway that on 7 August 1960 became the first standard-gauge steam-operated heritage line in the world to run a timetabled passenger service.

Since those early days a plethora of heritage railways – both standard- and narrow-gauge – and railway museums have opened to the public. Some have grown into large operations with some salaried staff while others still lead a fairly precarious existence manned totally by volunteers. However volunteer railway enthusiasts, both male and female, lie at the beating heart of all heritage railways – without their freely given time these railways just would not exist.

I can well remember a week I spent as a volunteer on the Ffestiniog Railway in North Wales in 1966. It was coming towards the end of the long school summer holidays and I had just returned from a steam safari in Scotland, the culmination of which was a ride on one of the last 'A4'-hauled Glasgow to Aberdeen 3-hour expresses. The last week of my holiday had already been booked some months before – my school chum, Richard, and I had volunteered our services to the Ffestiniog Railway in Porthmadog to assist them in track-laying in their push towards reopening their narrow-gauge line up to Blaenau Ffestiniog.

For the journey to North Wales Richard had already purchased an old banger (either an old Austin or Morris) for the princely sum of £25. However it was prone to overheating so our journey from Gloucester had to be carried out over two days, the first leg on 2 September took us as far as Welshpool. Here we obtained a fairly cheap B&B for the night and went off to discover the delights of this lovely market town. The evening was spent at a 'hop' in the Town Hall – you know, the kind where all the local girls congregate on one side of the dance hall and the young men gaze at them from the other.

Next day dawned bright and clear and our journey through the Welsh mountains was punctuated by numerous stops to allow our trusty steed to cool down – quite often we had to pull over as steam erupted from beneath the bonnet. At long last we reached our destination, a farmhouse B&B near Tan-y-Blwch, from where we would sally forth over the coming week to work on the Ffestiniog Railway's extension.

ABOVE
The author at Loughborough station on 18 June 2011 after driving BR Standard Class '2' 2-6-0 No 78019 on the Great Central Railway (see page 110).

RIGHT
In 1960 the Bluebell Railway became the first standard-gauge steam-operated heritage railway in the world to run a timetabled service. Here we see ex-SE&CR Class 'P' 0-6-0T No 323 Bluebell *at the head of a train at Horsted Keynes on 26 May 1970.*

Supplied with a packed lunch and soft drinks Richard and I would drive down each day to the permanent way depot at Minffordd where we were met by the foreman in charge of tracklaying further up the line. From Minffordd we were conveyed in a stately style on board a Wickham speeder up through Tan-y-Bwlch and along the mountainside ledge to the site of Campbell's Platform where tracklaying was in progress.

A private halt, Campbell's Platform had just been established to serve the hostel of Plas Dduallt, and was named after its owner, Colonel Andrew Campbell. He was not only allowed to run his own train down the line to Tan-y-Blwch but he was also later instrumental in the building of the Dduallt spiral deviation further up the line. During the week that we worked there the pointwork and siding for the halt was being laid, a laborious manual job in this remote part of Snowdonia. During one lunchbreak we walked further up the overgrown line as far as the western portal of the old Moelwyn Tunnel, soon to disappear beneath a hydro-electric scheme and the reason for the later building of the Dduallt spiral and deviation.

At the end of each day we would return down to Minffordd in the speeder before taking a well-earned dinner in a local hostelry. We even found time to walk down the trackbed and through the rock-cut tunnels of the old Welsh Highland Railway through the Aberglaslyn Pass, little knowing that this long-closed narrow-gauge line would come back to life 45 years later. Happy days.

Many years have passed since those idyllic days and now we in Britain are lucky to have over 100 of these heritage lines and museums, all of them totally dependent for their survival on a large band of volunteers.

Each feature is illustrated by a location map and a route diagram:

KEY

NEAREST NATIONAL RAIL NETWORK STATION

connecting route

HERITAGE RAIL STATION

heritage railway line

NATIONAL RAIL NETWORK STATION

national rail network line

STATION NOT SERVED

end of line

proposed extension

PROPOSED STATION

RAILWAY CENTRE/MUSEUM

SOUTHWEST ENGLAND

HELSTON RAILWAY

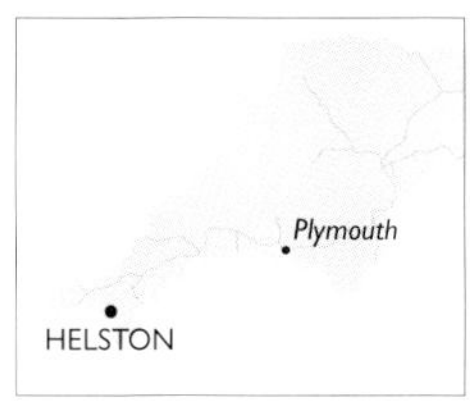

PROSPIDNICK HALT
TRUTHALL HALT
HELSTON

This standard-gauge branch line from Gwinear Road, on the Great Western Railway's Plymouth to Penzance mainline, to Helston was opened on 9 May 1887. Later taken over by the GWR, the 8¾-mile line became famous for the groundbreaking railway feeder bus service from Helston to The Lizard, which began operating in 1903 – an authorised light railway along this route had previously failed to materialise due to lack of funds. The passenger service on the line normally amounted to seven journeys each weekday between Helston and Gwinear Road and eight in the opposite direction with some trains passing at intermediate Nancegollan station. Goods traffic was particularly heavy especially during the Second World War when the Royal Naval Air Station was being built at nearby Culdrose and also for seasonal traffic such as broccoli and flowers – during the season special broccoli trains were run from the branch to supply Covent Garden Market in London.

Although the line was listed for closure in the 'Beeching Report', the end actually came over 5 months earlier on 3 November 1962 when passenger services, by then dieselised, ceased. Goods traffic continued until 3 October 1964 when NBL Type 2 diesel loco D6324 hauled the last official goods train on the branch. Any remaining wagons were collected by the same loco on 9 October and by mid-1965 the rails had been lifted.

THEN
'4500' Class 2-6-2T No 4570 departs from Nancegollan station on 23 July 1958.

Despite closure nearly 50 years ago much of the infrastructure of the line remains intact – most of the bridges and the viaduct over the River Cober north of Helston still stand. The Helston Railway Preservation Company was formed in 2005. The line was partially reopened in December 2011 and currently operates trains for just over 1 mile between Prospidnick and Truthall Halt – the latter was restored as a GWR halt and reopened in 2017. Trevarno Farm is the operational base and visitor car park. The long-term aim for the railway is to cross the 4-arch Cober Viaduct to a new station on the outskirts of Helston. Rolling stock on the railway, much of it being restored, includes a Park Royal Class 103 DMU, a BR Class 127 DMU, 2 industrial 0-4-0 diesels and a 0-4-0 Peckett industrial steam loco *William Murdoch*. The latter had originally worked at the Southern Gas Board's Hilsea Gasworks. Passengers are currently carried in a BR 20-ton standard brake van.

Trevarno Farm,
Prospidnick, Helston,
Cornwall TR13 0RY

07901 977597
www.helstonrailway.co.uk

LENGTH
1¼ miles

GAUGE
Standard

OPEN
Every Sunday, Thursday & Bank Holiday Mondays; additional days during school holidays

NOW
On loan from the Somerset & Dorset Railway Trust, Peckett 0-4-0ST Kilmersdon *arrives at Truthall Halt with its one-coach train from Prospidnick on 9 August 2018.*

BODMIN & WENFORD RAILWAY

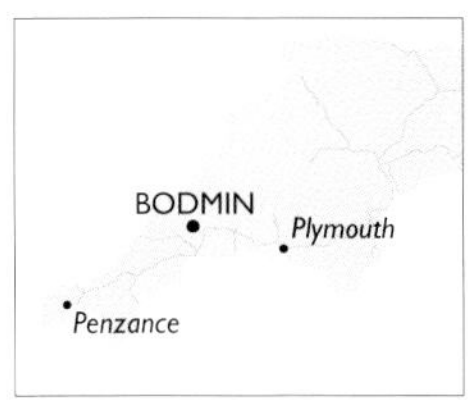

BODMIN GENERAL
BOSCARNE JUNCTION
COLESLOGGETT HALT
BODMIN PARKWAY

Bodmin General Station,
Bodmin, Cornwall PL31 1AQ

01208 73555
www.bodminrailway.co.uk

LENGTH
6½ miles

GAUGE
Standard

OPEN
Easter to end October & Santa Specials in December; see website for details

One of the earliest railways in Britain, the Bodmin & Wadebridge Railway (B&WR) opened between Wadebridge Quay, Bodmin and Wenfordbridge in 1834. Built primarily to carry sand, stone and agricultural goods, it was the first steam-operated line in Cornwall. Although taken over by the London & South Western Railway in 1846, it remained isolated from the rest of the expanding national rail network until as late as 1888 when the Great Western Railway (GWR) opened its branch line from Bodmin Road to Bodmin General with a link to the B&WR at Boscarne Junction.

However, the B&WR was only connected to its parent company, the LSWR, in 1895 when the line from Halwill and Delabole opened to Wadebridge. In the same year the LSWR realigned the approaches to the old B&W station at Bodmin and opened a new terminus here – it was renamed Bodmin North in 1949. To complete the railway picture in the area the LSWR opened its line from Wadebridge along the south shore of the Camel Estuary to Padstow in 1899.

Until the 1960s railway operations in the Bodmin area were fairly complicated. There was a shuttle service from the GWR mainline at Bodmin Road to Bodmin General with some trains reversing here and continuing on to Wadebridge and Padstow via Boscarne Junction. Other services operated between the LSWR terminus at Bodmin North, Wadebridge and Padstow. As a railway junction Wadebridge was a fairly busy place, not only with the comings and goings of trains between Bodmin and Padstow but also via the North Cornwall line to and from Okehampton and Exeter – hauled by Bulleid Light Pacifics after the Second World War there were also through coaches to and from Waterloo on the 'Atlantic Coast Express' (ACE).

China clay traffic along the Wenfordbridge branch from Dunmere Junction was in the charge of ancient Beattie 2-4-0 well tanks, based at Wadebridge, until as late as 1962 when ex-GWR 0-6-0PTs took over. These were replaced by diesel shunters in 1964 until closure of the branch in 1983.

By the early 1960s increased competition from road vehicles had led to a decline in both passengers and general freight carried on the line. As with all of Cornwall's branch lines, except Falmouth and Newquay, the Bodmin Road to Padstow passenger service was listed for closure in the 'Beeching Report'. While Wadebridge had already lost its service from the North Cornwall line in 1966, the end came for the rest of the railway on 30 January 1967. Four-wheel railbus W79977, carrying a wreath, operated the final service between Bodmin North and Wadebridge in the evening of 28 January. On the same day there were so many passengers wanting to travel that single-car diesel unit W55014 had to be replaced by D6309 and three coaches for the Bodmin Road to Wadebridge service. Goods traffic from Bodmin Road to Wadebridge lingered on until 1978 and china clay traffic from Wenfordbridge to Bodmin Road via Boscarne Junction continued until 1983 when the line closed.

The following year the Bodmin Railway Preservation Society was formed and in 1989 a Light Railway Order was granted with passenger services recommencing between Bodmin Parkway (previously named Bodmin Road) and Bodmin General in 1990. An intermediate station at Colesloggett Halt was also opened giving passengers access to Cardinham Woods with its waymarked trails, café, picnic area and cycle hire facilities. The line from Bodmin General to Boscarne Junction (for the Camel Trail footpath and cycleway) was re-opened in 1996. Trains are mainly steam-hauled along this scenic line which includes gradients as steep as 1-in-37. Motive power is provided by a selection of former GWR (Classes '4200', '5700', '4575', '6400'), LSWR (Classes '0298', 'T9') and industrial steam locomotives along with mainline diesel locos (Classes 08, 10, 33, 37, 47, 50) and a Class 108 DMU.

Future plans include a controversial extension of the railway from Boscarne Junction to Wadebridge alongside the existing Camel Trail. Known as the RailTrail project, it would extend the railway in three stages to Wadebridge via Nanstallon Halt and Grogley Halt but it has come under criticism from the cycling charity Sustrans and from environmentalists.

NOW

Preserved ex-LSWR Class '0298' 2-4-0WT No 30587 heads a short train of china clay wagons away from Boscarne Junction towards Bodmin during a photographers' charter on 26 August 2003.

MARSH MILLS
PLYM BRIDGE PLATFORM

Authorised by Parliament in 1854, the broad-gauge South Devon & Tavistock Railway opened from Tavistock Junction, on the South Devon Railway near Marsh Mills, to Tavistock in 1859. The company amalgamated with the South Devon Railway shortly afterwards. Involving the construction of 6 Brunel timber viaducts and 3 tunnels the single-track line was costly to build. In 1862 the separate Launceston & South Devon Railway was authorised to extend the line to Launceston – it opened on 1 June 1865 – and was amalgamated with the South Devon Railway in 1873. The South Devon was later amalgamated with the Great Western Railway (GWR) in 1876.

By 1876 the standard-gauge London & South Western Railway had reached Lydford from Okehampton and had obtained running powers over the GWR's Launceston line to Plymouth; to enable LSWR trains from Waterloo and Exeter to run over the line mixed-gauge track was laid. This state of affairs lasted until 1890 when its trains were able to travel over the newly-opened Plymouth, Devonport & South Western Junction Railway between Lydford and a terminus at Devonport – the GWR station at Tavistock was then renamed South and the new LSWR station, North.

Meanwhile a 10½-mile branch line had opened between Yelverton, just over 5 miles south of Tavistock, to the remote Dartmoor village of Princetown in 1883. Closure for this scenic line came in 1956. The GWR's line from Marsh Mills to Tavistock and Launceston was eventually converted to standard gauge in 1892 and, with the LSWR's trains out of the picture, the line settled down to a fairly quiet life. With both Tavistock and Launceston each served by 2 railway stations there was no doubt that the duplication of routes was never a recipe for financial success. Of course, in the end, both were listed for closure in the 'Beeching Report'. In order to reduce costs the GWR terminus at

THEN
Ex-GWR '4575' Class 2-6-2T No 5568 arrives at Marsh Mills Halt c.1960 with a two-coach train from Tavistock. Built at Swindon Works in 1929 this small prairie loco was withdrawn in 1963.

Launceston was closed in 1952 with trains from Tavistock South and Plymouth diverted into the former LSWR station.

Passenger services normally consisted of between 8 and 10 return trains each weekday between Tavistock South and Plymouth with 5 being extended to Launceston – the 34¾-mile journey taking some 1¾ hours to complete.

The end came on 31 December 1962 when all passenger services were withdrawn. The last day of operation, Saturday 29 December, saw blizzard conditions with the timetabled last train being unable to run. Although the section from Tavistock South to Marsh Mills closed completely on that day goods services continued along several stretches of the line for some years: Lydford to Tavistock South closed on 25 September 1964; Lydford to Launceston closed on 28 February 1966; china clay traffic from Tavistock Junction to Marsh Mills ended as recently as 2008.

Much of the line's impressive infrastructure such as Brunel's broad-gauge tunnels and viaducts survives today and can be seen by walking or cycling (NCN Route 27) along the 21-mile Drakes Trail on the trackbed between Plymouth and Tavistock via Marsh Mills.

Marsh Mills is now home to the Plym Valley Railway and at present the 1½-mile section from Marsh Mills to Plym Bridge sees steam-hauled trains on selected Sundays and Bank Holidays. Locomotives include former British Sugar Corporation 0-4-0ST *Albert*, Andrew Barclay 0-4-0ST No 705, ex-BR Class 08 0-6-0 diesel shunter No 13002 (the oldest working Class 08 diesel shunter in the country, built in 1952), Sentinel diesel shunter No 10077 *Sidney* and an ex-BR Class 117 DMU.

Marsh Mills Station,
Plymouth, Devon PL7 4NW

01752 345078
www.plymrail.co.uk

LENGTH
1½ miles

GAUGE
Standard

OPEN
Selected Sundays & Bank Holidays, April to October; Christmas Specials; see website for details

NOW
Preserved Andrew Barclay 0-4-0ST No 705 of 1937 makes a fine sight as it heads through the woods towards Plym Bridge Platform with its two-coach train.

LAUNCESTON
Plymouth
Penzance

LAUNCESTON
HUNT'S CROSSING
CANNA PARK
NEWMILLS

Despite the London & South Western Railway reaching the village of Halwill in 1872 the next stage in the company's tenuous 44-mile single-track route to Wadebridge was slow in coming. Meandering through sparsely populated rolling farmland, the LSWR-sponsored North Cornwall Railway opened from Halwill Junction to Launceston in 1886 and to Wadebridge in 1895. It was later extended along the south shore of the Camel Estuary to Padstow in 1899.

The coming of the railway to this isolated part of North Cornwall brought enormous benefits to farmers who could quickly transport their cattle and milk by rail to markets and bottling plants in London. Vast quantities of slate were also carried by rail from the giant quarry at Delabole along with fish from Padstow. Up to the early 1960s there was a passenger service of 4 return trains each day running along the route from Okehampton to Padstow plus through coaches from Waterloo on the 'Atlantic Coast Express'. Summer Saturdays saw extra trains from Waterloo including an overnight service that left Waterloo at 12.45 a.m., an early morning train that left at 7.28 a.m. and two portions of the 'ACE' – usually hauled along the North Cornwall line by Bulleid Light Pacifics.

In 1963 the Western Region took control of all ex-SR routes west of Exeter. The rot soon set in with all through trains including the 'ACE' being withdrawn on 7 September 1964 and any remaining local services dieselised in 1965 with stations becoming unmanned. On 5 September the very last down 'ACE' arrived at Halwill Junction from Exeter behind

THEN
Ex-SR 'N' Class 2-6-0 No 31839 waits patiently at Launceston with its train for Okehampton while a westbound goods train passes en route for Wadebridge, 11 June 1963.

'N' Class 2-6-0 No 31845. The train was then split with the Bude portion heading off behind 2-6-4T No 80037 while 31845 headed off for the last time to Padstow. Serving a small local population and unable to compete with road transport the line, much loved by future Poet Laureate John Betjeman, was listed for closure in the 'Beeching Report'. The end came on 3 October 1966 when it closed completely.

Opened in 1983, the Launceston Railway is a narrow-gauge line that runs along part of the trackbed of the old London & South Western Railway's line from Halwill Junction to Padstow. The railway was extended from Launceston to Newmills via Hunt's Crossing and Canna Park in 1995. Locomotives, including 0-4-0ST's *Lilian* and *Covertcoat*, built by Hunslet in 1883 and 1898 respectively, are beautifully restored examples that once worked in the North Wales slate quarries at Penrhyn and Dinorwic. *Dorothea* is also a 0-4-0ST, built by Hunslet in 1901 for the Dorothea Quarry in the Nanttle Valley. Passengers are conveyed through the scenic Kensey Valley in replicas of Victorian narrow-gauge carriages. The late-19th-century workshop at Launceston, once used by the Launceston Gas Company, is an example of a belt-driven machine shop in daily use, and the Transport & Engineering Exhibition gives an opportunity to view those locomotives not in service. The station features the canopy previously used at Launceston North station while the café and booking office are located in a building that was originally built in 1919 for the first Ideal Home Exhibition and then erected as a three-bedroom bungalow in Surrey.

St Thomas Road,
Launceston,
Cornwall PL15 8DA

01566 775665
www.launcestonsr.co.uk

LENGTH
2½ miles

GAUGE
1ft 11½in.

OPEN
Easter, May & Whitsun Bank Holiday weekends; Sunday, Monday & Tuesday in June; daily early July to late September; October half-term

NOW
Hunslet 0-4-0ST Lilian *of 1883 takes on water at Launceston while Hunslet 0-4-0ST* Covertcoat *of 1898 arrives with a train from Newmills.*

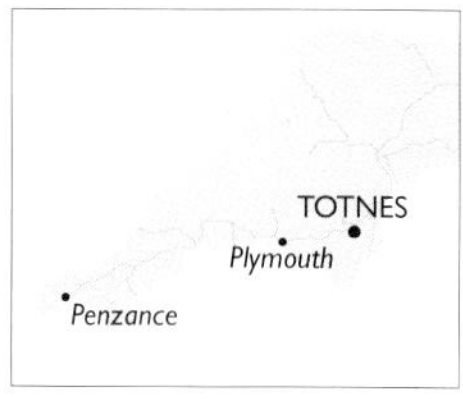

TOTNES
TOTNES (RIVERSIDE)
NAPPERS HALT
STAVERTON
BUCKFASTLEIGH

The Buckfastleigh, Totnes & South Devon Railway was incorporated in 1864 to build a single-track broad-gauge branch line up the picturesque Dart Valley between Totnes and Buckfastleigh. The following year an extension to Ashburton was approved. From its opening day on 1 May 1872 the 10½-mile line was worked by the South Devon Railway. Conversion to standard gauge came in 1892 before being taken over by the Great Western Railway in 1897. In its early years the railway depended heavily on the wool trade along the valley with Buckfastleigh station generating much of this traffic. However increasing competition from road transport before and after the Second World War saw the line in terminal decline – by 1950 the 8 return passenger services on the line (plus 1 extra on Saturdays) were carrying few passengers. The end came for these services on 3 November 1958 although freight traffic continued until 10 September 1962.

Fortunately for us today the track was not lifted following complete closure by BR and a group of enthusiasts calling themselves the Dart Valley Railway reopened the line on 5 April 1969 using restored GWR locomotives and rolling stock. Perversely, the reopening ceremony was honoured by Lord Beeching although, to be fair, BR had closed the line many years before his 'Beeching Report'.

Initially the Dart Valley Railway was able to occasionally use the section of line between Buckfastleigh and Ashburton but so-called improvements to the A38 severed this link just north of Buckfastleigh station. The last train to Ashburton was a special (1Z45) from London

THEN
Ex-GWR '4500' Class 2-6-2T No 4555 at Buckfastleigh station with a goods train for Totnes on 16 November 1960. Built at Swindon Works in 1924, this loco was withdrawn from Plymouth Laira at the end of 1963. The loco was later preserved and currently works on the East Somerset Railway.

Paddington hauled by Brush Type 4 diesel No 1660 as far as Totnes Riverside. From here preserved 0-6-0PTs Nos 6435 and 1638 took it to Ashburton before returning to Totnes behind 2-6-2T No 4588. Now operated by the South Devon Railway, the scenic line along the Dart Valley sees steam heritage trains running between a new station at Totnes Riverside, Nappers Halt, Staverton and Buckfastleigh between March and October. The only passing loop on the line is located just north of Staverton station. Motive power is currently provided by former GWR locos: '1366' Class 0-6-0PT No 1369 (formerly of Weymouth Quay and the Wenfordbridge branch), '4575' Class 2-6-2T No 5542, '5700' Class 0-6-0PT No 5786, and '6400' Class 0-6-0PT No 6412. Several other former GWR locos are currently being overhauled while 'Hall' Class 4-6-0 No 4920 *Dumbleton Hall* has recently moved to Carnforth and is being repainted in the 'Hogwarts Express' red livery. Operational mainline diesels include examples of BR Classes 20, 25, 33, and 37 while Class 50 D402 *Superb* is currently being restored.

Visitor attractions at Buckfastleigh include a railway museum and a miniature railway. In the museum is *Tiny*, a South Devon Railway vertical boilered locomotive that is the only surviving original broad-gauge loco still in existence in the UK.

At Ashburton the station building with its trainshed have survived and is a Grade II listed structure in use as a garage. The nearby goods shed has also survived.

The Station,
Dart Bridge Road,
Buckfastleigh,
Devon TQ11 0DZ

01364 644370
www.southdevonrailway.co.uk

LENGTH
7 miles

GAUGE
Standard

OPEN
February half-term;
March weekends;
April to October;
December weekends
& New Year

NOW
Preserved ex-GWR '2251' Class 0-6-0 No 3205 arrives at Buckfastleigh with its train from Totnes Riverside in June 2010.

DARTMOUTH STEAM RAILWAY

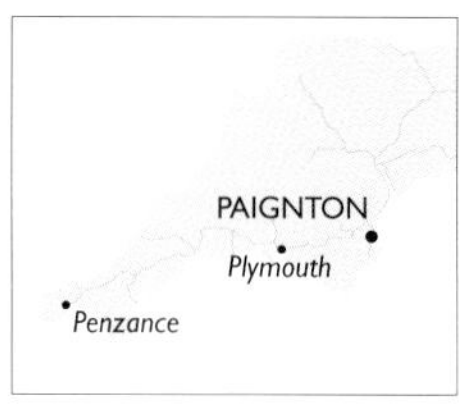

PAIGNTON

PAIGNTON (QUEEN'S PARK)
GOODRINGTON SANDS
CHURSTON
GREENWAY HALT
KINGSWEAR

Queen's Park Station,
Torbay Road, Paignton,
Devon TQ4 6AF

01803 555872
www.dartmouthrailriver.co.uk

LENGTH
7 miles

GAUGE
Standard

OPEN
Daily, April to end October;
Santa Specials in December

Preserved as a typical GWR seaside branch line the Dartmouth Steam Railway has a fascinating history. A broad-gauge line from Torquay was built by the Dartmouth & Torbay Railway Company, reaching Paignton in 1859 and Churston in 1861. A branch to Brixham was opened in 1867. Although originally intending to bridge the River Dart to reach Dartmouth, the railway was finally terminated at Kingswear in 1864, being converted to standard gauge by the Great Western Railway in 1892. A railway booking office also operated on the opposite side of the river at Dartmouth. Despite mainly being single-track the line was served by two named trains: 'The Devonian' from Bradford (introduced in 1927) and the 'Torbay Express' (introduced in 1923) from Paddington. During the days of steam haulage locomotives for these trains, such as GWR 'Castle' Class 4-6-0, were turned on a turntable at Kingswear station.

Scheduled for closure by British Rail on 28 October 1972 (the Brixham branch having closed in 1963) the line never actually closed and was taken over by the Dart Valley Light Railway Ltd at the end of that year – in the intervening 2 months BR operated a diesel multiple unit service on behalf of the DVLR. Services began in January 1973 and were worked by the company until 1991. Since then the operating company has been the Paignton & Dartmouth Steam Railway (now simply known as the 'Dartmouth Steam Railway') and it has the advantage of being linked with the national system at Paignton. A passing loop was opened at Churston in 1979 and 2 years later the BR turntable from Goodrington was moved there while the passing loop at Goodrington Sands was reinstated in 2007. At the other end of the line, Kingswear, passengers from the trains can take a ferry across to Dartmouth or take a pleasure cruise up the scenic River Dart. A journey along the line offers a variety of scenic attractions including 3 viaducts and a tunnel, passing sandy beaches and a river estuary. Motive power is provided by 3 ex-GWR steam locomotives – 2-8-0T No 4277 *Hercules*, 2-8-0T No 5239 *Goliath* and 4-6-0 No 7827 *Lydham Manor* – BR Standard Class '4' No 75014 *Braveheart* and a Class 37 ex-BR diesel. A service of regular trains operates along this attractive route, with an ex-'Devon Belle' observation car being attached to certain trains. The 'Dartmouth Express' dining train is also provided on certain evenings and for Sunday lunches.

THEN
Ex-GWR 'Hall' Class 4-6-0 No 4919 Donnington Hall *calls at Churston station with a train from Kingswear on 31 August 1959. On the left is the bay platform for the Brixham branch line. Built at Swindon Works in 1929, No 4919 was withdrawn in 1964.*

NOW
Ex-GWR '4500' Class 2-6-2T No 4555 Warrior *arrives at Kingswear with a train from Paignton on 8 June 2006.*

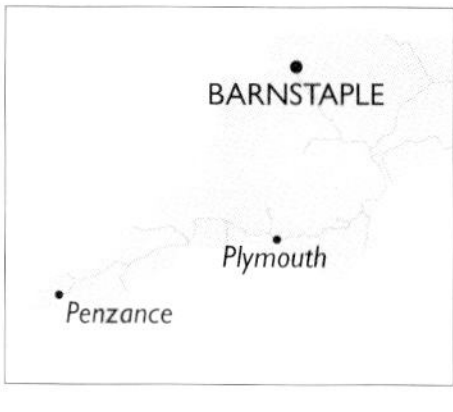

LYNTON
WOODY BAY
KILLINGTON LANE
PARRACOMBE HALT

What was to become a much-loved but short-lived institution, the Lynton & Barnstaple narrow-gauge railway opened in 1898. Financially backed by millionaire publisher Sir George Newnes, the 1ft-11½in.-gauge line ran from its standard-gauge interchange station alongside the River Taw at Barnstaple Town to the up-and-coming clifftop resort of Lynton. Winding its way up through the hills and valleys of North Devon this scenic line featured stations built in a Swiss-chalet style. The First World War brought an end to its popularity and with financial difficulties brought on by increasing competition from road transport it was taken over by the newly-formed Southern Railway in 1923. Despite much investment from its new owner the little Lynton & Barnstaple struggled to pay its way and succumbed to closure on 29 September 1935 – a wreath laid at Barnstaple Town on the very last day read 'Perchance it's not dead but sleepeth'. How very apt, as 60 years later the Lynton & Barnstaple Railway Association purchased the former Woody Bay station. Since 1995 about a mile of track has been laid to a temporary terminus at Killington Lane. With far-reaching views towards the North Devon coast most trains are steam-hauled during the period from April to October. Extensions to Lynton in the north and to Blackmoor Gate and Wistpoundland Reservoir in the south are serious long-term plans as the Lynton & Barnstaple Trust now owns much of the former trackbed. Chelfham station is currently being restored while Snapper Halt and Bratton Fleming station have also been secured for the railway.

THEN

Early-20th-century postcard of Woody Bay station, now the headquarters of the Lynton & Barnstaple Railway. The station was 2 miles via a steep road to Woody Bay itself.

The original locomotives and rolling stock were all sold off when the line closed in 1935. All the locos were scrapped or just disappeared, however a few passenger coaches survived in gardens as summer houses or sheds and have been acquired and restored by the railway. Modern replicas or versions of L&B steam locos have been built: 2-6-2T *Lyd* was built at Boston Lodge, Porthmadog, and operates on the Ffestiniog Railway (pages 140–2); 2-4-2T *Lyn* first steamed in 2017 and is now based at Woody Bay station.

Much of the route of the railway can still be followed today while the attractive Swiss-style former stations can still be seen at Chelfham, Blackmoor Gate and Lynton. The superb 70-ft-high Chelfham Viaduct has been waterproofed and will hopefully see steam trains crossing it once again in the future.

Woody Bay Station,
Martinhoe Cross,
Parracombe,
Devon EX31 4RA

01598 763487
www.lynton-rail.co.uk

LENGTH
1 mile

GAUGE
1ft 11½in.

OPEN
Most weekends throughout the year; most days April to October; see website for details

NOW
2-6-2T Lyd *hauls a 2-coach train towards Woody Bay station on 28 September 2010. This loco was built by the Ffestiniog Railway at Boston Lodge Works and is based on the design of Lynton & Barnstaple loco E188* Lew *which was built by Manning Wardle in 1925. After the railway closed in 1935* Lew *was shipped off to South America and never seen again.*

SEATON
RIVERSIDE HALT
WETLANDS HALT
COLYFORD
COLYTON

Riverside Depot,
Harbour Road, Seaton,
Devon EX12 2NQ

01297 20375
www.tram.co.uk

LENGTH
3 miles

GAUGE
2ft 9in.

OPEN
Selected days in February & March; daily April to October; Christmas & New Year week

The 4¼-mile branch line from Seaton Junction (originally named 'Colyton for Seaton'), on the London & South Western Railway's mainline, to the seaside town of Seaton was opened by the Seaton & Beer Railway on 16 March 1868. It was taken over by the LSWR in 1885. With intermediate stations at Colyton and Colyford the line sprang into life on summer Saturdays when holidaymakers descended on the town from London – even until 1963 there were through coaches carried on 3 separate trains from Waterloo. To cope with this seasonal traffic the Southern Railway had extended the platforms at Seaton in 1937. After being listed for closure in the 'Beeching Report' diesel multiple units were belatedly drafted in to work on the line but to no avail – after already losing its goods service the line closed along with Seaton Junction station on 7 March 1966.

In 1969 Modern Electric Tramways of Eastbourne took over the trackbed and stock was moved to Seaton in 1970. The present 2ft-9in.-gauge line from Seaton to Colyton was finally completed in 1980 and now miniature replica electric trams, taking their power from overhead wires (120 V DC), take passengers on a delightful trip firstly alongside the estuary of the River Axe and then, from Colyford station, along the valley of the River Coly to the present terminus (the original 1868 railway station) at Colyton. Here the original goods shed is now an antiques and craft shop. The tramway's fleet consists of 5 open-top double-deck trams, 2 enclosed trams, 1 toast-rack tram for disabled people and 1 illuminated tram for evening operating. A new Victorian tram-style terminus at Seaton was opened in 1995.

THEN
Ex-GWR '1400' Class 0-4-2T No 1442 restarts from Colyton station with its one-coach auto train for Seaton Junction on 27 February 1965. The Seaton branch line closed just over a year later. The last of its class to be withdrawn, No 1442 is preserved at Tiverton Museum in Devon.

NOW
Seaton Tramway replica tramcars alongside the Axe Estuary on 22 May 2004: Llandudno & Colwyn Bay car No 8, and Blackpool open-style Boat No 4 passing Freestyle car No 12.

SEATON
30 YEARS
SERVING
EAST DEVON
1970
2000

Following 10 years of railway proposals in west Somerset the broad-gauge West Somerset Railway was authorised in 1857 to build a 14¾-mile line from the harbour town of Watchet to the Bristol & Exeter Railway's mainline at Watchet Junction (later renamed Norton Fitzwarren) – from here WSR trains could travel 2 miles eastwards along the mainline to Taunton. The railway opened in 1862 with trains being worked by the Bristol & Exeter although the WSR remained independent until 1922 when it was taken over by the GWR. An extension from Watchet to the small harbour village of Minehead was authorised in 1857 but the line was never built. Eventually the separate Minehead Railway was authorised in 1871 to complete the 8-mile extension – it was opened in 1874 with trains being worked throughout from Taunton by the B&ER and from 1876 by the newly enlarged Great Western Railway. Curiously, while the WSR remained independent until 1922, the Minehead Railway was taken over by the GWR in 1897. Meanwhile, the entire branch line had been converted to standard gauge in 1882.

With the coming of the railway, the once small village of Minehead grew into a popular holiday destination and by the 1930s the GWR had introduced major improvements to cope with the increased traffic. The mainline between Taunton and Norton Fitzwarren was doubled from 2 to 4 tracks and the sections from the latter junction to Bishops Lydeard and from Dunster to Minehead were doubled. The latter terminus was enlarged to cope with longer holiday trains along with extended loops at Stogumber, Williton and Blue Anchor. Camping coaches were also installed at various stations along the line. The Second World War brought an end to this summer traffic and the post-war years saw retrenchment along the branch.

Despite cost-saving measures such as singling of track, the introduction of diesel multiple units, along with the opening of Butlin's holiday camp at Minehead in 1962, the branch line was listed for closure in the 'Beeching Report'. Minehead station featured in the filming of the Beatles' *A Hard Day's Night* in early March 1964. Along with supporting actors, such as Wilfred Bramble, the 'Fab Four' were hauled in their train along the branch by NBL diesel-hydraulic D6336 (Class 22). Goods traffic ceased in 1964 but despite record numbers of passengers still travelling to Butlin's during the summer months, many carried on through trains from Paddington, and strong local opposition to closure the end came on 4 January 1971.

The line was partly reopened, from Minehead to Williton, in 1976 by the newly-formed West Somerset Railway Company, who leased it from Somerset County Council – the council had had the foresight to purchase the closed line in 1973. By 1979 services had been extended southwards to the present 'terminus' at Bishops Lydeard. The section from here to Norton Fitzwarren is not currently used on a regular basis but there is a physical connection with the national network with a number of special through trains being run from the national system on to the WSR via the new turning triangle here. Plans to run a regular ▶

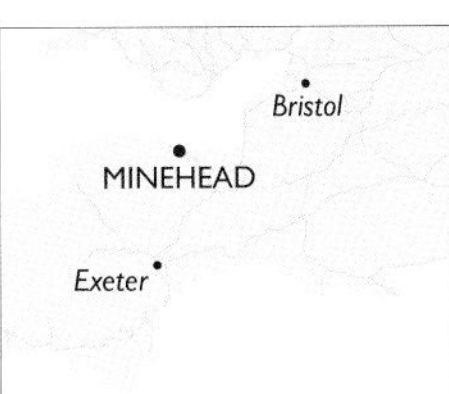

- NORTON FITZWARREN
- BISHOPS LYDEARD
- CROWCOMBE HEATHFIELD
- STOGUMBER
- WILLITON
- DONIFORD HALT
- WATCHET
- WASHFORD
- BLUE ANCHOR
- DUNSTER
- MINEHEAD

The Railway Station,
Minehead,
Somerset TA24 5BG

01643 704996
www.west-somerset-railway.co.uk

THEN
Ex-GWR '5101' Class 2-6-2T No 4110 departs from Watchet station with a train for Minehead on 25 August 1962. Built at Swindon in 1936, this large prairie locomotive was withdrawn in June 1965. It was later preserved and is currently being restored at the East Somerset Railway.

NOW
Preserved ex-GWR '2800' Class 2-8-0 No 3850 skirts the Bristol Channel near Blue Anchor with a train for Minehead on 2 February 2009.

LENGTH
22¾ miles

GAUGE
Standard

OPEN
Selected days February, March, December; daily April to October except selected Mondays & Fridays (see website); for numerous special events see website

service to Taunton have been obstructed for many years, originally by opposition from the National Union of Railwaymen and then by official state-run railway bureaucracy. Although a bus service currently links Bishops Lydeard with Taunton station it would be the 'icing on the cake' if WSR trains were once more allowed to run into the county town.

Britain's longest standard-gauge heritage railway, the West Somerset Railway is home to a wide variety of steam and diesel locomotives with the Diesel & Electric Preservation Group being based at Williton. Locos operating on the line include ex-GWR 'Manor' Class 4-6-0 No 7828 *Odney Manor*, GWR inspired 2-6-0 No 9351 (converted from '5100' Class 2-6-2T No 5193 in 2004), S&DJR 2-8-0 No 53808 and GWR '4500' Class 2-6-2T No 4561. Diesels based at Williton include Class 52 D1010 *Western Campaigner*, Class 35 'Hymek' D7017, 2 Class 33 D6566 and D6575 and Class 47 D1661 *North Star*.

Visiting locomotives can regularly be seen at work on the line on Gala Days (see website), making use of the turntable (originally from Pwllheli) that has been installed at Minehead. The 'Quantock Belle' dining train is very popular and advance booking is essential. The 10 picturesque stations on the line have all been painstakingly preserved and a journey through rolling Somerset countryside in the shadow of the Quantock Hills and along the coast to Minehead evokes all the atmosphere of a GWR country railway and must surely rate as one of the best heritage railway journeys in England.

NOW
Preserved ex-GWR 'Hall' Class 4-6-0 No 4936 Kinlet Hall *on the turntable at Minehead station, October 2015. The 65-ft turntable was moved from Pwllheli in North Wales and installed at Minehead in 2008.*

Operated by the South West Main Line Steam Company, the Yeovil Railway Centre was founded in 1993 when it was discovered that British Rail was about to remove the Southern Railway 70-ft turntable at Yeovil Junction. The turntable was built in 1947 by Cowans & Sheldon of Glasgow. Since 1993 a 99-year lease has been agreed for the site, the turntable restored to working order, a 15,000-gallon water tower and a 2-road engine shed erected and trackwork along the former GWR Clifton Maybank spur relaid. More recently the Centre has acquired the former GWR broad-gauge goods transfer shed, a listed building dating back to the 1860s, which now houses a café and art gallery.

Open days at the Centre see a variety of activities, including brake van rides behind beautifully restored Andrew Barclay 0-4-0 saddle tank *Lord Fisher*, a miniature railway and model railways. *Lord Fisher* was built in 1915 and worked at military establishments in the southeast before being bought by the Gas Board in 1950. After working at Hilsea Gasworks in Portsmouth it then moved to the Chapel Tramway near Southampton Docks. In 1967 it was purchased by preservationists and moved to Longmoor, then Radstock and finally to Cranmore where it operated trains on the fledgling East Somerset Railway. Its final move to the Yeovil Railway Centre came in 2011 when it was overhauled and returned to traffic in 2013.

The Centre's popularity vastly increases on days when visiting mainline steam locomotives from as far afield as Exeter and Weymouth make use of the only working locomotive turntable in the region.

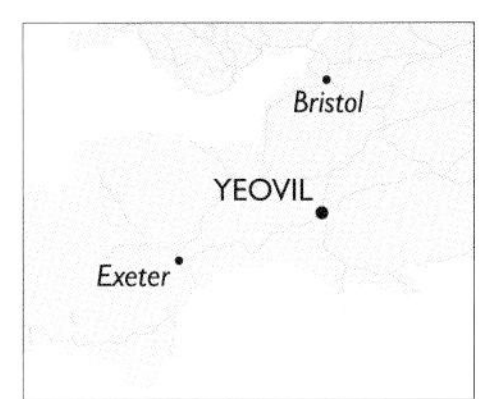

● **YEOVIL JUNCTION**

□ YEOVIL RAILWAY CENTRE

Yeovil Junction Station,
Stoford, Yeovil,
Somerset BA22 9UU

01935 410420
www.yeovilrailway.
freeservers.com

LENGTH
¼ mile

GAUGE
Standard

OPEN
Selected Sundays March to October; for Santa Specials & special events such as visiting mainline steam locomotives see website

NOW
Built in 1921 by Peckett & Sons of Bristol, 0-4-0ST Pectin *is seen here on the Southern Railway 70-ft turntable at Yeovil Railway Centre, adjacent to Yeovil Junction station.*

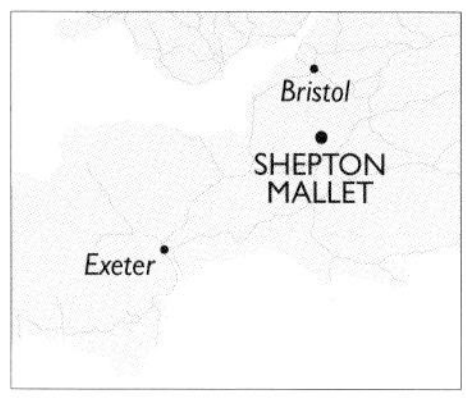

CRANMORE
CRANMORE WEST
MERRYFIELD LANE
MENDIP VALE

The first part of what became known as the 'Strawberry Line' opened in 1858 between Witham, on the Bristol to Weymouth line, and Shepton Mallet. Known as the East Somerset Railway, the broad-gauge line was extended westwards to the small city of Wells in 1862. The terminus here was named Wells East. From the west the broad-gauge Cheddar Valley & Yatton Railway opened between Yatton, on the Bristol & Exeter Railway's mainline, to Wells in 1870. Operated from the outset by the B&ER, the city terminus was named Tucker Street. Between these stations was a third terminus, the, by then standard gauge, Somerset & Dorset Railway's station of Priory Road at the end of their branch line from Glastonbury. Their 200 yards of standard-gauge track prevented through running between Witham and Yatton until 1875 when both the East Somerset (bought by the Great Western Railway in 1874) and the Bristol & Exeter's Cheddar Valley railways were converted to standard gauge. A year later the B&ER was amalgamated with the GWR.

With popular tourist destinations such as Cheddar, Wookey and Wells and important goods traffic such as strawberries and milk, the 'Strawberry Line' was kept fairly busy until the Second World War. Journey times for the 31¾-mile journey was around a leisurely 1½ hours. However, increased competition from road transport brought a serious decline in traffic after the war and this delightful rural railway was listed for closure in the 'Beeching Report'. Apparently the line had working expenses of £60,000 per year against receipts of £9,500 and a third of the passengers using it were schoolchildren. Closure soon followed on 9 September 1963 although goods traffic continued between Yatton and Cranmore until July 1964 with bitumen traffic from Ellesmere Port continuing to Cranmore via Witham until 1985.

However this was definitely not the end for the 'Strawberry Line'. Today a footpath and cycleway with the same name utilises the trackbed from Yatton station through to Cheddar via Shute Shelve Tunnel. An extension eastwards to Wells and Shepton Mallet is currently being

THEN
Class 35 Hymek diesel-hydraulic D7001 is seen here at Cranmore station with a train of bitumen wagons bound for Ellesmere Port on 20 July 1973.

planned. At the eastern end of the line the East Somerset Railway based at Cranmore station operates steam trains along 2½ miles of track to Mendip Vale on the eastern outskirts of Shepton Mallet. Modern Aggregates Industries stone trains operated by Mendip Rail continue to use the eastern end of the line between Merehead Quarry and the mainline at Witham.

The East Somerset Railway was founded in 1973 by David Shepherd, the wildlife and railway artist, to provide a home for his steam locomotives which included BR Standard Class '4MT' 4-6-0 No 75029 *The Green Knight* and Class '9F' 2-10-0 No 92203 *Black Prince* – these two locomotives have since found new homes at the North Yorkshire Moors Railway and the North Norfolk Railway respectively.

Trains presently operate from the attractive Cranmore station to Mendip Vale, on the outskirts of Shepton Mallet along part of the 'Strawberry Line'. Occasional specials once visited the railway from other parts of the system via the junction at Witham Priory, on the main Westbury to Taunton line, and the freight-only line currently used by stone trains from Merehead Quarry. This physical connection is not currently in use.

The 2-road engine shed at Cranmore, built to a traditional GWR design, was opened in 1976 and a new station building housing a restaurant and shop opened in 1991. The GWR signal box dates from 1904 and once housed an exhibition of David Shepherd's work. Future plans include extending the line westwards from Mendip Vale to the outskirts of Shepton Mallet at Cannards Grave. The East Somerset Railway also has a good reputation for restoring steam locomotives from other heritage lines: LMS Ivatt Class '2' 2-6-0 No 46447, Ivatt Class '2' 2-6-2T No 41313 and GWR '5205' Class No 5239 are among the recent examples. GWR '5101' Class 2-6-2T No 4110 is currently being restored.

Cranmore Station,
Shepton Mallet,
Somerset BA4 4QP

01749 880417
www.eastsomersetrailway.com

LENGTH
2½ miles

GAUGE
Standard

OPEN
Easter; weekends May to October; some Wednesdays June to Sept

NOW
Preserved ex-GWR '5600' Class 0-6-2T No 5637 at Cranmore station with a train for Mendip Vale in July 2019.

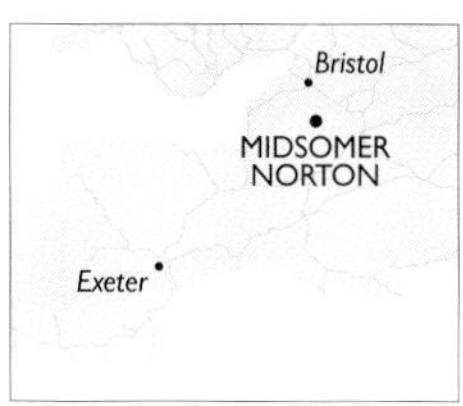

MIDSOMER NORTON

CHILCOMPTON

Midsomer Norton Station, Silver Street, Midsomer Norton, Somerset BA3 2EY

01761 411221
www.sdjr.co.uk

LENGTH
1 mile

GAUGE
Standard

OPEN
Sundays for all facilities including station tour; Monday afternoons for sales & viewing; see website for special events

The heavily engineered northerly extension of the Somerset & Dorset Railway from Evercreech Junction to Bath Green Park opened in 1874. Due to the high cost of building the line the S&D was already facing serious financial difficulties and a year later was bailed out by the London & South Western Railway and the Midland Railway who jointly took on a lease of the line for 999 years. Providing an important north-south freight route during both world wars, the steeply-graded line also became synonymous with numerous holiday trains between the North of England and the Midlands to Bournemouth, in particular the famous 'Pines Express', which could be seen passing through Midsomer Norton behind their double-headed steam locomotives on summer Saturdays until September 1962 when these through trains ended. Scheduled for closure in the 'Beeching Report', the S&D lingered a slow death by cuts until its delayed final closure on 7 March 1966. R.I.P.

Since then the Somerset & Dorset Railway Heritage Trust has restored the station at Midsomer Norton station, along with the former stable block, goods shed and has reconstructed the signal box, adjacent greenhouse and vegetable garden. Track has been laid southwards up the 1-in-50 gradient from the station towards Masbury and trains are operated by 2 diesel shunters, including BR Class 08 0-6-0 D4095, and a Sentinel 0-4-0 vertical boilered steam loco *Joyce* similar to one that once worked on the S&D. The station site is currently open to the public on Sundays and Mondays and public rides are operated on selected days (see website). Extension of the line to Chilcompton is seen as a long-term goal for the Trust. Available free to members, the S&D *Telegraph* is the Trust's excellent monthly magazine.

NOW
A hive of activity at Midsomer Norton station on 5 May 1964. The Wickham trolley has obviously stopped outside the signal box for the crew to have a cup of tea. Although destroyed in a suspicious fire after closure in 1966, the signal box and adjoining greenhouse have been reconstructed by the Somerset & Dorset Railway Heritage Trust.

Britain's only dockside steam railway, the Bristol Harbour Railway is operated by Bristol Museums, Galleries & Archives. With a network of about 5 miles the Bristol Harbour Railway originally opened between Temple Meads and the Floating Harbour in 1872. It was later extended to Wapping Wharf in 1876. Further extensions included a connection to the Portishead line which created the West Loop at Ashton Gate (1897) and new branches via the Ashton Swing Bridge to Canons Marsh and to Wapping (1906). The Bristol Harbour Railway closed in 1964 when the track from Temple Meads was lifted although the branch to Canons Marsh lingered on for another year.

Partially reopened in 1978 as a heritage railway, the Bristol Harbour Railway operates steam trains on certain weekends along the south side of Bristol Harbour between M Shed and the *SS Great Britain* or alongside the New Cut to Vauxhall footbridge. The two restored steam locomotives that originally worked at Avonmouth Docks are 0-6-0 saddle tanks No 1764 *Portbury*, built by Avonside in 1917, and No 1940 *Henbury*, built by Peckett in 1937. Passengers are carried in converted open wagons and a GWR 'Toad' brake van. Brunel's *SS Great Britain* is open to the public at the nearby Great Western Dry Dock.

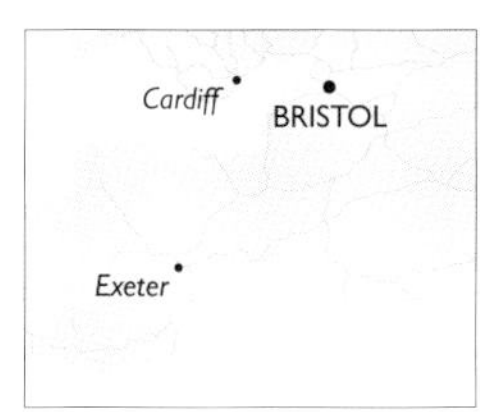

- **BRISTOL TEMPLE MEADS**
- M SHED
- SS GREAT BRITAIN

M Shed, Princes Wharf,
Wapping Road,
Bristol BS1 4RN

0117 352 6600
www.bristolmuseums.org.uk/m-shed/whats-on/train-rides

LENGTH
1 mile

GAUGE
Standard

OPEN
Some weekends April to October

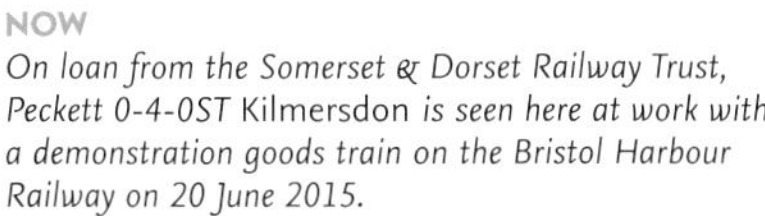

NOW
On loan from the Somerset & Dorset Railway Trust, Peckett 0-4-0ST Kilmersdon *is seen here at work with a demonstration goods train on the Bristol Harbour Railway on 20 June 2015.*

AVON VALLEY RAILWAY

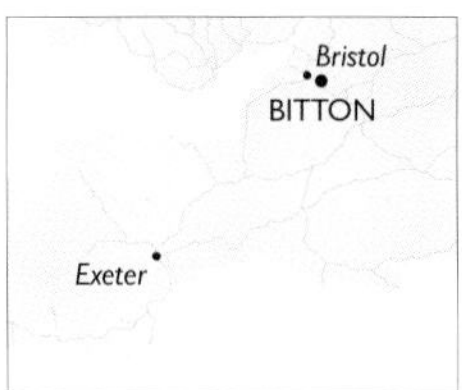

OLDLAND COMMON
BITTON
AVON RIVERSIDE

The broad-gauge Bristol & Gloucester Railway opened in 1844. It was taken over by the Midland Railway (MR) in 1845 and converted to standard gauge in 1854. An 8-mile double-track branch line from Mangotsfield, north of Bristol, to a temporary terminus at Queen Square, Bath, opened in 1869. A year later the MR opened its permanent terminus at Bath – known as the Midland station, it was renamed Green Park in 1951.

The line had two uses – the first was for MR local traffic between Bristol and Bath (the intermediate stations between Mangotsfield and Bath were Warmley, Oldland Common and Bitton); the second was for through trains between the North and the Midlands and Bournemouth via the Somerset & Dorset Joint Railway. The branch, and the S&DJR closed to passenger traffic on 7 March 1966 although goods trains continued to serve Bath gas works until 1971. Nearly the entire route, apart from a section between Mangotsfield and Warmley, was reopened as the Bristol & Bath Railway Path by Sustrans in 1984 while 3 miles of the line between Oldland Common, Bitton and Avon Riverside (for the Avon Valley Country Park) is now a heritage railway known as the Avon Valley Railway.

THEN
Ex-LMS Class '4F' 0-6-0 No 44466 heads the Wessex Downsman Rail Tour through Bitton station on 4 April 1965. The route of the rail tour was Waterloo–Reading–Newbury–Devizes–Bristol–Bath Green Park–Bournemouth West–Southampton–Basingstoke–Waterloo. What a great day out!

Initially set up to restore train services between Bristol and Bath, the Bristol Suburban Railway Society held its first open day at Bitton station in 1983. The first trains ran along a mile of line to Oldland in 1987. Oldland station opened in 1991 and in 2004 the section eastwards from Bitton to Avon Riverside was opened. The railway's long-term plan is to reach Bath once again, but this entails rebuilding 5 bridges over the meandering River Avon. Meanwhile, cyclists and walkers can take advantage of the Bristol & Bath Railway Path along most of the route of the closed railway, the first green traffic-free route to be opened for cyclists in Britain.

At its headquarters at Bitton the Avon Valley Railway has a mixed bag of steam and diesel locomotives, either operational or being restored. Although most of the steam locos are former industrial or military types, one brings back very many happy memories for me – currently being restored from Barry scrapyard condition LMS Fowler Class '4F' 0-6-0 No 44123 was a regular performer in my hometown of Gloucester in the 1960s. Ex-BR diesels on the AVR include examples of Classes 07, 08, 09 and 31 along with a 2-car Class 107 DMU.

Bitton Station, Bath Road,
Bitton, Bristol BS30 6HD

0117 932 5538
www.avonvalleyrailway.org

LENGTH
3 miles

GAUGE
Standard

OPEN
Selected days during school holidays February to October; most weekends April to October; see website for details

NOW
Seen here in steam at Bitton, preserved S&DJR Class '7F' 2-8-0 No 53809 visited the Avon Valley Railway in October 2010.

SWINDON & CRICKLADE RAILWAY

CRICKLADE
HAYES KNOLL
BLUNSDON
TAW VALLEY HALT
MOULDON HILL

Blunsdon Station,
Tadpole Lane,
Blunsdon, Swindon,
Wiltshire SN25 2DA

01793 771615
www.swindon-cricklade-railway.org

LENGTH
2¼ miles

GAUGE
Standard

OPEN
Weekends & Bank Holidays; Wednesdays during school holidays; see website for special events

Affectionately nicknamed as the 'Tiddley Dyke', the Midland & South Western Junction Railway was formed in 1884 by the amalgamation of two existing railway companies – the Swindon, Marlborough & Andover Railway and the Swindon & Cheltenham Extension Railway. Rescued from near bankruptcy by Sam Fay (later to become General Manager of the Great Central Railway) the railway offered an alternative north–south route between the North of England and the Midlands and Southampton. However, journey times on the single-track railway between Andoversford Junction (east of Cheltenham) and Andover Junction were painfully slow and by the 1950s saw only one through train each weekday between Cheltenham and Southampton – to reach Southampton the M&SWJR had obtained running powers over the LSWR's 'Sprat & Winkle Line' between Andover and Redbridge.

The end for this 'forgotten' rural railway came on 9 September 1961 when it was completely closed apart from a short section from Andover Junction to the military depot at Ludgershall for military trains. The depot closed in 2015 although the track is still *in situ* awaiting a possible reopening for passenger services from Andover.

Located on the old M&SWJR route between Swindon Town and Cirencester Watermoor, Blunsdon station actually closed as early as 1937. A preservation group took over the station site in 1979 and now operate mainly steam-hauled trains along two sections, north and south of the station. A northward extension from Blunsdon to South Meadow Lane was completed in 2008 while a southward extension from Blunsdon to Taw Valley Halt was opened in 2014. An extension further northwards to Cricklade is planned for the future.

Steam locomotives currently in service include resident Andrew Barclay 0-6-0ST *Swordfish* and guest locomotive ex-GWR '5600' Class No 5619. Diesels include examples of BR Classes 03, 08, 09 and a Class 73 electro-diesel E6003 *Sir Herbert Walker*. A number of vintage 19th- and early-20th-century coaches are also being restored including examples from the GWR, Taff Vale Railway, Cambrian Railways and the North London Railway.

THEN
Ex-SR 'N' Class 2-6-0 No 31816 halts at deserted Swindon Town station with once-daily Cheltenham St James to Southampton service, c.1960. This delightful but little-used route closed in 1961.

NOW
Preserved ex-GWR '5600' Class 0-6-2T No 5619 running round its train at Hayes Knoll station. The author is pleased to see that the loco carries a Gloucester Horton Road shed plate (85B).

WAREHAM
NORDEN
CORFE CASTLE
HARMAN'S CROSS
HERSTON HALT
SWANAGE

THEN
Built at Nine Elms Works in 1904, ex-LSWR 'M7' 0-4-4T No 30111 waits to depart from Swanage station with its train for Wareham on 9 June 1962. This veteran locomotive was withdrawn in 1964.

Operated from the outset by the London & South Western Railway, the Swanage Railway opened between Worgret Junction, just over a mile to the west of Wareham station, to Swanage on 20 May 1885. The 10¼-mile railway was taken over by the LSWR in 1886.

The arrival of the railway soon led to the former village of Swanage developing into a thriving seaside town while the clay extraction industry around Furzebrook provided the lion's share of goods traffic from the branch. Passenger services normally consisted of a push-pull service to and from Wareham with some trains being extended to and from Poole or Bournemouth Central. Until 1964 summer Saturdays saw several through trains running from Waterloo, routed along the Castleman's Corkscrew route via Ringwood and Wimborne Minster to avoid congested Bournemouth.

Despite carrying much summer holiday traffic the Swanage branch was not immune to closure threats, even as early as the 1950s. Surprisingly the railway was not listed for closure in the 'Beeching Report' but this did not guarantee its continuing survival. Steam haulage was replaced by diesel-electric multiple units in 1967 but the railway was seen by the then Government as surplus to requirements and closure was announced for 1968. Although a reprieve followed – the narrow roads on the Isle of Purbeck were not up to handling a replacement bus service – the end eventually came on 3 January 1972.

Despite an attempt by the Swanage Railway Society to reopen the line as a heritage railway, British Railways lifted the track with indecent haste, leaving only clay traffic from Furzebrook and, from 1978, oil traffic from a new terminal at Wytch Farm. A preservation group started to reopen the line from Swanage and first trains ran along a short section from the station in 1979. By August 1995 the line had been extended to Corfe Castle and Norden, and on its first week of extended operation packed trains carried over 20,000 passengers. A park-and-ride scheme is in operation from Norden which helps to ease road traffic congestion in the Corfe Castle and Swanage areas. Although the railway has now extended to Worgret Junction and thence into Wareham no regular trains run through at the moment, although the link is used by special trains from the national rail network. Trains are mainly steam-hauled by a variety of locomotives, and the 'Wessex Belle' Pullman dining train service is operated on certain Saturday evenings. Locomotives operating on the line include Southern Railway 'Battle of Britain' Class 4-6-2s No 34070 *Manston* and No 34072 *257 Squadron*, 'West Country' Class 4-6-2 No 34028 *Eddystone*, Class 'M7' 0-4-4 tank No 30053 and BR Standard Class '4' 2-6-4T No 80104.

Station House, Swanage,
Dorset BH19 1HB

01929 425800
www.swanagerailway.co.uk

LENGTH
6 miles

GAUGE
Standard

OPEN
February half-term; weekends March; daily April to October; weekends November, December & New Year

NOW
Overlooked by the 11th-century castle ruins, preserved ex-SR unrebuilt 'Battle of Britain' Class 4-6-2 No 34072 257 Squadron *makes a fine sight as it approaches Corfe Castle station with a train for Swanage on 4 March 2019.*

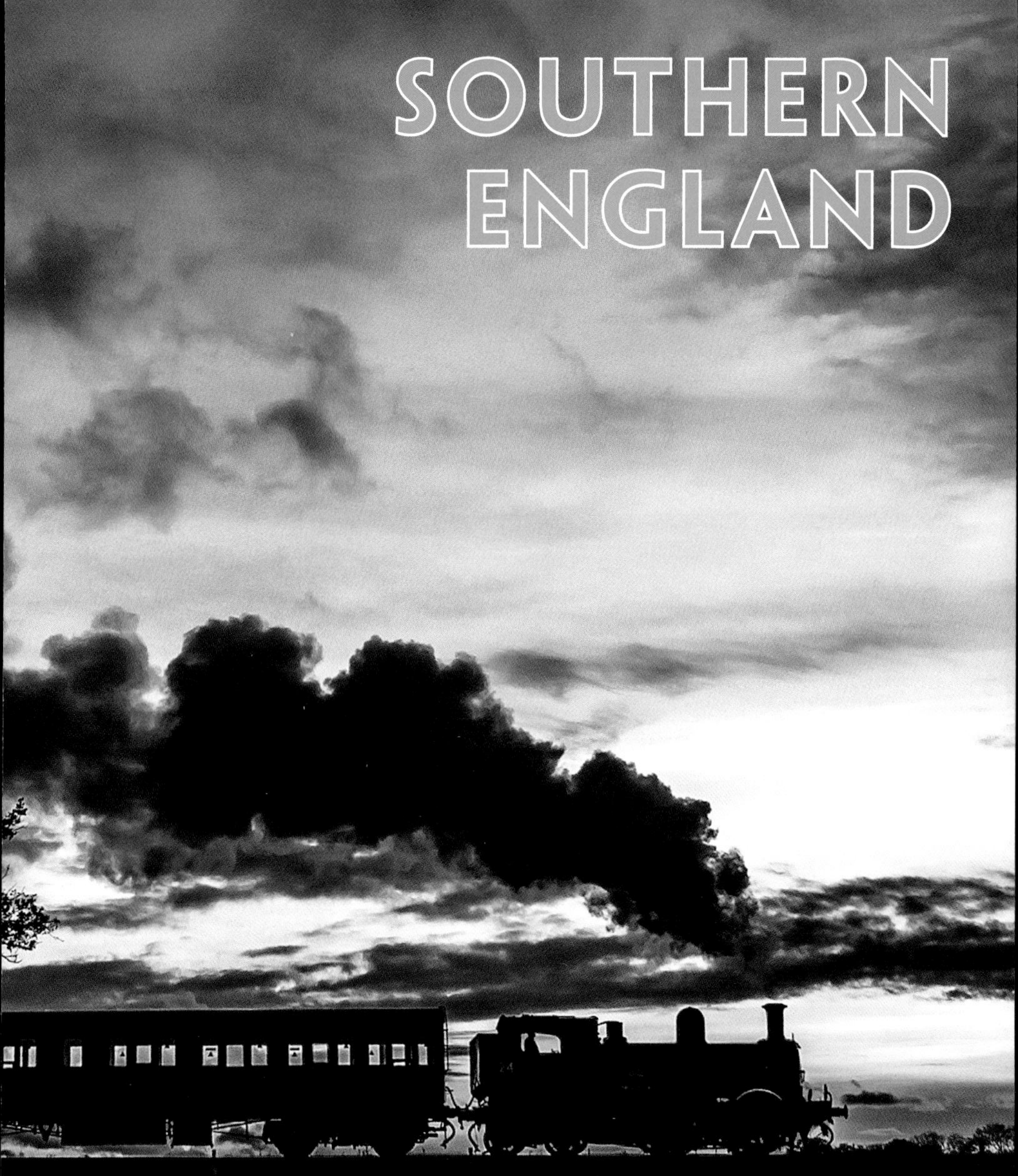
SOUTHERN
ENGLAND

DIDCOT RAILWAY CENTRE

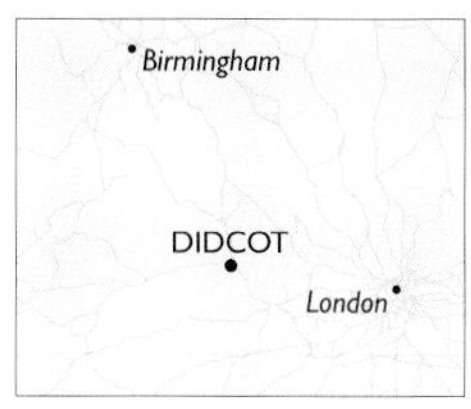

DIDCOT PARKWAY

DIDCOT RAILWAY CENTRE

Didcot,
Oxfordshire OX11 7NJ

01235 817200
www.didcotrailwaycentre.org.uk

LENGTH
¼ mile

GAUGE
Standard & broad

OPEN
Weekends all year except 25/26 December; daily during school holidays and from end May to mid-September; for steam days and special events see website

Strategically located on the GWR mainline between Paddington and Swindon at the junction with the mainline northwards to Oxford the engine shed at Didcot played an important part in the stabling and servicing of steam locos for 125 years. It eventually closed in June 1965 in the last months of steam traction on the Western Region of BR.

The Great Western Society, founded in 1961, moved its base to the engine shed at Didcot in 1967 and it now evokes all the atmosphere of a working 1930s GWR 4-road running shed with working 70-ft turntable and coaling stage. The 21-acre site is home to the largest collection of GWR locomotives and rolling stock in Britain and is also frequently visited by other locomotives employed on mainline steam specials. The site has been leased from Network Rail until 2061 thus securing the future of this important historic railway centre.

Locomotives on display include a wide range of GWR types including new-build '2900' Class 4-6-0 No 2999 *Lady of Legend*, 'Castle' Class 4-6-0s No 4079 *Pendennis Castle* and No 5051 *Drysllwyn Castle*, 'Hall' Class 4-6-0 No 5900 *Hinderton Hall*, blue-liveried 'King' Class 4-6-0 No 6023 *King Edward II*, 'Modified Hall' Class 4-6-0 No 6998 *Burton Agnes Hall*, 'Manor' Class 4-6-0 No 7808 *Cookham Manor* and steam railmotor No 93 along with former Wantage Tramway 0-4-0 well tank *Shannon*, built in 1857, and numerous other classes of former GWR tank locos. Early diesels are represented by streamlined GWR Railcar No 22 and the pioneering gas-turbine No 18000 (aka *Kerosene Castle*). The centre also boasts a large number of historic GWR passenger rolling stock and wagons in various stages of preservation.

Short rides are given on three demonstration lines within the site, which also boasts a rebuilt small country station (Didcot Halt) complete with working signal box that was originally used at Frome Mineral Junction. A short section of Brunel's broad-gauge (7ft 0¼in.), with a section of mixed-gauge trackwork, has also been built where replica broad-gauge locomotive *Firefly* can be seen in action on selected days. On Steam Days demonstrations are given using the restored Travelling Post Office. A library houses the Society's collection of books and papers relating to the Great Western Railway.

THEN
With 'Hall' Class 4-6-0 No 5988 Bostock Hall *in the foreground, several ex-GWR locomotives are seen parked outside Didcot engine shed on 6 February 1965, just over 10 months before the end of steam on the Western Region.*

NOW
A line-up of preserved Great Western Railway locomotives at Didcot Railway Centre on 1 May 2016. On the right is 'Modified Hall' Class 4-6-0 No 6998 Burton Agnes Hall.

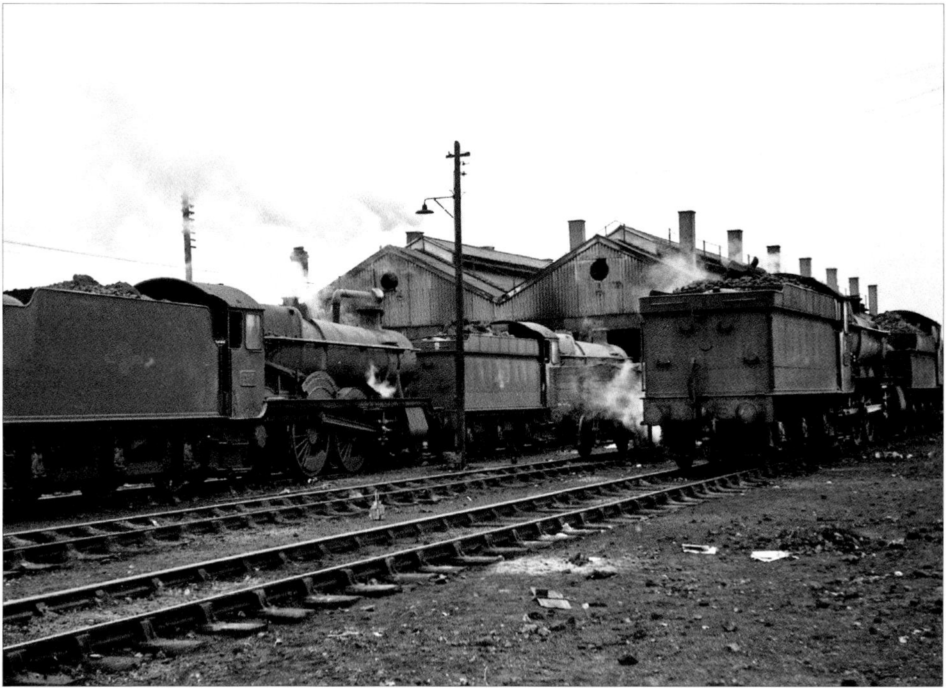

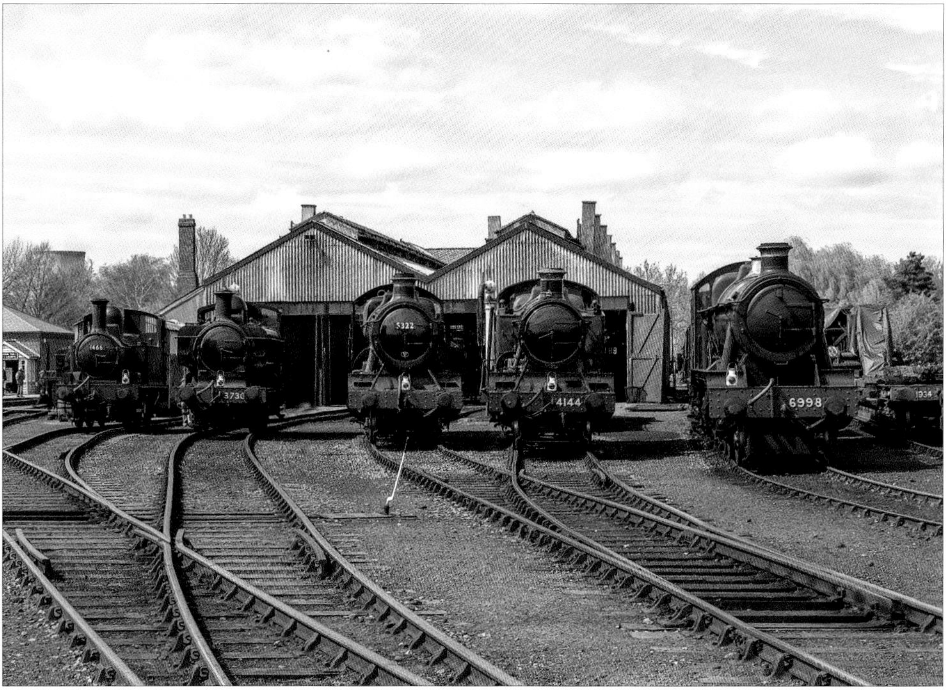
1466
3730
5322
4144
6998
1934

CHOLSEY & WALLINGFORD RAILWAY

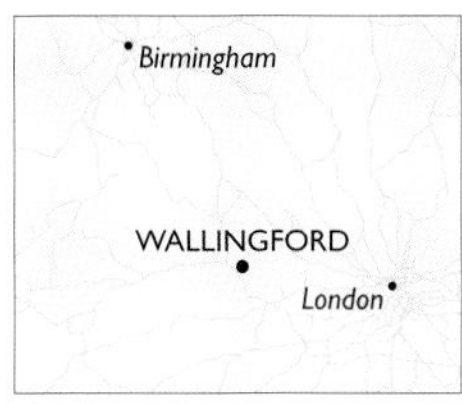

CHOLSEY
WALLINGFORD

5 Hithercroft Road,
Wallingford, Oxfordshire
OX10 9GQ

01491 835067
www.cholsey-wallingford-railway.com

LENGTH
2¼ miles

GAUGE
Standard

OPEN
Selected weekends & Bank Holidays April to October; weekends, December

In 1861 a branch line was proposed to run from Cholsey, on the GWR mainline, to Wallingford, Benson, Watlington, Chinnor and Princes Risborough. In the end this did not come to pass although the two unconnected ends of this route were eventually built (see also Chinnor & Princes Risborough Railway). The line from Wallingford Road to Wallingford opened on 26 June 1865 and was the first branch to be built off the GWR mainline to a narrow or standard gauge, the mainline by then having been converted to a mixed gauge. Trains on the Wallingford Railway were worked by the GWR from the start until 1871 when the line was purchased outright by that company. In 1892 to make way for a quadrupling of track on the mainline Wallingford Road was closed and a new junction station at Cholsey was opened. The line remained busy and well-served until after the Second World War and even in 1947 the single auto coach and a '1400' Class 0-4-2T operated 14 trains each way on weekdays. However falling passenger numbers finally led to the passenger service being withdrawn on 15 June 1959 although general goods traffic lasted until 13 September 1965. After that part of the line was left open to serve a mill until 1981 but the station at Wallingford was demolished to make way for a housing estate.

Since complete closure a preservation society, the Cholsey & Wallingford Railway, reopened the line – nicknamed 'The Bunk' – in 1985, and limited services with a borrowed locomotive ran until 1990, when the line bought its first locomotive. A Light Railway Order was granted in 1995 and trains now connect with the national network at Cholsey on the mainline to Paddington. Although the railway does not currently own a resident steam loco, visiting ex-GWR locomotives are a regular feature, however the railway is home to three BR Class 08 diesel shunters. The original station at Wallingford was demolished in 1981 but the society has now built a new terminus on the outskirts of the town using the Victorian station canopy from Maidenhead.

THEN
Ex-GWR '1400' Class 0-4-2T No 1407 is seen here at Wallingford station with its auto-coach service to Cholsey in the late 1950s. Built at Swindon Works in 1932 this loco was withdrawn from Reading shed in June 1960.

NOW
On loan from the Bressingham Steam Museum ex-LBSCR Class 'A1X' 0-6-0T No 662 of 1875 vintage visited the Cholsey & Wallingord Railway on 30 August 2008. Following withdrawal in 1963 it was sold to Butlins at Heads of Ayr and put on display before being bought by Bressingham Steam Museum.

PRINCES RISBOROUGH
CHINNOR
ASTON ROWANT

Station Road, Chinnor, Oxfordshire OX39 4ER

07979 055366
www.chinnorrailway.co.uk

LENGTH
3½ miles

GAUGE
Standard

OPEN
Certain Bank Holiday Mondays, Saturdays &/or Sundays, end March to end October; weekends, December

The 8¾-mile single-track branch line from Thame Junction, Princes Risborough, to the Oxfordshire village of Watlington was originally planned to be part of the Wallingford & Watlington Railway but the latter only opened in 1866 between Cholsey, on the GWR London to Bristol mainline, and Wallingford. The line got no further due to lack of funds and the need to bridge the River Thames. Eventually the locally-promoted Watlington & Princes Risborough Railway was authorised to build the branch line which opened for business on 15 August 1872. Serving 6 intermediate stations and halts, the railway was taken over by the GWR in 1883.

Running beneath the Chiltern escarpment this delightful rural branch line led a fairly quiet life until 1927 when sidings were laid at Chinnor station to serve a large cement works. Its 175-ft-high concrete chimneys were a local landmark and could be seen from miles away. Business commuters who lived along the line were lucky to be served by a through slip coach from London (each evening in summer, Fridays and Saturdays in winter), slipped at Princes Risborough, that was conveyed on an evening Paddington to Birmingham express until this ceased to operate in 1956 – leaving bustling Paddington at 7.10 p.m. they would arrive at sleepy Watlington at 8.46 p.m.

Sadly passenger numbers had gone into decline by the early 1950s and services were withdrawn on 1 July 1957. Goods traffic continued until 2 January 1961 when the line was cut back to the cement works at Chinnor. This traffic continued until 1989 when the remaining section to Princes Risborough was closed completely.

Since 1990 the Chinnor & Princes Risborough Railway, one of the newer preservation projects, has reopened part of the closed GWR Watlington branch from Chinnor to its connection with the national rail network at Princes Risborough.

Trains run from Chinnor to Platform 4 at Princes Risborough station via the junction with the former Thame branch. The line parallels the Icknield Way and passes through attractive countryside with views across the Vale of Whiteleaf. Now that the link with the Chiltern line has been made at Princes Risborough (completed in 2018) the long-term plan is to extend the line back to Aston Rowant. A new ticket office and waiting room, using a grounded Cambrian Railway 6-wheel coach dating from 1895, was opened at Chinnor station in 1995. The station here has been used as a location for filming TV series such as *Midsomer Murders* and *Miss Marple*. Motive power on the railway is provided by two ex-BR diesel shunters, representatives of Classes 17, 31 and 37 diesels and two 1960-vintage Class 121 'Bubble Cars'. Visiting steam locomotives such as GWR '6400' Class 0-6-0PT No 6412 also provide haulage.

NOW
Preserved ex-GWR '6400' Class 0-6-0TPT No 6412 enters Chinnor station with an engineers' train on 19 July 2020. Built at Swindon Works in 1934 it was withdrawn from Gloucester Horton Road shed in November 1964.

6412

QUAINTON ROAD

BUCKINGHAMSHIRE RAILWAY CENTRE

This 25-acre working steam museum incorporates 2 demonstration lines based on the former Metropolitan Railway country station at Quainton Road, where that railway originally met the Great Central Railway (see page 110). Opened in 1899, the London Extension of the Great Central Railway from Marylebone to Nottingham, Leicester and Sheffield closed in 1966, although trains still operate between Marylebone and Aylesbury Vale Parkway.

Opened in 1969, the centre houses a very large collection of steam and diesel locomotives which operate trains along two short sections of track within the site. The station itself has been restored to its condition of 1900 while the smaller building on the Brill platform houses an exhibition of the Brill Tramway, which closed in 1935. The former LNWR station at Rewley Road in Oxford was dismantled in 1999 and re-erected at Quainton Road in 2002 to provide new visitor facilities and office accommodation. Occasional specials also work from Quainton Road to Aylesbury Town along the freight-only line still operated by Network Rail. This line sees regular landfill freight trains travelling from London to former brick pits at Calvert.

THEN

Minus its front number plate and nameplates of Anzac, dishevelled BR Standard Class '7' 4-6-2 No 70046 speeds past Quainton Road signal box with a Great Central line train for Leicester and Nottingham, c.1962. This loco was later transferred to Carlisle Kingmoor and withdrawn in November 1967.

Locomotives and rolling stock are restored to working order in well-equipped workshops which are open to public viewing. Locomotives on site include Metropolitan Railway 0-4-4T No 1 (London Transport L44), London & South Western Railway 2-4-0 Beattie well tank No 0314 (BR No 30585), ex-GWR/London Transport 0-6-0 pannier tank No L99, WR/BR 'Modified Hall' Class 4-6-0s No 6984 *Owsden Hall* and No 6989 *Wightwick Hall*, GWR 7200 Class 2-8-2T No '7200' and South African Class '25NC' 4-8-4 No 3405. There are also many industrial steam and diesel locos in various states of preservation on the site. Historic rolling stock includes a London & North Western Railway first class royal dining car and vintage coaching stock examples from the London Chatham & Dover Railway, Great Northern Railway, Manchester South Junction & Altrincham Railway, Manchester, Sheffield & Lincolnshire Railway and its successor the Great Central Railway. Future plans include a proposed reconnection to the national network which will enable steam trains to operate between Aylesbury and Calvert via Quainton.

Station Road, Quainton, Aylesbury, Bucks HP22 4BY

01296 655720
www.bucksrailcentre.org

LENGTH
½ mile

GAUGE
Standard

OPEN
February half-term; most days late March to end October; weekends, December

NOW
A line-up of preserved steam locos at the Buckinghamshire Railway Centre. From left to right: ex-LSWR Class '0298' Beattie 2-4-0WT No 30585, Andrew Barclay 0-4-0ST No 699 Swanscombe *and Peckett 0-4-0ST No 2087.*

PAGE'S PARK
STONEHENGE WORKS
DOUBLE ARCHES

Opened to transport sand from quarries to Grovebury interchange sidings on the standard gauge Dunstable branch line, the 2ft-gauge Leighton Buzzard Light Railway opened on 20 November 1919. The line was built using surplus equipment from the War Department Light Railways. Although steam locomotives were initially used these were found to be unsatisfactory and were replaced in 1921 by internal combustion locomotives made by Motor Rail. Following the end of the Second World War much of the sand traffic from the quarries was diverted to road transport until only Arnold's Quarry used the railway. A group of railway enthusiasts started running passenger services in 1968 and the following year the last sand train ran.

Currently the 3-mile route starts at Page's Park station and now runs mainly through modern housing estates via several level crossings until open countryside is reached for the last ½-mile. The northern terminus is at Stonehenge Works where the railway has its workshops. The line is currently being extended another ¾-mile from Stonehenge to Double Arches. The railway has a large and varied collection of both steam and internal combustion industrial locomotives. The steam collection includes examples from Penrhyn slate quarry in Wales, India, Cameroon, Spain, South Africa, Germany and Portugal. The internal combustion collection includes examples that previously worked at sand and gravel pits, brickworks, a bottle company and sewage works.

Page's Park Station,
Billington Road,
Leighton Buzzard,
Bedfordshire LU7 4TG

01962 733810
www.buzzrail.uk

LENGTH
3 miles

GAUGE
2ft

OPEN
see website for details

NOW
During a 'Tracks to the Trenches' photographic charter event on the Leighton Buzzard Light Railway on 3 May 2019, recreating War Department Light Railway operations of the First World War in France, 60cm (2ft) -gauge 4-6-0 tanks, (left) No 778 built by Baldwin in 1917 and (right) No 303 built by Hunslet in 1916, stand in the Leedon Loop.

ALTON
MEDSTEAD & FOUR MARKS
ROPLEY
ALRESFORD

THEN
Ex-SR Class 'S15' 4-6-0 No 30837 and 'U' Class 2-6-0 No 31639 approaching Medstead & Four Marks station with the LCGB 'S15 Commemorative Rail Tour' on 16 January 1966.

Railways first reached the town of Alton in Hampshire in 1852 when the London & South Western Railway (LSWR) opened its extension from Ash Junction, near Aldershot. Alton remained the end of the line until the Mid-Hants Railway opened its 17-mile line from Alton to Winchester Junction (2 miles north of Winchester) via Alresford in 1865. Worked from the outset by the LSWR it was taken over by that company in 1884. Between Alton and Alresford the switchback line became known as 'The Alps' due to the steep gradients encountered either side of the 644-ft-high summit at Medstead & Four Marks station.

The line provided an alternative route for Waterloo to Southampton trains and was heavily used for military trains between Aldershot and Southampton during both world wars. Locally produced watercress was also conveyed to market in London from stations along the line. Two other railways once branched off the Mid-Hants Railway at Butts Junction to the west of Alton: the Basingstoke & Alton Light Railway opened in 1901, closed to passengers in 1932 and to goods in 1936; the Meon Valley line to Knowle Junction near Fareham opened in 1903, closed to passengers in 1955 and to goods (to Farringdon) in 1968.

Despite Southern Railway third-rail electrification reaching Alton from Waterloo in 1937, the Mid-Hants line remained steam-hauled until the introduction of diesel-electric multiple units and a regular-interval service between Alton and Southampton Terminus in the late 1950s. Sundays often saw diverted Waterloo to Southampton and Bournemouth expresses struggling over 'The Alps' behind Bulleid Pacifics during engineering work on the mainline. Although it was listed for closure in the 'Beeching Report', a long-running battle from objectors saw the line reprieved for nearly another 10 years – however, the inevitable finally happened on 5 February 1973 when it closed.

Following closure the current section of the line was bought by a preservation group in 1975 which started services, initially from Alresford to Ropley, 2 years later. Services to Alton, where there is an important link with the national rail network, started in 1985. Steam-hauled trains operate over this steeply-graded line, necessitating the use of large and impressive steam locomotives. Visiting locomotives can also be regularly seen hard at work on special event days through the year. The stations along the line are all beautifully restored to different periods in the history of the railway, and of special note is the carefully pruned 60-year-old topiary at Ropley station, where the Mid-Hants also has its extensive workshops and engine shed. The former station building from Lyme Regis was re-erected at Alresford in 1979, the footbridge from Cowes station on the Isle of Wight was rebuilt at Medstead & Four Marks station, as was the signal box from Wilton South.

The Railway Station,
Alresford,
Hampshire SO24 9JG

01962 733810
www.watercressline.co.uk

LENGTH
10 miles

GAUGE
Standard

OPEN
February half-term; most days late March to end October; weekends, December

NOW
Preserved ex-SR 'West Country' Class 4-6-2 No 34007 Wadebridge *enters Medstead & Four Marks station with a train for Alresford on 11 September 2009. This fine loco was built at Brighton works in 1945 and withdrawn from BR service in October 1965.*

ONGAR
NORTH WEALD
EPPING FOREST

Ongar Station, Station Approach, Ongar, Essex CM5 9BN

01277 365 200
www.eorailway.co.uk

LENGTH
6½ miles

GAUGE
Standard

OPEN
Weekends & Bank Holidays

An extension of the Great Eastern Railway's Stratford to Loughton line was opened from Loughton to Ongar in 1865. The section from Loughton to Epping was later doubled. Following the end of the Second World War, London Transport's Central Line had reached Loughton by 1948 although steam trains continued to operate from there to Ongar until 1949 when the section to Epping was electrified – at the same time the London Transport Executive took over the Epping to Ongar steam push-pull service from British Railways. Eventually this last section was electrified in 1957 but passenger numbers had declined so much – only carrying 80 passengers each day – that it was finally closed in 1994. The intermediate station of Blake Hall had closed in 1981 after it was revealed that it served only 6 passengers a day! Some say that the line was kept open to enable the Cabinet to be evacuated to a nearby nuclear bunker in time of war.

The line was purchased by the Epping Ongar Railway Volunteer Society in 1994 and it ran a diesel multiple unit service on Sundays from 2004 to 2007. Following a change in ownership in 2007 train services were suspended to allow engineering work prior to eventually reopening the line with steam haulage. Services were reintroduced between Ongar, North Weald and the site of Coopersale Halt, just short of the London Underground station at Epping, on 25 May 2012 and the railway now has a fleet of diesel locomotives, some undergoing overhaul or restoration (including BR Classes 03, 20, 25, 31, 37, 45, 47), Class 117 DMU and a Class 205 'Thumper'. Steam locos include GWR 'Hall' Class No 4953 *Pitchford Hall* and former ICI Hawthorn Leslie 0-6-0ST *Isabel*. The Epping Ongar Railway is the closest heritage line to London and within easy reach of the M11 and A12. On operating days there is a frequent heritage bus service (running RT's, RM's & RF's) from Epping Tube station (on the Central Line) to North Weald station, with combined bus and rail tickets available.

NOW
Preserved English Electric Type 3 (Class 37) diesel electric locomotive D6729, built at Vulcan Foundry in 1961, and diesel electric multiple unit No 205205 at North Weald station. Nicknamed 'Thumper' the Class '205' unit was built in 1957 and withdrawn from service in 2004.

SITTINGBOURNE & KEMSLEY LIGHT RAILWAY

This industrial railway was originally built in 1906 by Edward Lloyd Ltd to carry paper from a wharf on Milton Creek to a mill at Sittingbourne and was later extended to carry logs and wood pulp from a wharf on the River Swale at Ridham to the paper mill. In 1924 a further paper mill, served by the railway, was opened at Kemsley and more locomotives were purchased to cope with the extra traffic.

In 1948 the Bowater Group purchased the company and its railway, with further locomotive acquisitions, and continued to run it until 4 October 1969 when road transport was introduced. The Locomotive Club of Great Britain took over, on loan from Bowaters, the 2 miles of track between Sittingbourne and Kemsley in 1969 and by Easter 1970 the line was open for passengers. Trains are now mainly steam-hauled using industrial locomotives and coaches, many from the original railway, including 4 coaches from the former Chattenden & Upnor Military Railway on the Isle of Grain.

An interesting narrow-gauge locomotive line-up includes Kerr Stuart 0-4-2STs *Premier*, *Mellor* and *Leader*, Bagnall 0-6-2Ts *Alpha*, *Triumph* and *Superb*, Bagnall Fireless *Unique* and three diesels *Victor*, *Edward Lloyd* and *Barton Hall*. Several of these can still be seen at work on the line today.

The railway survived a closure threat in 2008/9 as the owners of Sittingbourne Paper Mill were closing the mill and selling off the land. Fortunately the railway has since been saved from extinction and limited services recommenced in 2011. Full services recommenced in 2012 and the railway now operates passenger trains from Sittingbourne Viaduct to Kemsley Down via Milton Regis Halt.

London
SITTINGBOURNE
Brighton

- KEMSLEY DOWN
- MILTON REGIS HALT
- SITTINGBOURNE VIADUCT

Viaduct Station,
off Milton Road,
Sittingbourne,
Kent ME10 2XD

01795 424 899
www.sklr.net

LENGTH
2 miles

GAUGE
2ft 6in.

OPEN
Sundays, Easter to October; for other dates see website

NOW
Surrounded by industrial relics Kerr Stuart 0-4-2ST Melior crosses Sittingbourne Viaduct with a train on the Sittingbourne & Kemsley Railway on 13 October 2012.

London
ROBERTSBRIDGE
Brighton

ROBERTSBRIDGE
BODIAM

Station Road, Robertsbridge,
East Sussex TN32 5DG

01580 881 833
www.rvr.org.uk

LENGTH
3½ miles

GAUGE
Standard

OPEN
Railway Visitor Centre only, weekends & Bank Holidays

The missing 3½-mile link from Robertsbridge (on the national rail network) to Bodiam (western terminus of the Kent & East Sussex Railway – see pages 62–3) is being rebuilt by volunteer members of the Rother Valley Railway, which was formed in 1991. Track laying has already commenced from both ends although the major challenges will be the crossing of the A21 and the B2244 roads. A Visitor Centre at Robertsbridge RVR station is housed in the former Venice-Simplon-Orient reception lounge from London's Victoria station. Rolling stock at Robertsbridge includes two 0-4-0 Drewry diesels and a BR Class 03 0-6-0 diesel No 03 112. Also based there, the Hastings Tramways Club is currently restoring two early-20th-century ex-Hastings electric tram cars for static display.

THEN
A scene from the past on the Rother Valley Railway – ex-LBSCR 'A1X' Class 0-6-0T No 32678 is seen at the head of a mixed train at Robertsbridge on 14 November 1953.

As part of what was to become the London, Brighton & South Coast Railway's Three Bridges to Tunbridge Wells Central line the East Grinstead, Groombridge & Tunbridge Wells Railway opened in 1866. A connecting line from Eridge, on the Uckfield line, was opened in 1868. Listed for closure in the 1963 'Beeching Report' (the author of which lived in nearby East Grinstead), the section between Three Bridges and Groombridge was closed at the beginning of 1967. However, the section from Groombridge to Tunbridge Wells West remained open for trains to and from Eridge until 6 July 1985 when that, too, closed.

Formed soon after closure of the line in 1985, the Tunbridge Wells & Eridge Preservation Society (TWERPS) began their long campaign to reopen the line. From early beginnings in 1996 when the Society established their base at Tunbridge Wells West locomotive shed the line was completely reopened in 2011 when passenger trains on the new Spa Valley Railway ran for the first time in 26 years between Tunbridge Wells West and Eridge. Here, Spa Valley trains connect with national network services on the London to Uckfield line. Heritage steam and diesel locomotives convey passengers through the picturesque Kent and Sussex Weald, stopping off at Groombridge and High Rocks stations for a visit to one of the local pubs. The railway is currently home to 12 steam locos and a collection of diesels including GWR '6400' Class 0-6-0PT No 6435, rebuilt 'Battle of Britain' Class 4-6-2 No 34053 *Sir Keith Park*, Class 33 diesel No 33063, Class 73 electro-diesel 73140 and Class 20 diesel D8188. A miniature railway operates most Saturdays alongside Tunbridge Wells West engine shed. Groombridge station is also a good starting point to follow the very pleasant and peaceful 10-mile 'lost railway' Forest Way footpath and cycleway to East Grinstead, followed by the 7-mile Worth Way to Three Bridges.

- **TUNBRIDGE WELLS**
- TUNBRIDGE WELLS WEST
- HIGH ROCKS
- GROOMBRIDGE
- **ERIDGE**

West Station, Nevill Terrace,
Royal Tunbridge Wells,
Kent TN2 5QY

01892 300141
www.spavalleyrailway.co.uk

LENGTH
5½ miles

GAUGE
Standard

OPEN
Weekends & Bank Holidays, April to October & December; selected Thursdays & Fridays, April to October; numerous special events (see website)

THEN
A scene from the past on the Spa Valley Railway – watched by a young trainspotter ex-SR 'D1' Class 4-4-0 No 31470 prepares to depart from Groombridge station on 15 June 1957. Built at Ashford Works in 1926 this loco was withdrawn in June 1959.

ISFIELD
WORTH HALT

What became known as the Wealden Line between Lewes and Tunbridge Wells started life as the Lewes & Uckfield Railway which was authorised in 1856 to build a railway between the two towns. Lewes had already been reached by the London, Brighton & South Coast Railway (LBSCR) as early as 1846 and the new line would branch off from that company's existing route from Lewes to Keymer Junction via Plumpton, at a junction 1½ miles northwest of Lewes. The Uckfield branch opened in 1858 and the Lewes & Uckfield Railway was taken over by the LBSCR in 1864. The junction on the Plumpton line was taken out of use in 1868 when the line from Uckfield was rerouted via a 3½-mile diversion so that trains from the branch entered Lewes station from the opposite direction and could then continue unhindered to Brighton.

Meanwhile, the Brighton, Uckfield & Tunbridge Wells Railway had been authorised in 1861 to extend the Uckfield branch in a northerly direction to Eridge and Tunbridge Wells. Involving the building of two viaducts between Buxted and Crowborough and the 1,022-yd-long Crowborough Tunnel, construction was expensive and slow and the railway was taken over by the LBSCR before completion. Opening on 5 August 1868 and with the new diversion at Lewes also open, trains could travel directly from Tunbridge Wells to Brighton via Eridge and Uckfield for the first time.

With its eventual connections via East Croydon, Hurst Green and Ashurst the Wealden Line was also used as an alternative through route between London and Brighton. Up until the 1950s passenger numbers held up well, no doubt helped by a regular interval service introduced in 1956 with though trains between London and Brighton operating during rush hours. While the Lewes to Crowborough section was listed for closure in the 'Beeching Report' the line northwards from

THEN
BR Standard Class '4MT' 2-6-4T No 80153 hurries through Isfield station on 13 April 1958. Built at Brighton Works in 1957 this versatile loco had a very short life, being withdrawn in June 1965.

Crowborough to Hurst Green appeared to be safe – it is shown on Map 9A and in the Appendices of the Report as being retained. However, the closure of the southerly section appeared inevitable especially when a proposed relief road in Lewes would effectively sever the line. A plan to reinstate the original route out of Lewes via the former junction on the Plumpton line was turned down by the Government in 1966. By then the northern section from Hurst Green to Crowborough had also been added to the closure list and the whole of the Wealden Line was now under threat. Following a public enquiry in 1967 closure of the line between Uckfield and Lewes was confirmed although the line northwards was fortunately saved. Closure finally came on 24 February 1969 – the replacement bus service via the former stations at Isfield and Barcombe Mills only lasted until 4 May!

Today, while there are serious proposals afoot to reopen the Uckfield to Lewes line, the restored station at Isfield is home to the Lavender Line, a short heritage railway that runs for a mile southwards to Little Horsted. The other intermediate station at Barcombe Mills is now a private residence.

Isfield station was bought by David Milham in 1983 and, along with the Saxby & Farmer signal box, was restored to its former Victorian glory. In 1992 it was sold to a preservation group, the Lavender Line Preservation Society, who operate both steam and diesel trains along a mile of track – during quiet times an ex-British Railways Wickham railbus carries passengers along the line. The former coal office of a certain Mr Lavender now houses a model railway. Current stock includes a 1962 BR-built diesel-electric multiple unit (or 'Thumper'), 1920-built Cockerill 0-4-0 vertical boilered tank loco *Lady Lisa* and three 0-6-0 diesel shunters.

Isfield Station, Uckfield,
East Sussex TN22 5XB

01825 750515
www.lavender-line.co.uk

LENGTH
1 mile

GAUGE
Standard

OPEN
Sundays throughout the year; Bank Holidays & some weekdays during summer months (see website)

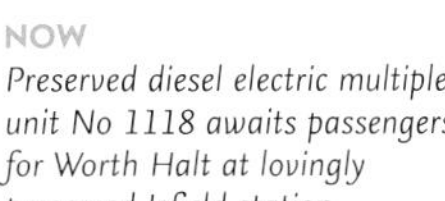

NOW
Preserved diesel electric multiple unit No 1118 awaits passengers for Worth Halt at lovingly preserved Isfield station.

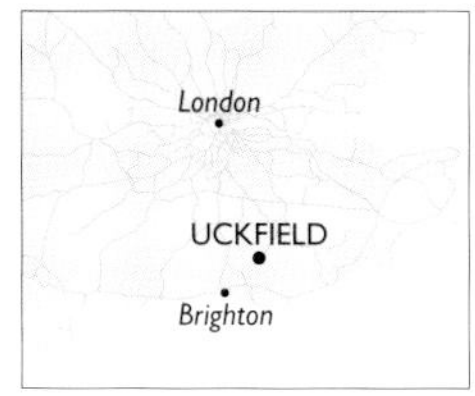

EAST GRINSTEAD
KINGSCOTE
HORSTED KEYNES
SHEFFIELD PARK

Sheffield Park Station,
Uckfield,
East Sussex TN22 3QL

01825 720800
www.bluebell-railway.co.uk

LENGTH
11 miles

GAUGE
Standard

OPEN
Daily, May to September, half-term holidays & weekends all year; Santa Specials in December months (see website)

The Lewes & East Grinstead Railway was authorised in 1877 to build a double-track railway between East Grinstead and Culver Junction, north of Lewes, in Sussex. From Horsted Keynes a branch was also authorised to Haywards Heath to connect with the London Brighton & South Coast Railway's (LBSCR) mainline to Brighton. The required capital to build the line was not forthcoming so the LBSCR agreed to back and build the line. The 'mainline' was opened on 1 August 1882 and the Horsted Keynes to Haywards Heath branch on 3 September 1883. Only the section from East Grinstead to Horsted Keynes was laid with double-track, the section south of here was built to accommodate it but in the end only single-track with passing loops was built.

Traffic was always light on this rural railway backwater, a situation aggravated by the fact that many of the 6 intermediate stations served no useful purpose other than being built close to the homes of the railway's financial backers. On the 4½-mile double-track branch from Horsted Keynes an intermediate station was opened at Ardingly. A physical connection was laid north of Haywards Heath at Copyhold Junction in 1931 and in 1935 the branch was electrified by the Southern Railway. It held out longer than the 'mainline', closing to passengers on 28 October 1963. The section from Copyhold Junction to a Hanson Aggregates depot at Ardingly is still in use today while the remainder of the trackbed is now owned by the Bluebell Railway, which has long-term plans to reopen it.

The 'mainline' from East Grinstead to Culver Junction was due to close on 15 June 1955 but a railwaymen's strike brought that forward to 29 May. However local residents, angered by the closure, discovered that the original Acts of Parliament authorising the building of the line included a clause that imposed a legal requirement to provide passenger services – in effect this meant that British Railways had to get a new Act passed to remove this. On 7 August 1956 the line was reopened! There then followed a public enquiry before the obligation was repealed by Parliament. The line eventually closed on 17 March 1958.

However, waiting in the wings was a group of preservationists eager to reopen the line as a steam-operated heritage railway. The Bluebell Railway Preservation Society was thus born in 1959 and in 1960 had managed to start running trains between Sheffield Park and Bluebell Halt, just short of Horsted Keynes, and the railway became the first standard-gauge steam-operated heritage line in the world to run a timetabled passenger service. Services were extended from Bluebell Halt to Horsted Keynes in 1962.

The push northwards from Horsted Keynes to East Grinstead took many years to complete with the society faced with buying back pockets of land that by then were privately owned and removing vast amounts of landfill that had been used to infill Imberhorne Cutting. Imberhorne Viaduct was given to the society and work gathered pace from 2008 onwards with much of the spoil from the cutting being removed by rail via the national rail network link at East Grinstead. Opening day came on 7 March 2013 thus allowing passengers to travel once more from London's Victoria station to Sheffield Park (changing trains at East Grinstead) for the first time in 55 years.

With one of the largest collections of preserved steam locomotives in Britain, trains of beautifully restored vintage carriages now terminate at East Grinstead. A wide range of historic steam locomotives operate on the line including examples from the LBSCR, SECR, LSWR, NLR, GWR, SR and BR. The Bluebell Railway is widely used by film and TV companies seeking authentic period locations, and this in turn has led to a great public awareness of the line.

The Bluebell Railway Museum (www.bluebell-railway-museum.co.uk) at Sheffield Park station houses a large railway archive and ephemera collection, while at Horsted Keynes station the Carriage Works has a visitor centre where coach restoration can be viewed.

NOW
Ex-LB&SCR Class 'A1X' 0-6-0T No 672 Fenchurch *passes the remains of Town House bridge, near Freshfield, with an Autumn Tints Special returning to Sheffield Park on 13 August 2006.*

London

TENTERDEN

Brighton

TENTERDEN TOWN
ROLVENDEN
WITTERSHAM ROAD
NORTHIAM
BODIAM

The first railway to be authorised under the Light Railways Act of 1896, the Rother Valley Light Railway opened the 12 miles between Robertsbridge, on the Tonbridge Wells to Hastings line, and Tenterden in Kent on 2 April 1900. A 1½-mile extension eastwards to Tenterden Town opened on 16 March 1903 and the original Tenterden station was renamed Rolvenden. A year later an 8-mile northerly extension to Headcorn, on the Tonbridge to Ashford line, was authorised and the company changed its name to the Kent & East Sussex Railway. Managed by Colonel Holman F. Stephens the railway opened to Headcorn on 15 May 1905 but a planned extension to Maidstone never materialised.

The railway's guiding light, Colonel Stephens, died in 1931 and the company went into liquidation the following year to be managed by his successor W. T. Austen. This ramshackle rural railway struggled on using secondhand locomotives and rolling stock until it was nationalised in 1948. By 1950 passenger services consisted of 3 trains between Robertsbridge and Tenterden Town and 5 between the latter station and Headcorn although none of them allowed reasonable connections. In the opposite direction there was 1 train that travelled the whole length of the line and 4 between Headcorn and Tenterden Town, again with no reasonable connections – the two sections were virtually run as two separate railways.

THEN
Ex-LB&SCR Class 'A1X' No 32655 and its one-coach train vainly wait for passengers at Tenterden station in August 1953. Built at Brighton Works at the end of 1875, this veteran loco was finally withdrawn in 1960 at the age of 85.

The loss-making line was closed to passengers on 4 January 1954 although hop-pickers' specials were run from London to Bodiam until 1959. Goods services north of Tenterden Town ceased at the same time as passenger services and this section was lifted in 1956. Goods trains continued to operate on the western section until 12 June 1961.

Following closure a preservation group, the Kent & East Sussex Railway based at Tenterden, was quickly formed but it was not until 1974 that services started running. Wittersham Road station was opened in 1978, Northiam in 1990 and Bodiam in 2000. Trains are mainly steam-hauled and the railway owns a collection of superbly restored 4- and 6-wheeled Victorian coaches. Locomotives include the diminutive former SECR 'P' Class 0-6-0 tank No 753, built in 1909, 2 Stroudley LBSCR 'Terrier' 0-6-0Ts No 3 *Bodiam* and No 8 *Knowle*, 2 'USA' 0-6-0Ts formerly of Southampton Docks, 2 powerful Hunslet ex-War Department 'Austerity' types, GWR '1600' Class 0-6-0PT No 1638, GWR '5600' Class 0-6-2T No 6619, GWR '4200' Class 2-8-0T No 4253 and a 1919-built Norwegian 2-6-0 tender engine. The award-winning Colonel Stephens Museum is located at Tenterden Town station.

A separate railway preservation group, the Rother Valley Railway (see page 56), is currently restoring the line west of Bodiam from Robertsbridge where it will once again connect with the national rail network.

Tenterden Town Station,
Station Road, Tenterden,
Kent TN30 6HE

01580 765155
www.kesr.org.uk

LENGTH
10½ miles

GAUGE
Standard

OPEN
March to December,
see website for details

NOW
Built in 1917 for working in an ironstone quarry, Manning Wardle 0-6-0ST No 14 Charwelton *hauls a mixed train near Rolvenden on 16 March 1998.*

EAST KENT RAILWAY

SHEPHERDS WELL

SHEPHERDSWELL

EYTHORNE

Station Road,
Shepherdswell, Dover,
Kent CT15 7PD

01304 832042
www.eastkentrailway.co.uk

LENGTH
2½ miles

GAUGE
Standard

OPEN
Sundays, April to October; Saturdays in mid-summer; Easter, May, Whitsun & August Bank Holidays

The East Kent Light Railway (EKLR) was a ramshackle affair and part of the cheaply built rural light railway empire run by Colonel Holman F. Stephens. Authorised in 1911, the 10¼-mile single-track railway was opened between Shepherdswell, adjacent to the South Eastern & Chatham Railway's mainline between Canterbury and Dover, and Wingham Colliery in 1916. Primarily a coal-carrying line serving collieries at Wingham, Woodnesborough and Tilmanstone, the EKLR also offered a sparse passenger service which by 1922 consisted of 2 return trains on weekdays along the whole length of the line (journey time around 45 minutes) and 2 which terminated at Eastry. In 1925 the railway was extended by 1 mile from Wingham Colliery to Canterbury Road, a terminus which apparently served no useful purpose.

Also in 1925 a 2¼-mile branch from Eastry northwards to Sandwich Road was opened and in 1928 this was connected to Richborough Port. However the expected traffic did not materialise and passenger services ended on 1 November that year. Wingham Colliery closed in 1935 and the eccentric railway struggled to exist with just a skeleton passenger service and coal-carrying from Tilmanstone Colliery, near Eythorne, to Shepherdswell. The EKLR was nationalised on 1 January 1948 and British Railways lost no time in withdrawing the passenger service, which came on 30 October of that year. The track beyond Eythorne had been lifted by 1951 but coal traffic continued from Tilmanstone Colliery until the latter's closure in 1986.

Today the 2½ miles of the EKLR between Shepherdswell and Eythorne via 477-yd-long Golgotha Tunnel is a heritage railway operated by the East Kent Railway Trust. Operating on most Sundays from its base at Shepherdswell the railway also features a passenger-carrying miniature railway, an extensive model railway located in a restored LMS Stanier carriage, woodland walks and a visitor centre in the restored signal box from Barham station on the Elham Valley Line. Shepherds Well [sic] station, on the mainline between Canterbury and Dover, is still open and served by Southeastern trains to and from London Victoria and Dover Priory. At Eythorne the old signal box from Selling contains an exhibition that tells the history and present story of the railway. Motive power includes a diesel multiple unit, a Class 142 'Pacer' and various diesels while Avonside 0-6-0 colliery engine *St Dunstan* is currently awaiting restoration.

THEN
Built at Ashford Works in 1894 ex-SE&CR Class 'O1' 0-6-0 No 31258 departs from Shepherdswell with a special train on 23 May 1959. This veteran loco was withdrawn in 1961, aged 67, the last of its class along with No 31065 which has since been preserved on the Bluebell Railway.

NOW
Built in 1948 for shunting at Courtaulds' Aber Works in Flintshire, preserved Peckett 0-4-0ST Achilles *heads a train on the East Kent Railway near Eythorne on 24 March 2019.*

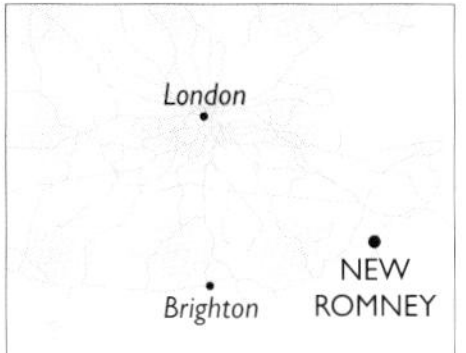

HYTHE
BURMARSH ROAD
DYMCHURCH
ST MARY'S BAY
WARREN HALT
NEW ROMNEY
ROMNEY SANDS
DUNGENESS

During the 1920s Count Louis Zborowski and Captain Jack Howey were not only both wealthy racing drivers but they also shared a passion for miniature railways. Their first attempt to build a 15in.-gauge passenger-carrying railway along the narrow-gauge Ravenglass & Eskdale Railway (see pages 172–3) in Cumbria fell through, but not before they had ordered two miniature LNER Pacific locomotives from railway engineers Davey Paxman of Colchester. Tragically, before a new home for their railway could be found, Zborowski was killed in a motor racing accident at Monza in Italy. Howey then teamed up with miniature locomotive designer Henry Greenly and chose a level 8-mile stretch of coast between Hythe and New Romney in Kent which was already becoming popular with holidaymakers.

Opened between Hythe and New Romney in 1927 by the Duke of York (later King George VI), the Romney, Hythe & Dymchurch Railway (RH&DR) is a one-third scale fully signalled double-track mainline with express trains operating at up to 25 mph hauled by scale versions of LNER and Canadian steam locomotives. A 5½-mile single-track extension was opened in 1928 from New Romney to Dungeness where the line makes a 360° loop.

Proving popular during the 1930s, the onset of war placed the RH&DR on the front line. Train services were suspended while the railway, operated by the Somerset Light Infantry, played its part employing an armoured train and transporting materials for the D-Day landings. The railway was reopened by Laurel and Hardy in 1947 but declining passenger numbers and Howey's death in 1963 led to its sale in 1968. The new owners also struggled to make ends meet and the railway was only saved from extinction when it was purchased and then restored by a consortium led by Sir William McAlpine in 1973. Today, while goods traffic such as shingle is no longer carried, the railway is still popular with local residents and tourists and operates a train for school children during term time. Intermediate stations between Hythe and Dungeness are at Dymchurch, St Mary's Bay, Romney Warren, New Romney and Romney Sands. The railway is also unique as it still operates a postal and parcels service and issues its own stamps.

The RHDR currently boasts 11 magnificent steam locomotives (including 7 of Henry Greenly's built by Davey Paxman in the 1920s), 2 diesels (used on the regular school train during term time), and over 65 assorted coaches including the unique buffet observation car. To add to the authentic mainline atmosphere the railway boasts a large engine shed, turntable and workshop at New Romney, and an overall roof covers the 3 platforms at Hythe terminus. Also at New Romney, an extensive model railway exhibition and museum is open most days. During peak periods trains run every 45 minutes, at speeds of up to 25 mph.

New Romney Station,
New Romney,
Kent TN28 8PL

01797 362353
www.rhdr.org.uk

LENGTH
13½ miles

GAUGE
15in.

OPEN
Daily, Easter to end October; weekends January to March & December, for numerous special events see website

NOW
Designed by Henry Greenly and built by Davey Paxman in 1927, 'Mountain' Class 4-8-2 Hercules *approaches Dungeness with a train from Hythe on 6 September 2019. This loco hauled the inaugural train on the opening of the Romney, Hythe & Dymchurch Railway on 16 July 1927.*

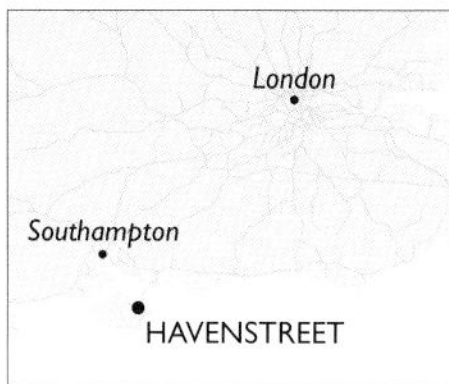

SMALLBROOK JUNCTION
ASHEY
HAVENSTREET
WOOTTON

The first railway to be built on the Isle of Wight was the Cowes & Newport Railway (C&NR), which opened in 1862. However, it remained isolated from the island's other railways for some years. While the Isle of Wight (Newport Junction) Railway opened between Newport and Sandown in 1875 it was another 4 years before it was physically joined to the C&NR via a viaduct at Newport, by which time it had gone bankrupt. A short goods-only branch line was opened to Medina Wharf near Cowes in 1875. To the east of Newport, the Ryde & Newport Railway opened its line from Smallbrook Junction, on the Isle of Wight (Eastern Section) Railway's line from Ryde to Shanklin, in 1875. All three railways (C&NR, the bankrupt IoW(NJ)R and IoW(ES)R) amalgamated to form the Isle of Wight Central Railway in 1887.

By 1900 the island's railway system was in place and remained so for another 52 years. In 1923 the island lines became part of the newly-formed Southern Railway which set about modernising the by then antiquated Victorian system. With the exception of a few ex-LBSCR 'Terrier' tanks, all of the ancient steam locomotives and worn out coaching stock were replaced by modern carriages and newly-built Class 'O2' 0-4-4 tanks. Under SR management passenger traffic continued to grow, especially during the busy summer season when holidaymakers in their hundreds of thousands descended on the island each year. Apart from a lull during the Second World War, this rosy picture continued until the early 1950s when competition from road transport started to make inroads into passenger traffic.

With new British Railways' management looking to prune uneconomic branch lines the first closure on the island came in 1952 when the Merstone to Ventnor West line closed. A year later the Brading to Bembridge and Newport to Freshwater lines closed, followed in 1956 by

THEN
Single-line token exchange at Havenstreet station between Hughie White and the crew of ex-L&SWR Class 'O2' 0-4-4T No 24 Calbourne *on 31 August 1965. The train is the 9.30 a.m. from Ryde to Cowes. No 24 has since been restored and works on the Isle of Wight Steam Railway.*

the Newport to Sandown line. What was left (Ryde to Ventnor and Ryde to Cowes) struggled on with ageing locomotives and coaching stock until both lines were listed for closure in the 'Beeching Report' of 1963. Despite numerous objections, especially from islanders worried about more traffic clogging up their narrow roads, the end for virtually all the island's railways came in 1966. First to close was the Smallbrook Junction to Newport and Cowes line on 21 February 1966 while the Shanklin to Ventnor line went on 18 April although Ryde to Shanklin was reprieved and converted to third rail electrification. Meanwhile goods trains continued to operate to Newport and Cowes until May 1966 after which all of the island's withdrawn steam locomotives and coaching stock were stored awaiting disposal at Newport station.

The Isle of Wight Steam Railway preservation group moved into Havenstreet station on the former Ryde & Newport Railway's line between Smallbrook Junction and Newport in 1971. Services to Wootton restarted in 1977 and to Ashey and a new station at Smallbrook Junction in 1991, where connection can be made with the electrified Island Line. The veteran and beautifully preserved locomotives and rolling stock, some dating back to the 19th century, all contribute to the Victorian atmosphere that pervades the railway. Included in the line-up are former London Brighton & South Coast Railway Class 'A1X' 0-6-0 tanks, No W8 *Freshwater* and No W11 *Newport*, built in 1876 and 1878 respectively, and Southern Railway Class '02' 0-4-4 tank No W24 *Calbourne* recently restored in SR malachite green livery. Also on the books are 1877-built LB&SCR 'E1' Class 0-6-0T No W2 *Yarmouth*, LMS Ivatt Class '2' 2-6-2Ts Nos 41298 and 41313, LMS Ivatt Class '2' 2-6-0 No 46447 and 5 industrial and WD 0-6-0 tanks.

Havenstreet,
Isle of Wight,
Hampshire PO33 4DS

01983 882204
www.iwsteamrailway.co.uk

LENGTH
5½ miles

GAUGE
Standard

OPEN
Selected days, February to December (see website); daily June to September

NOW
An atmospheric early-morning photo of preserved ex-L&SWR Class 'O2' 0-4-4T No 24 Calbourne *near Ashey on 16 November 2010. This loco was built at Nine Elms Works in 1891 and was shipped to the Isle of Wight in 1925.*

EASTERN ENGLAND

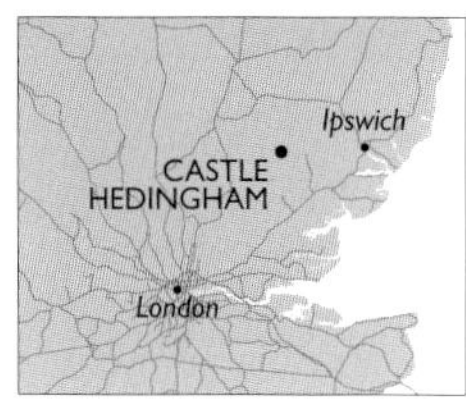

CASTLE HEDINGHAM

The 19½-mile single-track line through rural Essex between Chappel & Wakes Colne and Haverhill was built in stages by the Colne Valley & Halstead Railway (CV&HR). The first section to be completed was from Chappel & Wakes Colne, on the Eastern Counties Railway's line from Marks Tey to Sudbury, to Halstead on 16 April 1860. It was then extended up the Colne Valley reaching Sible & Castle Hedingham in 1861, Yeldham in 1862 and Haverhill in 1863. Here the railway had its own terminus and a physical link with the Great Eastern Railway's cross-country line between Cambridge and Sudbury.

Always a quiet rural backwater, the CV&HR led a precarious existence serving small villages and farming communities along its route during its early years. The company went bankrupt in 1874 and an official receiver was appointed until 1885 when debts were finally repaid. The beginning of the 20th century saw an upturn in the railway's fortunes when a large rail-served brickworks was opened at Hedingham followed by another at Halstead where the CV&HR also established a small railway works. The immediate years following the First World War saw the railway back in financial trouble with passenger traffic hit by the introduction of local bus services. Sunday services ceased for a while but in 1923 the still independent CV&HR was absorbed by the newly-formed London & North Eastern Railway. The railway's separate station at Haverhill was closed to passenger traffic on 14 July 1924 and all trains diverted to the former GER station.

The Second World War brought a massive increase in traffic along the line when several US Air Force airfields were opened along its route.

THEN
A deserted Earls Colne station on 21 January 1961. The line closed to passenger traffic less than a year later.

Peaking in 1944, huge tonnages of bombs and fuel along with military personnel were despatched to White Colne, Earls Colne, Halstead and Birdbrook to aid the war effort. The railway resumed its peaceful rural life after the war and, following Nationalisation in 1948, continued to provide a passenger service of 4 return trains on weekdays and 2 on Sundays despite rapidly dwindling traffic. The eleventh-hour introduction of diesel multiple units and railbuses at the beginning of 1959 was too late and the line closed to passenger traffic on 1 January 1962 with the section from Haverhill to Yeldham closing completely. Freight services continued to Yeldham until 28 December 1964 and to Halstead until 19 April 1965.

However the Colne Valley Railway did not completely disappear. In 1973 a group of railway preservationists moved to a site just west of Castle Hedingham. One mile of track was relaid and the original station building from Sible & Castle Hedingham was re-erected on the new site. Today the Colne Valley Railway operates passenger trains either side of the station where there are also other visitor attractions including a miniature railway, an extensive model railway, a garden railway and a working signal box. Steam locomotives including those being restored include military and industrial 0-6-0STs WD 190, WD 200 and *Jupiter*. Diesels include BR Class 03 diesel shunters D2041 and D2184 and Class 121 'Bubble Car' W55033.

Chappel & Wakes Colne is still served by diesel trains on the Marks Tey to Sudbury branch line while the East Anglian Railway Museum (see page 78) is also based at the station.

Castle Hedingham Station,
Yeldham Road,
Castle Hedingham,
Halstead, Essex CO9 3DZ

01787 461174
www.colnevalleyrailway.co.uk

LENGTH
1 mile

GAUGE
Standard

OPEN
Weekends & Bank Holidays; also Wednesdays & Thursdays in August

NOW
Built in 1960, unpowered Pressed Steel Driving Trailer Second No 56287 surrounded by period railway artefacts at Castle Hedingham station on the Colne Valley Railway.

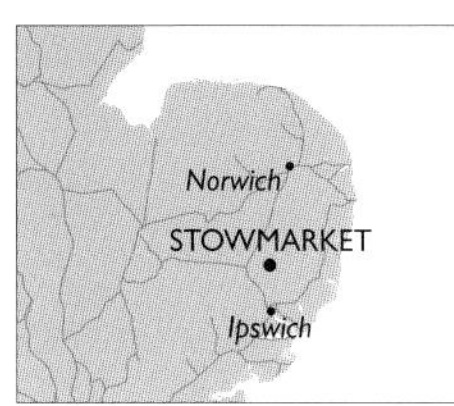

BROCKFORD & WETHERINGSETT

WILBY HALT

ASPALL

In 1901 the Mid-Suffolk Light Railway was given authorisation to build a 28-mile 'mainline' between Haughley and Halesworth along with a 14-mile branch from Kenton to Westerfield (near Ipswich). In the end the line was never completed but what did open was the 19-mile meandering single-track line between Haughley, on the Great Eastern Railway's mainline between Ipswich and Norwich, and the village of Laxfield. Goods services only commenced running on 20 September 1904 but receipts were disappointing in this rural corner of Suffolk which was then suffering from the general agricultural recession sweeping the country. Debts mounted and in 1907 an Official Receiver was appointed to run the line. By then a 2¼-mile extension from Laxfield to Cratfield had been opened along with 2½ miles of the branch south from Kenton to Debenham. The lines never went any further.

In a bid to increase income the 'Middy', as it was affectionately known, introduced an infrequent passenger service between Haughley and Laxfield on 29 September 1908. However traffic was always light as most of the stations were some distance from the villages they purported to serve. The Cratfield extension was closed in 1912 and the stub of the branch line a few years later.

Following the First World War the financial situation of the railway became even worse with the few mixed trains, limited to a maximum speed of 25 mph and journeys that involved shunting wagons and opening and closing numerous level crossing gates, unable to compete with newly-introduced buses and lorries. In 1924 the London & North Eastern Railway came to the rescue and the Official Receiver was withdrawn. Life on this sleepy rural line continued as before until the Second World War when it had its busiest period providing an important link for two new US airbases that had opened near Horham and Mendlesham stations.

THEN
Less than a year before the closure of the Mid-Suffolk Light Railway this delightful scene at Horham station was saved for posterity by famous railway photographer Henry Casserley on 1 September 1951.

The end of the war found the 'Middy' in a neglected state but it struggled on to become part of the nationalised British Railways in 1948. By 1950 the passenger service consisted of just 2 return trains each weekday, the 19 miles being covered in around 1 hr 30 mins. The few passengers carried rode in vintage coaches hauled by equally vintage steam locomotives along a rickety weed-strewn track – the end was nigh. The inevitable total closure came on 26 July 1952 with the last train hauled by Class 'J15' 0-6-0 No 65447. The track was lifted in 1953 and the trackbed of the 'Middy' slowly disappeared into the Suffolk landscape.

Nearly 40 years later a railway preservation society opened a small museum dedicated to the railway on the site of Brockford & Wetheringsett station. Since then members of the Mid-Suffolk Light Railway have started to recreate this much-loved railway, bringing former station buildings from Mendlesham, Brockford and Wilby on to the site and restoring 19th-century Great Eastern Railway coaches. A steam-operated passenger service also runs along about ½-mile of the 'Middy' trackbed and there are proposals to extend this route in the future. Steam locomotives on the line include late-19th-century North Eastern Railway Class 'Y7' 0-4-0T No 985 (on loan from the North Norfolk Railway), 1936-built Bagnall 0-4-0ST No 2565 and 1906-built Cockerill 0-4-0 vertical boilered tram engine No 2525. Several industrial diesel shunters and a Wickham railmotor complete the roster.

Visitors can use the Trackbed Walk of about 1 mile and also the waymarked Middy Light Railway Long Distance Path between Haughley and Brockford. Future plans include an extension of the running line to Blacksmith's Green.

Brockford Station,
Wetheringsett, Stowmarket,
Suffolk IP14 5PW

01449 766899
www.mslr.org.uk

LENGTH
½ mile

GAUGE
Standard

OPEN
Museum open Sundays from Easter to end September & Wednesdays in August; trains operate on Special Event days throughout the year (see website)

NOW
An idyllic rural scene on the Mid-Suffolk Light Railway – the farmer on his ancient Fergie stops to watch the progress of 0-6-0ST Wissington *haul a short goods train at Brockford, 1 September 2012. Built by Hudswell-Clarke in 1938 for the British Sugar Corporation this diminutive loco was withdrawn in 1978 and preserved on the North Norfolk Railway.*

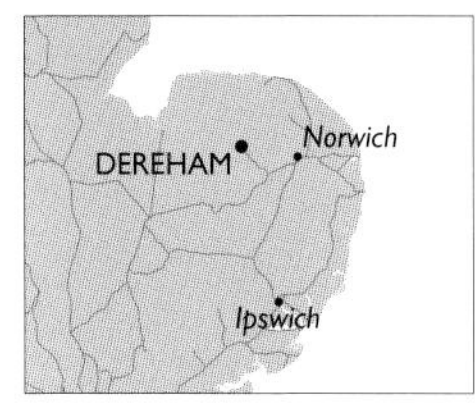

WYMONDHAM
WYMONDHAM ABBEY
KIMBERLEY PARK
THUXTON
YAXHAM
DEREHAM
COUNTY SCHOOL

Dereham Station, Station Road, Dereham, Norfolk NR19 1DF

01362 851723
www.mnr.org.uk

LENGTH
11½ miles

GAUGE
Standard

OPEN
Most weekends, March to October & December; Bank Holidays; more frequent services (excepting some Mondays, Tuesdays & Fridays) June to September, see website for full details

The 11½-mile branch line from Wymondham, on the Norwich to Ely mainline, to Dereham was opened by the Norfolk Railway in 1847. It was later extended northwards to Fakenham in 1849 and to Wells-next-the-Sea by the Wells & Fakenham Railway in 1857. While the line northwards from Dereham to Wells was listed for closure in the 'Beeching Report' (closing to passengers on 5 October 1964), Dereham was also served by the line from King's Lynn and saw a through service between King's Lynn and Norwich. None of this route was listed for closure in the 'Beeching Report' but the various cost savings introduced such as the use of diesel multiple units, unmanned stations and conductor/guards were all to no avail. While the King's Lynn to Dereham line closed on 9 September 1968, the Wymondham to Dereham line lingered on as a branch for just over another year until closure on 6 October 1969 although freight continued to use the line, as far north as Fakenham, into the 1980s. Since 1997 the railway between Wymondham and Dereham has been reopened as a heritage line – the Mid-Norfolk Railway also owns the trackbed north of Dereham to County School station.

The northerly section of line between Walsingham and Wells is now operated by the 10¼in.-gauge Wells & Walsingham Light Railway (see pages 84–5).

Opening as a tourist line in 1997, the Mid-Norfolk Railway today operates steam and diesel services along the 11½-mile section between Wymondham Abbey and Dereham with intermediate stations at Yaxham (where there is also a short 2ft-gauge line), Thuxton and Kimberley Park. Visiting locomotives are often seen at work on the line. The railway also owns a further 6 miles of track northwards from Dereham to the restored County School station and once this opens the Mid-Norfolk will be the third-longest heritage railway in England. Track has already been laid at County School where there is a visitor centre and miniature railway. Charter and excursion trains along with commercial freight traffic and MOD military traffic also use the line via the connection with the national rail network at Wymondham. Numerous special events such as vintage rallies are also held by the railway. Although predominately diesel-operated the MNR also regularly hires in steam locomotives from other heritage railways. Diesel locos include examples of BR Classes 04, 31, 33, 37, 47 and 50 as well as an extensive collection of diesel multiple units.

THEN
Class 31 diesel-electric No 31177 and its freight train wait for the level crossing gates to open at Dereham, 2 September 1982.

NOW
Class 101 diesel multiple unit in Dereham station on 26 March 2017. The Mid-Norfolk Railway has a large collection of diesel multiple units and railcars including examples of Classes 100, 101, 108, 117, 142/0, 142/1, and 144.

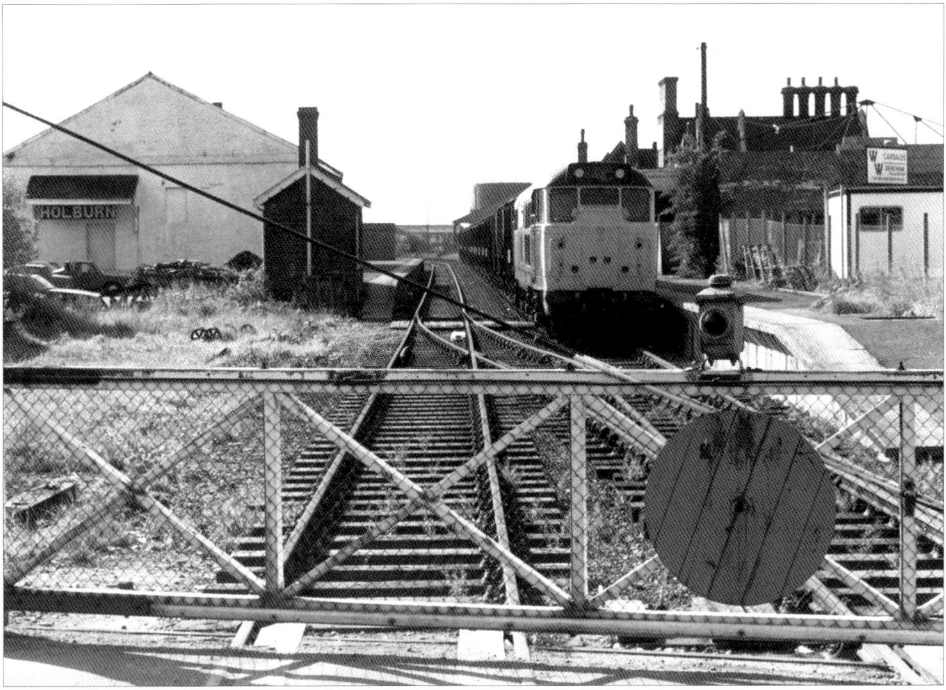
HOLBORN

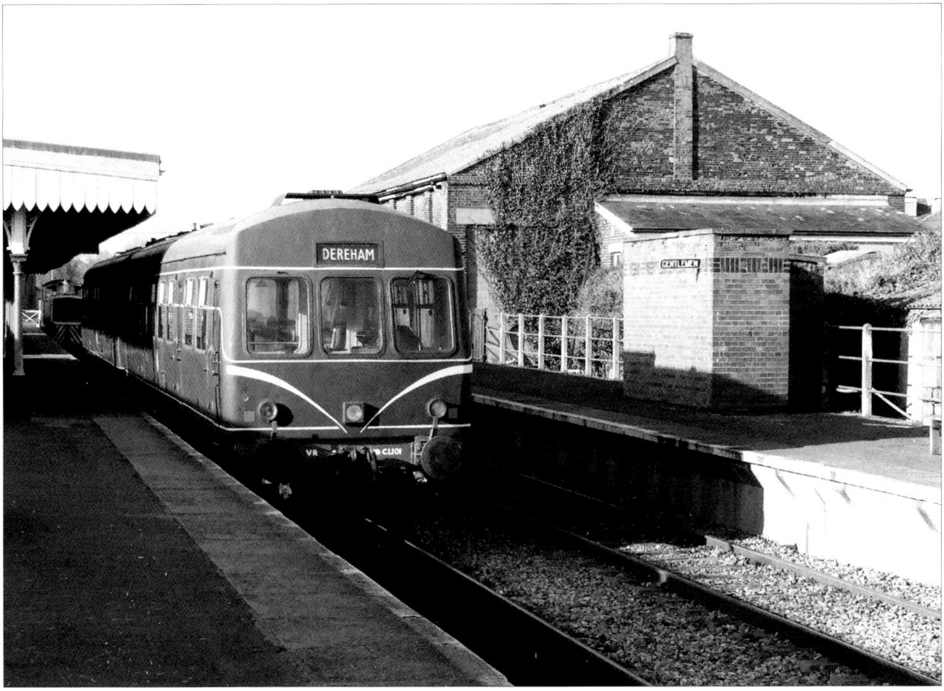
DEREHAM
GENTLEMEN

EAST ANGLIAN RAILWAY MUSEUM

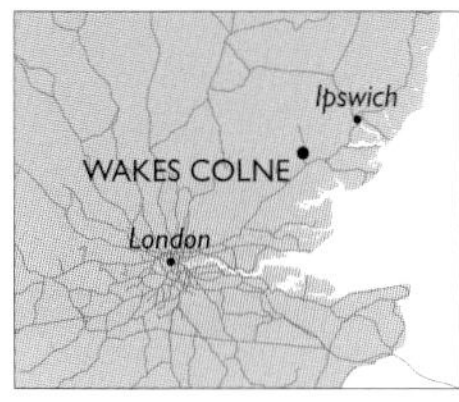

CHAPPEL & WAKES COLNE

EAST ANGLIAN RAILWAY MUSEUM

Chappel & Wakes Colne Station, Wakes Colne, Essex CO6 2DS

01206 242524
www.earm.co.uk

OPEN
Museum open daily throughout year; see website for dates of special events & when trains are operating

This working museum contains a comprehensive collection of railway architecture, engineering and relics representing over 100 years of railways in the Eastern Counties. It was formed in 1968 as the Stour Valley Railway Preservation Society to preserve a section of the Stour Valley Railway when closure was threatened. When closure did not take place the museum, a registered charity, was formed in 1986. Chappel & Wakes Colne station is situated on the former GER branch line from Marks Tey to Cambridge via Haverhill. It opened in 1849 and is still open today as far as Sudbury. Built in the 1890s the station building is a classic example of GER architecture and is restored to its original condition with a heritage centre situated in the storage arches underneath. Two restored signal boxes include the original one and one that was moved from Mistley, near Manningtree, now controls train movements within the site. A restored Victorian goods shed is now used for functions. Running days, vintage train events, beer festivals and a miniature railway day are held at various weekends throughout the year.

Operational steam locomotives at the museum include 1936-built Bagnall 0-4-0ST *Jubilee*, 1905-built Andrew Barclay 0-4-0ST *Storefield* and 1941-built Robert Stephenson & Hawthorns 0-6-0ST *Pen Green* (converted into a 'Thomas the Tank Engine') while LNER 'N7' Class 0-6-2T No 69621 is currently under overhaul. Several industrial diesels and a Class 101 diesel multiple unit completes the roster.

The museum is situated close to Chappel Viaduct which was opened in 1849 and is still used by trains on the Sudbury branch today. It is the longest viaduct in East Anglia and is reputed to be the largest brick structure in Europe, containing over 7 million bricks, with each of the 32 arches being 30 ft wide.

NOW
Opened in 1849, Chappel Viaduct is located close to the East Anglian Railway Museum. It is reputed to be the second largest brick structure in Europe.

Located on the former Midland & Great Northern Joint Railway's line from Melton Constable to Norwich City, Whitwell & Reepham station opened in 1882 and closed to passengers in 1959. Freight continued along the line via Themelthorpe Curve to the Lenwade concrete factory until 1985. From 1993 the Marriott's Way long-distance path was opened along the old trackbed of the railway adjacent to the station. The derelict station was purchased in 2007 and since then the Whitwell & Reepham Railway Preservation Society has laid track within the site, converted the old goods shed into an engine shed, resurfaced the platform and built a replica signal box. A caravan and camping site is located next to the station site.

The first steam gala at the restored station was held on 28 February 2009 – exactly 50 years since the M&GN closed to passengers. Steam locomotives based at Whitwell & Reepham are Andrew Barclay 0-4-0STs *Annie* and *Victory* and Robert Stephenson & Hawthorns 0-4-0ST *Agecroft No. 3*. In addition the Claud Hamilton Locomotive Group are based here where they are building a replica GER Class 'H88' (LNER Class 'D16/2') 4-4-0 locomotive No 8783 *Phoenix*.

O WHITWELL & REEPHAM

Whitwell & Reepham Station,
Whitwell Road, Reepham,
Norfolk NR10 4GA

01603 871694
www.whitwellstation.com

GAUGE
Standard

OPEN
Daily

NOW
Andrew Barclay 0-4-0ST No 4 Victory and 4-wheeled Baguley-Drewry diesel No 7 engaged in a spot of shunting at Whitwell & Reepham station.

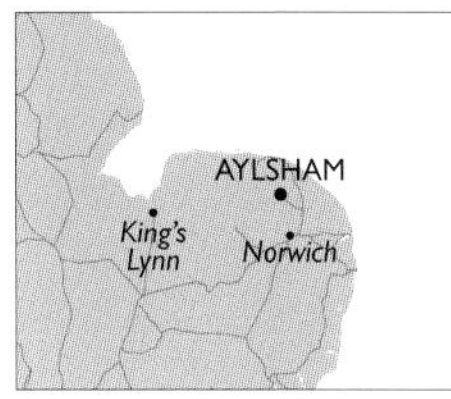

AYLSHAM
BRAMPTON
BUXTON
COLTISHALL
WROXHAM
HOVETON & WROXHAM

The 23¾-mile single-track line between Wroxham and County School was opened in stages by the East Norfolk Railway and throughout on 1 May 1882, by which time the company had been absorbed by the Great Eastern Railway. County School station, 1 mile south of the junction between the ENR's line from Wroxham and the GER's Dereham to Wells-next-the-Sea line, did not open until 1886, primarily to serve the nearby Norfolk County School.

The 6 intermediate stations along the line, of which Aylsham South was the busiest, were served by a passenger service that took a circuitous 38½-mile route between Norwich and Dereham. During the Second World War the line became busy when several RAF airfields were opened nearby – Buxton Lamas station served RAF Coltishall which was in fact nearer this station than Coltishall station, and Foulsham station was near to the RAF Bomber Command base of the same name. By 1950 there were 6 passenger services between Norwich and Dereham with 5 in the opposite direction. By then increased competition from road transport had brought a decline in traffic and the line closed to passengers on 15 September 1952.

Freight trains continued to use the line until 31 October 1964 when it was closed between County School and Themelthorpe. Here a connection had been laid to connect with the M&GNJR's freight-only line to Norwich City in 1960 – Themelthorpe Curve was the sharpest radius curve on the BR network. This enabled goods trains to run the 40 or so miles from Norwich Thorpe to Norwich City (geographically less than a mile apart!) via Wroxham and Aylsham while the M&GN section north to Melton Constable was completely closed. The goods traffic to Norwich City ceased in 1969 but trains continued to carry concrete products from a factory at Lenwade until 1985 when the entire route from Wroxham was closed completely.

THEN
Having brought a freight train down from Aylsham the driver of Class 31 diesel-electric D5847 passes the single-line token to the signalman at Wroxham on 4 August 1969. The 120-year-old signal box at Wroxham has been restored and is open to the public on special event days.

Some of the original stations still survive between Wroxham and County School: Coltishall station is a bed and breakfast establishment; Cawston station building is a private residence; Reepham station with its platforms and goods shed is now a tea room and cycle hire centre; Foulsham station is a private residence. At the western end County School station is being restored in readiness for the extension of the 17-mile Mid-Norfolk Railway from Wymondham Abbey (see pages 76–7).

Running along the trackbed of this former branch line between Wroxham and Aylsham, the 15in.-gauge Bure Valley Railway cost £2.5 million to build and was opened as a miniature passenger-carrying line in 1990. The Bure Valley station at Wroxham is adjacent to that of the national rail network station and has a 3-track layout with a turntable at one end. As the line meanders along the valley of the River Bure, alongside the Bure Valley Walk, it passes through 3 other stations, at Coltishall, Brampton and Buxton, before arriving at Aylsham – formerly Aylsham South – through a ¼-mile-long tunnel, where the railway has its overall-roofed terminus, engine sheds and workshops. Five steam locomotives and 1 diesel operate the line and visiting locos from the Romney Hythe & Dymchurch Railway and the Ravenglass & Eskdale Railway can occasionally be seen at work. The Bure Valley Railway's steam locos are as follows: 2-6-2T No 1 *Wroxham Broad*, 2-6-2 No 6 *Blickling Hall*, 2-6-2 No 7 *Spitfire*, 2-6-2T No 8 *John of Gaunt* and 2-6-4T No 9 *Mark Timothy*. Combined rail and Broads boat excursions are available in the summer as is local cycle hire. The magnificent 120-year-old Great Eastern Railway signal box at Wroxham, with its 50 levers, has been beautifully restored by the Wroxham Signalbox Trust and is open to the public on special events days (www.wroxhamsignalbox.org.uk).

Beyond Aylsham station the trackbed survives as the Marriott's Way long-distance footpath to the outskirts of Norwich.

Aylsham Station,
Norwich Road,
Aylsham,
Norwich NR11 6BW

01263 733858
www.bvrw.co.uk

LENGTH
9 miles

GAUGE
15in.

OPEN
Daily, April to October & during school holidays; weekends during March, November & December

NOW
Bure Valley Railway 2-6-2 No 6 Blickling Hall *on the turntable at Wroxham station before hauling its train back to Aylsham. Built by Winson Engineering in 1994 this 15in.-gauge loco is based on the Indian Railways 'ZB' Class.*

NORTH NORFOLK RAILWAY

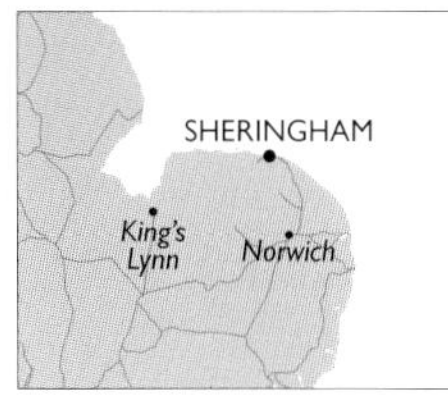

SHERINGHAM

SHERINGHAM
WEYBOURNE
KELLING HEATH PARK
HOLT

The seaside village of Sheringham was first reached by the Eastern & Midlands Railway which opened its steeply-graded 15¼-mile branch line from its important hub junction at Melton Constable to Cromer Beach in 1887. In 1893 the E&MR was in a parlous financial position and it was taken over by the Midland Railway and the Great Northern Railway to form the Midland & Great Northern Joint Railway (M&GNJR). The mainly single-track M&GNJR via Bourne in Lincolnshire, South Lynn and Fakenham was a popular route for holiday trains from the Midlands during the summer months but it fell on hard times after the Second World War and almost the whole system including lines to Peterborough, Norwich City and Yarmouth Beach was closed on 2 March 1959. The only exception were passenger services between Cromer Beach (reached by through diesel trains from Norwich via Wroxham and North Walsham) and Melton Constable which were retained for a further 5 years until closure east of Sheringham on 6 April 1964 – on that date trains to and from Norwich reversed direction at Cromer Beach to continue along the coast to Sheringham. Today, the 3¾-mile section between Cromer Beach and Sheringham (served by trains from Norwich on the 'Bittern Line') is the only part of the M&GNJR to remain open as part of the national rail network.

After several rather optimistic preservation plans on other parts of the Midland & Great Northern system were rejected as being impractical, a preservation group moved in, initially at Weybourne, and now has its headquarters at Sheringham. In 1969, the year John Betjeman became the North Norfolk Railway's president, the railway became the first of the preservation societies in Britain to be floated as a Public Company,

THEN
Ex-LNER Class 'J39/1' 0-6-0 No 64761 of Norwich shed heads through Sheringham station with a freight train, c.1958. This freight loco was built at Darlington Works in 1928 and withdrawn in November 1959.

and by 1989 the present route, known as the 'Poppy Line', had been fully re-opened. The restored period stations, particularly at Weybourne where the railway has its large locomotive and carriage works, have often been used as TV and film locations – these include *Dad's Army*, *Swallows and Amazons* and *Love on a Branch Line*. In addition to Weybourne there is an intermediate halt at Kelling Heath Park. The present station building at Holt was removed from nearby Stalham brick-by-brick in 2002 and re-erected in its present position. Here there is a museum dedicated to the M&GNJR while there is also a railway museum and museum signal box open to the public at Sheringham. In 2010 the railway was reconnected to the national rail network via a level crossing at Sheringham.

A journey along the line provides passengers with views of the Norfolk coastline and heathland, and a large collection of restored steam and diesel locomotives and ex-LNER rolling stock operate the trains. The star of the railway is ex-LNER Class 'B12' 4-6-0 No 8572, built in 1928, which was returned to traffic in early 1995 after a major 3½-year rebuild at Mansfeld locomotive works in Germany. Other steam locomotives include 1912-built GER Class 'J15' 0-6-0 No 65462, 1921-built GNR Class 'N2' 0-6-2T No 1744, 1925-built S&DJR Class '7' 2-8-0 No 53809, 1943-built 'WD' 2-10-0 No 90775 *The Royal Norfolk Regiment*, 1957-built BR Standard Class '4' 2-6-0 No 76084 and 1959-built BR Standard Class '9F' 2-10-0 No 92203 *Black Prince*. Mainline diesels include examples of BR Classes 08, 11, 20, 31 and 37 along with Class 101 diesel multiple units and Waggon und Maschinenbau 4-wheeled railbus E79960.

Sheringham Station,
Station Approach,
Sheringham,
Norfolk NR26 8RA

01263 820800
www.nnrailway.co.uk

LENGTH
5¼ miles

GAUGE
Standard

OPEN
Daily, April to October & during school holidays; weekends, March & November; Santa Specials, December; for special event days see website

NOW
Built by English Electric at Vulcan Foundry in 1962, preserved BR Class '37' diesel-electric loco D6732 hauls a demonstration goods train through Weybourne station on the North Norfolk Railway.

WELLS & WALSINGHAM LIGHT RAILWAY

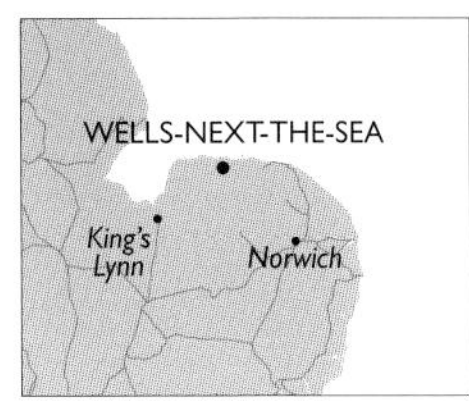

WELLS ON SEA
THE MIDDEN HALT
WARHAM
WIGHTON HALT
WALSINGHAM

Stiffkey Road,
Wells-next-the-Sea,
Norfolk NR23 1QB

01328 711630
www.wwlr.co.uk

LENGTH
4 miles

GAUGE
10¼in.

OPEN
Daily, early April to end October

Built by the Norfolk Railway, the first railway to reach the town of Dereham was opened from Wymondham, on the Norwich to Thetford mainline, in 1847. Although an extension northwards to Wells-next-the-Sea had been authorised, construction stopped at Fakenham and the 12-mile line from Dereham opened in 1849. The remaining 9½ miles to Wells was built by the Wells & Fakenham Railway which had been part-funded by the Earl of Leicester of Holkham Hall. The line opened in 1857 with a short branch to Wells Harbour being added 2 years later. The entire route from Wymondham to Wells became part of the Great Eastern Railway in 1862.

Two other railways branched off the Dereham to Wells line: the 18¼-mile West Norfolk Junction Railway from Wells to Heacham, on the King's Lynn to Hunstanton branch, opened in 1866 and closed to passengers in 1952 and completely in 1964; the 23¾-mile line from County School to Wroxham opened in 1882 and also closed to passengers in 1952. Parts of it remained open for goods until 1981.

Popular with holidaymakers in the summer heading for Wells and pilgrims to the shrine of Our Lady of Walsingham, the line also carried vast quantities of milk to London, imported potash and exported corn via Wells Harbour and was extensively used during the Second World War when it was guarded by an armoured train. Traffic declined after the war and despite the introduction of diesel multiple units in 1955 the line became increasingly uneconomic and was listed for closure in the 'Beeching Report'. Despite this a fairly healthy service of 11 return trains each weekday, the majority starting or ending their journey at Norwich, continued up until closure which came on 5 October 1964.

Today the longest 10¼in.-gauge railway in the world operates trains between Wells and Walsingham. It also operates the most powerful steam locomotive of that gauge in the world – a 20ft-long 'Garratt' 2-6-0+0-6-2 *Norfolk Hero*, built in 1986. This unique little line opened in 1982 and was owned, built and operated by retired naval commander Roy Francis until his death in 2015. Intermediate halts are provided at Warham St Mary and Wighton, and a former Great Eastern Railway signal box, originally sited at Swainsthorpe, has been preserved at Wells station where it is used as a shop and tearoom.

THEN
Ex-GER Class 'J19' 0-6-0 No 64644 with a short goods train at Wells-on-Sea in September 1958. Built at Stratford Works in 1912 this freight loco was withdrawn from Norwich shed in 1959.

NOW
Introduced in 1987, 2-6-0+0-6-2 'Garratt' locomotive Norfolk Hero *arrives at Wells-on-Sea station with a train from Walsingham. The signal box here was moved from Swainsthorpe on the mainline from Norwich to London.*

NENE VALLEY RAILWAY

PETERBOROUGH
PETERBOROUGH NENE VALLEY
ORTON MERE
OVERTON FOR FERRY MEADOWS
WANSFORD
YARWELL JUNCTION

Wansford Station, Stibbington, Peterborough, Cambridgeshire PE8 6LR

01780 784444
www.nvr.org.uk

LENGTH
7½ miles

GAUGE
Standard

OPEN
Weekends, Bank Holidays & most days (except Mondays) during school holidays, March to October; for special events & Santa Specials see website

The 51-mile cross-country railway between Rugby and Peterborough was opened in several stages. First on the scene was the London & Birmingham Railway's Rugby & Stamford branch line which ran from Rugby via Market Harborough, Seaton and Luffenham Junction and opened throughout in 1851. From Luffenham Junction trains for Peterborough were forced to use the Midland Railway's route via Stamford. This unsatisfactory arrangement lasted until 1879 when the London & North Western Railway opened a direct route from Seaton to Peterborough along the Nene Valley through Wansford.

As a cross-country route the railway from Rugby to Peterborough also saw through trains between Birmingham and East Anglia, becoming the major route for this holiday traffic after the Midland & Great Northern Joint Railway closed in 1959. Listed for closure in the 'Beeching Report', the entire route closed on 6 June 1966. Since then the 7½-mile section from Yarwell Junction to Peterborough has been opened as a heritage railway by the Nene Valley Railway.

The Nene Valley Railway is well known for its international flavour and location filming for TV and cinema. Since 1974, with assistance from Peterborough Development Corporation, the Peterborough Railway Society has had its headquarters at Wansford, which has become the main centre for foreign locomotives and rolling stock in Britain. Trains started operating in 1977 and a new NVR station at Peterborough (Nene Valley) was opened in 1986 adjacent to a site which is being developed into an international railway museum. From Peterborough the line runs through Nene Park along the banks of the River Nene, crossing the river twice, and into open countryside, before passing through Wansford and the 616-yd Wansford Tunnel. Current restored stock on the NVR consists of examples from Germany, Denmark, Sweden, France and Belgium as well as many from Britain, including the line's first locomotive, former BR Class '5MT' 4-6-0 No 73050 *City of Peterborough*. Other steam locos based on the NVR are BR 'Battle of Britain' Class 4-6-2 No 34081 92 *Squadron*, 1949-built Danish 0-6-0T No 656, Polish 0-8-0T No 5485, Swedish 'B' Class 4-6-0 No 101 and the latest arrival Swedish Class 'S' 2-6-2T No 1178. Diesels include 2 BR Class 14 diesel-hydraulics (D9520 and D9529), Class 45 No 45041 and Swedish railcar No 1212.

Film-makers have taken advantage of the continental flavour and the NVR stations have often been cleverly disguised as foreign locations for films such as the James Bond classics *Octopussy* (1982) and *Goldeneye* (1995), television dramas (*Eastenders, Casualty, Silent Witness* and *Poirot*) and TV commercials. A Travelling Post Office demonstration train with mailbag exchange apparatus can also be seen in action. A museum exhibiting the railway's extensive collection of TPO and Wagons-Lit rolling stock can be visited at Ferry Meadows.

NOW
Preserved ex-LNER Class 'D49/1' 4-4-0 No 62712 Morayshire *makes a fine sight with its train of 'blood and custard' coaches on the Nene Valley Railway. Built at Darlington Works in 1928 this loco was withdrawn in 1961 and subsequently preserved at the Bo'ness & Kinneil Railway* *(see pages 192–3).*

62712
63
A
CLASS
D49

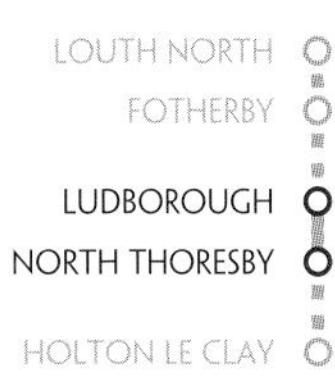

The 47½-mile railway from Grimsby Town to Boston via Louth was built by the East Lincolnshire Railway (ELR) but before completion in 1848 it had already been leased by the Great Northern Railway (GNR) as part of an eventual through route to Peterborough and King's Cross. The ELR remained independent until the 'Big Four Grouping' in 1923 when it became part of the newly-formed London & North Eastern Railway.

With through running over Manchester, Sheffield & Lincolnshire Railway's lines between Grimsby and New Holland the GNR could ostensibly offer a direct service between King's Cross and Hull, the latter reached by ferry across the River Humber. However, this slow route never fully developed and depended mainly on local traffic to survive along with seasonal holiday traffic to Cleethorpes and, via branch lines, to the resorts of Mablethorpe and Skegness. By far the most important intermediate town on the line was Louth which was not only a major agricultural centre but home to an enormous maltings complex built near the station in 1870 – destroyed by German bombing in 1940, the 90-ft-high storage chambers were subsequently rebuilt in the early 1950s – much of the freight traffic along the line was generated at Louth.

The through service of passenger trains to and from King's Cross continued until the early 1960s – even in 1961 there were two through buffet car services (one to Cleethorpes and one to Grimsby) to and from the capital on weekdays. In a bid to reduce ever increasing losses diesel multiple units had been introduced for local services as early as 1955 but these failed to stem a decline in passenger usage caused by slow journey times and increasing ownership of cars. The 1963 'Beeching Report' was a bombshell for the inhabitants of East Lincolnshire – all railways were to be closed leaving only Grimsby in the north and Boston in the south to serve as railheads. Closure, not only for the East

THEN
Nicknamed 'Pom-Poms', ex-GCR Class 'J11' 0-6-0 No 64320 and a stablemate wait in the loco yard at Louth for their next turn of duty in September 1954. Built by Neilson, Reid in 1902 this loco was withdrawn from Immingham shed in 1958.

Lincolnshire line but also for the branches to Mablethorpe and Skegness and lines from Lincoln to Boston and Woodhall Junction to Little Steeping, was scheduled for 1964 but a hard-fought campaign by the county and local councils brought a reprieve except for the Woodhall to Boston line which closed on 17 June 1963.

Despite this hard-won battle, the East Lincolnshire line only survived another 7 years and, amidst continuing protest from local councils, closed between Grimsby and Firsby and between Boston and Spalding on 5 October 1970 – the section south of Firsby to Boston along with the branch to Skegness was reprieved and is still open today. Goods traffic continued to use the line between Grimsby and Louth until 1980 when it closed completely.

Today, a 1½-mile stretch of the Grimsby to Firsby section from Ludborough to North Thoresby is operated as a heritage railway by the Lincolnshire Wolds Railway. Starting in 1984, the station, platforms and signal box at Ludborough have since been rebuilt and track relaid to North Thoresby. The present route reopened in 2009 – the first train to work on this line for 47 years. At Ludborough there are working Great Northern Railway signals while a collection of Lincolnshire railway artefacts and a model railway are housed in a small museum on the site. Steam trains now operate between Ludborough and North Thoresby making the railway the only standard-gauge steam railway open to the public in Lincolnshire. Steam locos include 1949-built Robert Stephenson & Hawthorns 0-6-0T *Zebedee*, 1928-built Peckett 0-4-0ST *Fulstow*, 1914-built Peckett 0-4-0ST *Lion* and 1929-built Barclay 0-4-0ST *Spitfire*. Diesels include BR Class 08 diesel shunter D3167. Track laying has already commenced from Ludborough towards Utterby and future plans feature extending the line northwards to Holton-le-Clay and southwards to Louth.

Ludborough Station,
Station Road,
Ludborough,
Lincolnshire DN36 5SQ

01507 363 881
www.lincolnshirewoldsrailway.co.uk

LENGTH
1½ miles

GAUGE
Standard

OPEN
For steam operating days and special events see website

NOW
Restored Peckett 0-4-0ST Fulstow No. 2 *at the end of the line at North Thoresby on 30 March 2013. Built in 1928, this loco worked at Cawdor Quarry in Matlock until 1970.*

THE
ROYAL SCOT
46233

CENTRAL ENGLAND

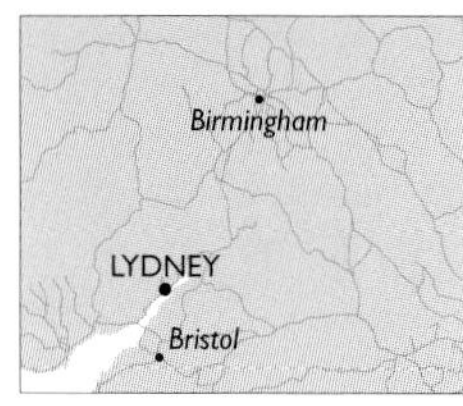

LYDNEY JUNCTION
LYDNEY TOWN
NORCHARD
WHITECROFT
PARKEND

Norchard Station,
Forest Road, Lydney,
Gloucestershire GL15 4ET

01594 845840
www.deanforestrailway.co.uk

LENGTH
4¼ miles

GAUGE
Standard

OPEN
Most Sundays, end February to December, Bank Holidays, Easter to August; most Wednesdays & Saturdays, Easter to October, see website for details

By the early 19th century the Forest of Dean on the west bank of the River Severn in Gloucestershire had become a small, but significant, player in Britain's Industrial Revolution. The mining of coal and iron ore was especially important but transporting these raw materials to local ironworks or the nearest rivers for onward shipment was a slow process. Enter the Severn & Wye Railway & Canal Company (S&WR), which in 1809 began the construction of a tramway through the forest between Lydney and Lydbrook and a 1-mile canal linking Lydney with the River Severn. The steeply-graded 3ft-6in.-gauge horse-drawn tramway, or plateway, opened in 1810 and the canal in 1813, both enterprises speeding up the transport of raw materials.

In 1851 the broad-gauge (7ft 0¼in.) South Wales Railway, engineered by Isambard Kingdom Brunel, opened along the west bank of the River Severn between Gloucester and Chepstow via Lydney. However, the change of gauge between the railway and tramway at Lydney was to become an ever increasing problem. By the 1860s the tramway was worn out after over 50 years of service and in 1868, after successfully experimenting with steam haulage, a broad-gauge line was laid alongside it between Lydney and Speech House Road. Broad-gauge steam locomotives replaced horsepower but more changes were soon looming when the mainline between Gloucester and Chepstow was converted from broad to standard gauge (4ft 8½in.) by the Great Western Railway. By 1874 both the broad-gauge section of the S&WR and the rest of the tramway had been rebuilt to standard gauge. An extension was also built over the impressive Lydbrook Viaduct to Lydbrook Junction where the S&WR met the newly opened Ross & Monmouth Railway. In the same year a mineral loop line was opened between Drybrook Road Junction and Tufts Junction, just south of Whitecroft, and a year later a 2¾-mile branch line from Parkend to Coleford was opened. The latter met the Coleford Railway from Wyesham Junction, near Monmouth, when it opened in 1883.

In 1879 the S&WR amalgamated with the Severn Bridge Railway on the day that the bridge opened, 17 October. Over a mile in length, the single-track bridge was built primarily to carry coal from the Forest of Dean to Sharpness Docks but also provided a route for a passenger service between Lydney and Berkeley Road station on the Midland Railway's (MR) mainline between Gloucester and Bristol. However, the looming opening of the Severn Railway Tunnel and a miners' strike in the Forest was a serious blow to the joint company which went bankrupt in 1885. The company was sold to the GWR and the MR and the railway became the Severn & Wye Joint Railway (S&WJR) in 1894. Along with several short colliery branches and the opening of a short branch line from Drybrook Road to Cinderford in 1900 the S&WJR finally reached its maximum extent of 39 route miles.

The years following the First World War brought a decline in passengers using the S&WJR north of Lydney and the services to Coleford,

Lydbrook Junction and Cinderford all ceased on 8 July 1929. All that remained was the passenger service over the Severn Bridge between Lydney Town and Berkeley Road but this finished on 25 October 1960 following a collision by two barges in thick fog – the damaged bridge was never reopened and was demolished in 1967.

Despite the loss of passenger services the S&WJR was kept busy transporting minerals and freight for many more years. The beginning of the end came when the Serridge Junction to Lydbrook Junction section closed in 1956. With the closure of the last collieries in the area the line northwards from Coleford Junction to Speech House Road and beyond closed completely on 12 August 1963 but the Coleford branch via Parkend remained open for stone traffic from Whitecliff Quarry until 26 March 1976.

The Dean Forest Railway first set up its base at Norchard, north of Lydney, in 1978, having been running steam open days at Parkend since 1972. The scenic 4¼-mile railway from Lydney to Parkend was purchased from British Rail in 1985 and since then has been progressively reopened. Restored steam locomotives operating on the line or under overhaul include GWR 2-6-2 tank No 5541 and BR 0-6-0 pannier tanks Nos 9681 and 9682 along with several ex-WD and industrial examples. There are a number of diesel locos either awaiting restoration or operational including 2 BR Class 14 0-6-0s diesel-hydraulics D9521 and D9555, 2 Class 08, 2 Class 31 and a Class 37. Diesel multiple units are represented by 5 Derby-built Class 108 railcars. A new intermediate station at Whitecroft & Bream was opened in 2012 while future plans include extending the line northwards from Parkend to Speech House Road. North of Parkend the Forest of Dean Family Cycle Trail follows an 11-mile circular route along the trackbed of the Severn & Wye Railway.

NOW

Resident preserved ex-British Railways (WR) '5700' Class 0-6-0PT No 9681 hard at work on the Dean Forest Railway at Upper Forge on 20 December 2012 with an engineers' train. Built at Swindon Works in 1949 this loco was withdrawn in 1965.

SEVERN VALLEY RAILWAY

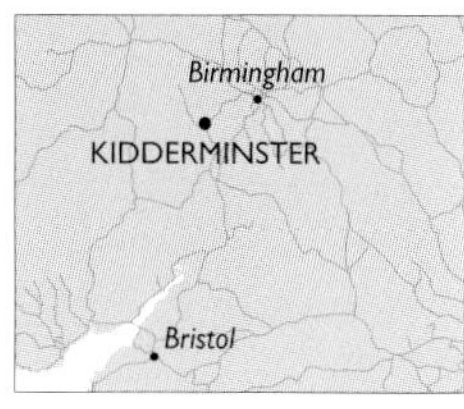

BRIDGNORTH
HAMPTON LOADE
COUNTRY PARK HALT
HIGHLEY
ARLEY
NORTHWOOD HALT
BEWDLEY
KIDDERMINSTER

The 40¾-mile Severn Valley Railway (SVR) between Shrewsbury and Hartlebury, north of Droitwich, was incorporated in 1853. As its name suggests the railway was built along the valley of the River Severn, closely following the west bank of the river for much of its route, and crossing it only once at Victoria Bridge north of Bewdley. Leased from its opening in 1862 by the West Midland Railway, the SVR was eventually taken over by the Great Western Railway (GWR) in 1872. A 3-mile connection from Bewdley to Kidderminster was opened by the GWR in 1878.

Traffic was never heavy on this long rural line – goods consisted mainly of coal from mines at Highley and Alveley, along with some agricultural traffic. Up to the Second World War passenger services consisted of some 5 return journeys each weekday between Shrewsbury and Worcester – journey times for the 52-mile journey were around 2 hrs 45 mins, at a leisurely pace of 19 mph. With increasing competition from road transport, traffic declined considerably in the post-war years – this was certainly not helped by British Railways' timetabling which forced passengers to change trains at Bridgnorth on most through journeys. Inevitably, closure between Shrewsbury and Bewdley followed in 1963 and between Bewdley and Kidderminster/Hartlebury in 1970.

Since then the 16 miles of the Severn Valley Railway south of Bridgnorth to Kidderminster has been reborn as a heritage railway. From the early days in 1970 when a preservation group ran its first train to Hampton Loade, the current Severn Valley Railway now runs a mainly steam-operated service throughout the year between Bridgnorth and Kidderminster where it connects with the national rail network. With

THEN

End of the line – ex-LMS Ivatt Class '2MT' 2-6-2T No 41207 at Bridgnorth with its train to Kidderminster on 6 September 1963 – the Shrewsbury to Bewdley line closed 3 days later. This loco was built at Crewe in 1946 and withdrawn at the end of 1966.

its 6 beautifully restored stations, historic steam locomotives, vintage rolling stock, well-equipped workshops and Engine House Museum, the railway is today one of the most attractive heritage lines in Britain. Intermediate stations are provided at Hampton Loade, Country Park, Highley, Arley, Northwood Halt and Bewdley. The tunnel at Bewdley is 480 yds long.

Train services, mainly steam-hauled, along the Severn Valley Railway are operated by a team of full-time staff and a large band of volunteers. Steam locomotives based on the SVR include 1900-built Hudswell Clarke ex-Port Talbot Railway 0-6-0ST No 813, 1932-built GWR '1400' Class 0-4-2T No 1450, 1949-built BR(WR) '1500' Class 0-6-0T No 1501, 1918-built GWR '2800' Class 2-8-0 No 2857, 1944-built GWR 'Modified Hall' Class 4-6-0 No 6960 *Raveningham Hall*, 1930-built GWR '5700' Class 0-6-0T No 7714, 1945-built SR 'West Country' Class 4-6-2 No 34027 *Taw Valley*, 1951-built Ivatt Class '4' 2-6-0 No 43106 and 1957-built BR Standard Class '4' 4-6-0 No 75069. Diesels are represented by examples of BR Classes 08, 09, 11, 14, 17, 33, 35, 40, 42, 50, 52 and a Class 108 diesel multiple unit.

The railway is open most weekends and during school holidays and most days from Easter to September. Housed in a 19th-century GWR warehouse in the Station Approach, the Kidderminster Railway Museum houses a vast range of railway artefacts. National rail network trains to and from Birmingham and Worcester to Kidderminster are operated by West Midland Trains.

The Railway Station,
Bewdley,
Worcestershire DY10 1QX

01562 757900
www.svr.co.uk

LENGTH
16 miles

GAUGE
Standard

OPEN
Most weekends & during all School Holidays; daily with a few exceptions (see website), Easter to end September; see website for details of numerous special events days

NOW
Preserved ex-GWR 'Manor' Class 4-6-0 No 7812 Erlestoke Manor *with a train of LNER teak carriages arrives at Bewdley station on the Severn Valley Railway. Built at Swindon Works in 1949 this fine loco was withdrawn in late 1965 and was sold for scrap to Dai Woodham of Barry where it stayed for 9 years before being bought for preservation.*

TELFORD STEAM RAILWAY

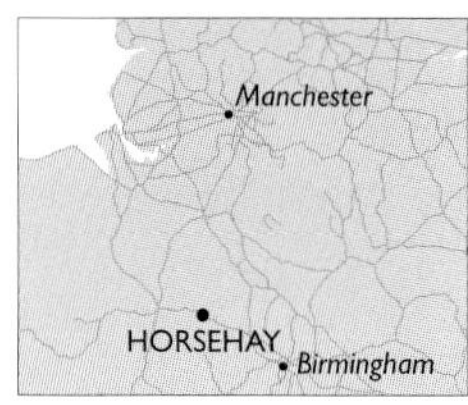

LAWLEY VILLAGE
SPRING VILLAGE
HORSEHAY & DAWLEY

The Old Loco Shed,
Bridge Road,
Horsehay, Telford,
Shropshire TF4 2NF

07816 762790
www.telfordsteamrailway.co.uk

LENGTH
1 mile

GAUGE
Standard

OPEN
Sundays & Bank Holidays,
Easter to September

THEN
Ex-GWR '5101' Class 2-6-2T No 5167 at Buildwas Junction on 21 August 1959. Buildwas was an interchange station with no access by road – the lower level serving the Severn Valley Railway and the upper level, shown in this photo, served by trains from Wellington to Much Wenlock. Behind are the chimneys of coal-fired Ironbridge power station.

NOW
Stars of the Telford Steam Railway at Horsehay in 2008 – much-travelled preserved ex-GWR '5600' Class 0-6-2T No 5619 and 1926-built Peckett 0-4-0ST Rocket. *No 5619 was built at Swindon in 1925 and withdrawn in 1964. After spending 8 years at Dai Woodham's scrapyard in Barry it was bought for preservation.*

A convoluted tale of many railway companies! The branch line from Ketley Junction, to the east of Wellington, to Lightmoor was opened by the Wellington & Severn Junction Railway as far as Horsehay in 1857 and extended to Lightmoor in 1858. The section between Lightmoor and Coalbrookdale had already opened in 1854 as part of a branch line from Madeley Junction. Initially worked by the Coalbrookdale Iron Company the branch from Ketley Junction to Coalbrookdale was leased to the GWR in 1861 and taken over by that company in 1892. To the west, the Much Wenlock & Severn Junction Railway was opened between Buildwas (on the Severn Valley Railway's line from Hartlebury to Shrewsbury) and Much Wenlock in 1862. This line was worked by the West Midlands Railway until taken over by the GWR in 1863. The intervening gap over the River Severn between Coalbrookdale and Buildwas was opened by the Much Wenlock, Craven Arms & Coalbrookdale Railway in 1864. From Much Wenlock the latter company extended westwards beneath Wenlock Edge to Marsh Farm Junction, north of Craven Arms on the Shrewsbury & Hereford Railway, opening in 1867.

The Wellington (Ketley Junction) to Craven Arms (Marsh Farm Junction) railway operated as a 24-mile cross-country route until 1951 when passenger services between Much Wenlock and Craven Arms were withdrawn. Goods trains continued to use the line between Buildwas and Longville until 1963. The remaining stretch of line between Ketley Junction, Buildwas and Much Wenlock reverted to branch line status and was served by 6 return trains each day, the 11¼-mile journey from Wellington to Much Wenlock taking 45–50 minutes. Despite the introduction of diesel multiple units passenger numbers continued to decline and the branch was marked on Map 9 of the 'Beeching Report' as recommended for closure – in fact this came on 23 July 1962, 8 months before publication of the 'Report'.

The Telford Horsehay Steam Trust was founded in 1976 to restore locomotives and rolling stock. It is planned to operate these on the Horsehay to Lightmoor branch, part of the former GWR line from Wellington to Buildwas which closed in 1962. Services along ½-mile of track started in 1984 and a ¼-mile length of 2ft-gauge tramway operated by a 0-4-0 steam tram opened at Horsehay in 1991. Lawley Village was reached from Horsehay & Dawley via Heath Hill Tunnel in 2015. Trains are normally operated by Peckett 1926-built 0-4-0ST *Rocket* while former resident GWR 0-6-2T No 5619 has been away visiting other heritage railways. The railway also has on site several stored steam locomotives, 2 diesel multiple units and 6 small diesel shunters. Future plans for the Telford Steam Railway include an extension southwards to Ironbridge and Buildwas.

CHASEWATER RAILWAY

CHASETOWN
CHASEWATER HEATHS
NORTON LAKESIDE HALT
BROWNHILLS WEST

Chasewater Country Park,
Brownhills West Station,
Pool Road, Brownhills,
Staffordshire WS8 7NL

01543 452623
www.chasewaterrailway.co.uk

LENGTH
2 miles

GAUGE
Standard

OPEN
Trains run on Sundays from Easter to mid October

Situated on part of the old Midland Railway's Brownhills branch line, a colliery line north of Birmingham, which was opened in 1883 and closed by the LMS in 1930, is the Chasewater Railway. One of the earliest preservation projects in Britain, it was founded in 1959 as a static museum run by the Railway Preservation Society. The railway had its first steam day in 1968 and was represented at the Stockton & Darlington Railway 150th anniversary celebrations in 1975. However, by 1982 the line had almost closed and it was not until 1988 that it re-opened with a new terminus at Brownhills West, the original station at Brownhills being demolished due to the building of the M6 toll motorway. A short extension was opened in 1992 with a further one in December 1995, which took the railway over the ¼-mile causeway in Chasewater Pleasure Park, forming a horse-shoe-shape route around Chasewater Lake (built in 1797 as a canal feeder reservoir). Since then the line has been further extended to a new easterly terminus at Chasetown (Church Street). The railway is home to 11 steam and 4 diesel industrial locomotives and passenger services on the line are handled by locomotive-hauled trains and a more recently arrived Class 142 'Pacer' unit. The railway also has a large collection of Wickham trolleys. A 2-ft narrow-gauge railway is currently being built close to the museum at Brownhills West.

NOW
Built in 1964, Hunslet 'Austerity' 0-6-0ST No 66 arrives at Chasewater Heath sidings with former 'Merry-Go-Round' wagons while Hunslet diesel No 6678, built in 1969, waits with National Coal Board mineral wagons.

Located south of Birmingham Snow Hill, the large steam engine shed at Tyseley was opened by the Great Western Railway in 1908 to service locos operating on the new North Warwickshire Line to Stratford-upon-Avon, Honeybourne and Cheltenham. A total of 72 mainly tank engines and freight locomotives were allocated to the shed then and this grew to about 100 by the mid-1950s. The shed's Western Region code was 84E until September 1963 when it was transferred to the London Midland Region with the new code of 2A. Although steam operations ended in 1967 the shed continued to be used by diesel shunters and diesel multiple units until the late 1980s.

BR had already started to demolish the passenger loco roundhouse in 1968 when railway photographer and preservationist Patrick Whitehouse – new owner of 'Castle' Class 4-6-0 No 7029 *Clun Castle* – stepped in and negotiated a lease with BR for the remaining buildings and servicing facilities at Tyseley.

Formerly known as the Birmingham Railway Museum Trust, the Tyseley Locomotive Works houses a large collection of locomotives and rolling stock based in the former GWR repair shop. The site is fully equipped for locomotive preservation and overhaul and is home to many steam locomotives, both operational, being restored or stored, including GWR 'Castle' Class 4-6-0s No 7029 *Clun Castle*, No 5043 *Earl of Mount Edgcumbe* and No 5080 *Defiant*, GWR 'Hall' Class 4-6-0 No 4965 *Rood Ashton Hall*, GWR 'Manor' Class 4-6-0 No 7812 *Erlestoke Manor*, new-build 'Grange' Class 4-6-0 No 6880 *Betton Grange*, BR Standard Class 8 4-6-2 No 71000 *Duke of Gloucester* and LMS 'Jubilee' Class 4-6-0 No 5593 *Kolhapur*. There are also various diesel and industrial locos based here including examples of BR Classes 20, 40, 47 and 50. A varied collection of rolling stock includes a travelling post office and a steam crane. The museum also arranges driving and firing lessons on steam locomotives, which operate along the 600-yd track within the site.

Open Days feature train rides, locomotive line-ups, demonstrations with locomotive cavalcades, turntable operation and shunting. Vintage Trains also operate out of Tyseley with the steam-hauled 'Shakespeare Express' to Stratford-upon-Avon.

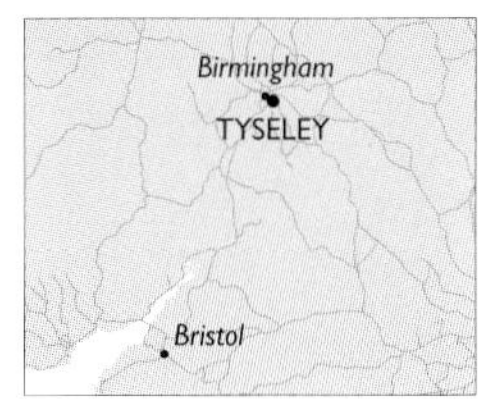

• **TYSELEY**

□ TYSELEY LOCOMOTIVE WORKS

670 Warwick Road, Tyseley, Birmingham B11 2HL

0121 707 4696
www.vintagetrains.co.uk/shakespeare-express

GAUGE
Standard

OPEN
On selected Open Days, see website for details

NOW
An impressive line-up of preserved ex-GWR locos at Tyseley Locomotive Works on 28 June 2008. From left to right are 'Castle' Class 4-6-0s Nos 5029 Nunney Castle, *5043* Earl of Mount Edgcumbe *and 7029* Clun Castle *and 'Hall' Class 4-6-0s Nos 4936* Kinlet Hall *and 4965* Rood Ashton Hall.

GLOUCESTERSHIRE WARWICKSHIRE RAILWAY

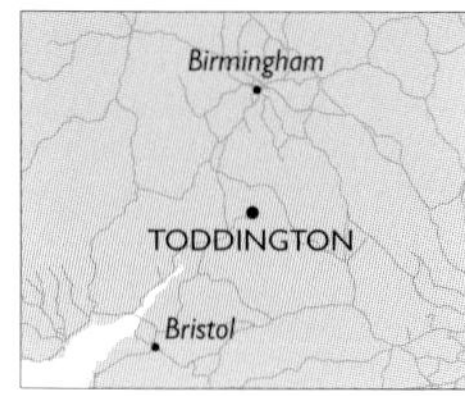

BROADWAY
TODDINGTON
HAYLES ABBEY HALT
WINCHCOMBE
GOTHERINGTON
CHELTENHAM RACECOURSE

The north-south railway between Stratford-upon-Avon and Cheltenham was a very belated attempt by the Great Western Railway to win back traffic from the Midland Railway's route between Birmingham and Bristol. Opened throughout in 1908 it was one of the last stretches of double-track mainline to be built in Britain until the Selby cut-off on the East Coast Main Line in 1983. During the 1930s the line was used by the highly successful GWR's streamlined diesel railcar express between Birmingham and Cardiff. After the Second World War the route saw the introduction of 'The Cornishman' express from Wolverhampton (LL) to Penzance and iron ore trains bound for South Wales from the Northamptonshire open cast mines via Stratford-upon-Avon. Summer Saturdays also saw a continual stream of steam-hauled holiday specials – a veritable feast for railway photographers during the last year of steam in 1965. Decline soon followed with the remaining spartan passenger service ceasing in 1966 leaving only freight traffic until 1976 when a derailment north of Cheltenham brought about complete closure between Stratford and Cheltenham. The track had been lifted by 1979.

A preservation group moved into Toddington in 1984 and have since relaid the line southwards to Cheltenham Racecourse and northwards to Broadway. Trains currently run southwards from Toddington to Cheltenham Racecourse with intermediate stations at Hayles Abbey Halt, Winchcombe (originally the station building at Monmouth Troy) and Gotherington via the 693-yd Greet Tunnel. Northwards from Toddington trains run to Broadway, which was reached in 2018. Motive

THEN
Ex-GWR 'Castle' Class 4-6-0 No 5021 Whittington Castle *passes through Hayles Abbey Halt with a Wolverhampton to West of England express on 25 July 1959. Built at Swindon Works in 1932 this loco was withdrawn in September 1962.*

power is drawn from a fleet of GWR steam locos: 'Manor' Class 4-6-0 No 7820 *Dinmore Manor*, 'Modified Hall' 4-6-0 No 7903 *Foremarke Hall* and '4200' Class 2-8-0T No 4270 (plus SR 'Merchant Navy' Class 4-6-2 No 35006 *Peninsular & Oriental S. N. Co.*) – all 4 locomotives were rescued from Dai Woodham's scrapyard in Barry. A large fleet of BR diesel locomotives is also based at Toddington including examples of Classes 20, 24, 26, 37, 45 and 47 while electro-diesel No E6036 (73 129) is also active. A 3-car Class 117 diesel multiple unit completes the roster. Visiting mainline locomotives from other heritage railways are also a common sight on the railway.

A journey along the line takes passengers through the picturesque North Gloucestershire countryside with fine views of the Cotswold escarpment, past the reopened Hayles Abbey Halt to the beautifully restored station at Winchcombe, and then through the 693-yd Greet Tunnel to the terminus at Cheltenham Racecourse. The future northward extension from Broadway to Honeybourne (where a new island platform has already been built) to provide connection with the national rail network is the long-term goal for the railway as is a short southward extension from Racecourse Station into Cheltenham.

The 2ft-gauge North Gloucestershire Railway operates along a ½-mile of track adjacent to the GWR station site at Toddington. The restored Midland Railway signal box from California Crossing in Gloucester (100 yards from my childhood home) has been re-erected here.

The Railway Station, Toddington, Gloucestershire GL54 5DT

01242 621405
www.gwsr.com

LENGTH
14 miles

GAUGE
Standard

OPEN
Weekends & Bank Holidays, April to November; Tuesdays to Thursdays, April to October; Santa Specials in December (see website)

NOW
Preserved BR-built 'Manor' Class 4-6-0 No 7820 Dinmore Manor *passes through the newly reopened Hayles Abbey Halt on the Gloucestershire Warwickshire Railway in 2017. Built at Swindon in 1950 this loco had a short life before being withdrawn in 1965. It then spent 14 years at Dai Woodham's scrapyard at Barry before being bought for preservation.*

BATTLEFIELD LINE RAILWAY

SHACKERSTONE
MARKET BOSWORTH
SHENTON

Shackerstone Railway Station,
Shackerstone,
Leicestershire CV13 6NW

01827 880754
www.battlefieldline.co.uk

LENGTH
4¾ miles

GAUGE
Standard

OPEN
Weekends, Easter to October; Wednesday afternoons, July & August, Christmas Specials on December weekends

The 5-mile Battlefield Line, named after the nearby site of the Battle of Bosworth (1485), is situated on the old LNW & Midland Joint Railway Charnwood Forest line between Nuneaton and Coalville, opened in 1873 and closed to passengers in 1931. It continued to be used by freight and excursion trains into the 1960s until the Coalville Junction to Shackerstone was closed completely in 1964. The Ashby to Nuneaton section lingered on for freight until 1968 when it was also closed.

A preservation group took over in 1969 and has since opened the operating line from Shackerstone to Shenton via Market Bosworth. A collection of diesel multiple units and diesel locomotives are based on this typical English rural railway, which runs through delightful countryside alongside the Ashby Canal which originally opened in 1804. Steam locos visiting from other heritage railways make regular appearances while examples of privately-owned BR mainline diesels (Classes 33, 37, 47) and railway-owned diesel multiple units (Classes 116, 118 and 122) are based here.

The 'Tudor Rose' dining train runs on the third Sunday of each month and the Bosworth Battlefield Country Park can be reached on foot from Shenton station, this building being originally situated at Leicester Humberstone Road.

NOW
Preserved ex-GWR '4575' Class 2-6-2T No 5542 heads out of Shackerstone station with diesel railcars Class '118' No 51131 and Class '122' No 55005 in tow, 4 January 2020.

The Rushden Historical Transport Society aims to partly reopen the former Midland railway branch line from Wellingborough to Higham Ferrers. Passenger services were withdrawn on 15 June 1959 and the line closed completely in 1969. The society is currently based at Rushden station where there is ½-mile of running track. Motive power at Rushden includes BR Class 31 diesel No 31206, a Sentinel shunter, Class 121 'Bubble Car', Class 142 'Pacer' 2-car diesel unit and 2 industrial steam saddle tank locos awaiting restoration. Rushden station is a transport museum which has a collection of many railway artefacts, buses, an Andrew Barclay 0-4-0 steam locomotive and signalling equipment. The former waiting rooms have been converted into a social club with a Victorian-style real ale bar complete with gas lighting.

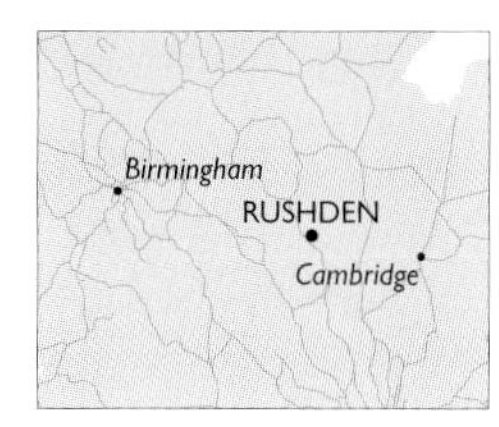

RUSHDEN

The Railway Station,
Station Approach, Rushden,
Northants NN10 0AW

01933 318988
www.rhts.co.uk

LENGTH
¼ mile

GAUGE
Standard

OPEN
Museum: Saturday afternoons & Sundays, Easter to end October; special events days see website

THEN
BR Standard Class '2MT' 2-6-2T No 84006 at Rushden station with a train from Wellingborough on 28 May 1959. This loco was built at Crewe in 1953 and withdrawn in 1965. Rushden station is now the headquarters of the Rushden, Higham & Wellingborough Railway.

NORTHAMPTON & LAMPORT RAILWAY

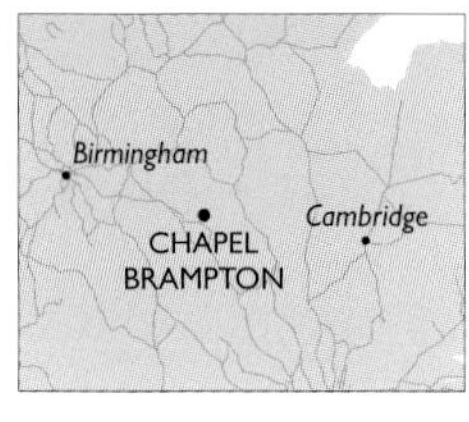

PITSFORD & BRAMPTON
BOUGHTON

Pitsford & Brampton Station,
Pitsford Road,
Chapel Brampton,
Northampton NN6 8BA

01604 820327
www.nlr.org.uk

LENGTH
2 miles

GAUGE
Standard

OPEN
Bank Holiday weekends; Sundays, March to November; Santa Specials on three weekends in December

When large deposits of iron ore were discovered in Northamptonshire in 1851 the London & North Western Railway (LNWR) put forward a proposal to build a railway to tap into this lucrative trade. Involving the boring of tunnels at Kelmarsh and Oxendon the 18-mile single-track railway between Market Harborough and Northampton was opened in 1859. In addition to the tunnels there were 4 intermediate stations (from north to south: Kelmarsh, Lamport, Brixworth and Pitsford & Brampton) and 5 level crossings. A station was also planned for Boughton but the 5th Earl Spencer of nearby Althorp had insisted on a more convenient station at Pitsford & Brampton. Two further stations were later opened: Clipston & Oxenden, in 1863 and Spratton in 1864. At about this time the entire route was doubled along with additional single-bore tunnels at Kelmarsh and Oxendon.

Although passenger traffic was never heavy on the line it did carry large quantities of locally grown sugar beet from Pitsford & Brampton and also served a large opencast ironstone quarry at Scaldwell near Brixworth. A large cold store was built by the Ministry of Food as a supply depot adjacent to Pitsford & Brampton station during the Second World War.

By the early 1920s passengers were served by 8 southbound trains and 7 northbound trains all of which apart from 1 service in each direction stopped at all of the intermediate stations. By 1948 this had dropped to 5 southbound and 6 northbound, in both cases 3 trains started or ended their journeys at Nottingham – the 64¾ miles between Northampton and Nottingham taking up to a leisurely 3 hours!

The railway's final years were marked by a series of closures and reopenings. While Spratton station closed in 1949 and Pitsford & Brampton in 1950, the line remained open until 4 January 1960 when it closed to passenger traffic. Freight trains continued to use the route for many more years and it was reopened to through passenger trains on 6 January 1969, closed again on 1 May 1972, reopened for a northbound service on 10 July 1972 and permanently closed to passenger services on 26 August 1973. Freight services continued until 16 August 1981 when the line closed completely.

Following closure of the railway the track was lifted. Thirteen miles of the trackbed were sold to Northampton County Council and 1 mile at the northern end to Leicestershire County Council in 1987. It was reopened as a linear park known as the Brampton Valley Way in 1993 and now also forms part of National Cycle Network Route 6 and the Midshires Way Long Distance Path. South of Brixworth the Brampton Valley Way meets up with the Northampton & Lamport Railway which now shares the trackbed (separated by heavy-duty fencing) for 2 miles through its headquarters at Pitsford & Brampton station to a new southern terminus at Boughton. This heritage railway opened to the public in 1996 and is currently planning to extend northwards over the River Nene to Brixworth.

The headquarters of the railway at Pitsford & Brampton is made up of a single through platform with portable buildings and the LNWR working signal box which was moved from Little Bowden Crossing south of Market Harborough and rebuilt on its present site. The booking office is the top half of the signal box from Lamport station. The railway is home to 7 steam locomotives, many of them awaiting restoration, including 5 industrial examples and GWR '2800' Class 2-8-0 No 3862 and GWR 'Hall' Class 4-6-0 No 5967 *Bickmarsh Hall*. Diesels are represented by BR Classes 31 and 47 and 2 industrial shunters.

South of the station the Way and the railway keep company past Pitsford Sidings signal box which was moved from its original location at Wolverton Works on the West Coast Main Line. Still following the Nene Valley the railway reaches its southern terminus at Boughton where there is car parking and a pub.

NOW

The working signal box at the headquarters of the Northampton & Lamport Railway at Pitsford & Brampton station. Built by the London & North Western Railway, the box was originally sited at Little Bowden level crossing south of Market Harborough and rebuilt on its present site.

CAMBRIAN HERITAGE RAILWAYS

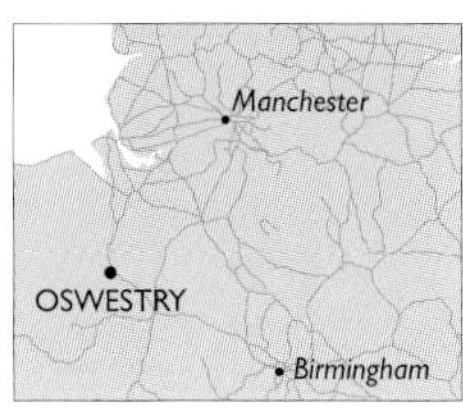

OSWESTRY
LLYNCLYS SOUTH
PENYGARREG LANE HALT

Old Station Building,
Oswald Road, Oswestry,
Shropshire SY11 1RE

01691 728131
www.cambrianrailways.com

LENGTH
1 mile

GAUGE
Standard

OPEN
Weekends & Bank Holiday Mondays, April to October

The 2½-mile single-track branch line from Gobowen, on the Shrewsbury to Wrexham mainline, to Oswestry was opened by the Shrewsbury & Chester Railway in 1848 – the company was amalgamated with the Great Western Railway (GWR) in 1854. From 1864 Oswestry was also served by the Cambrian Railway's line from Whitchurch to Welshpool – the town also became the headquarters and main workshops of that railway. Following the CR's absorption by the GWR in 1922 all trains from Gobowen were then diverted to the former company's station in 1924.

Both listed for closure in the 'Beeching Report', the CR line closed on 18 January 1965 while the branch from Gobowen survived until 7 November 1966. Despite closure to passenger services the branch, along with the former CR line south of Oswestry to Llynclys Junction and Llanddu Quarry near Blodwell (on the closed Llangyog branch line along the Tanat Valley) remained open for stone traffic until 1989 when it was mothballed. The intact line was purchased by Shropshire County Council from Network Rail in 2008 and an umbrella organisation known as the Cambrian Heritage Railway plan to reopen the entire route as a heritage railway.

Cambrian Heritage Railways is the umbrella banner for the Cambrian Railways Society and the Cambrian Railways Trust. The former plans to reopen the ex-CR Tanat Valley line from Blodwell to Llynclys Junction; the latter plans to reopen the ex-CR line from Oswestry to Llynclys, where the two railways will link up. At Oswestry, the Cambrian Railways Trust's railway museum and depot were once part of a major railway complex in the town that, until takeover by the GWR in 1922, was the headquarters of the Cambrian Railways. As late as the 1960s, Oswestry was the headquarters for the Central Wales Division of BR Western Region and the workshops were one of the last locations to undertake steam locomotive repairs. On display in the old railway building are artefacts from the Cambrian Railways with some also arranged in a former GWR autocar.

Trains currently operate at weekends from two separate locations: at Oswestry station and for ¾-mile from Llynclys South station to Penygarreg Lane.

THEN
The sad remains of a once grand station at Oswestry, the headquarters of Cambrian Railways, seen here after closure in 1966.

NOW
Seen here on 16 May 2015, short brake van rides are provided by Cambrian Heritage Railways from their imposing station at Oswestry.

MIDLAND RAILWAY – BUTTERLEY

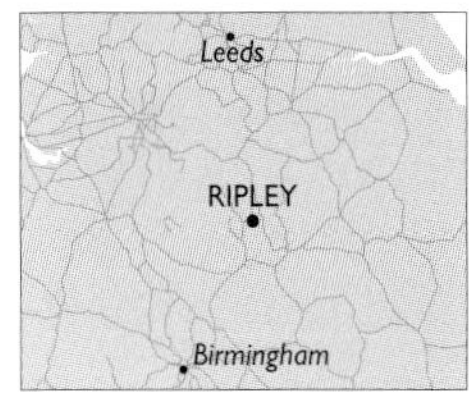

HAMMERSMITH
BUTTERLEY
SWANWICK JUNCTION

Butterley Station, Ripley, Derbyshire DE5 3QZ

01773 570140
www.midlandrailway-butterley.co.uk

LENGTH
3½ miles

GAUGES
Mainline: standard; narrow gauge: 2ft; miniature: 3½in. and 5in.

OPEN
Every weekend March to October & December; every Wednesday April to October; daily August & most school holidays

Situated on part of the former Midland Railway line from Pye Bridge to Ambergate, which was opened in 1875 and closed by British Railways in 1968, is the Midland Railway – Butterley (formerly known as the Midland Railway Centre). Re-opened by a preservation group in 1973, the first passenger trains ran in 1981. With its headquarters at Butterley, the centre, famous for its quality restoration work, occupies a 57-acre site and operates trains along a 3½-mile section of track including crossing a viaduct over Butterley Reservoir. The centre is home to 3 registered charities, 39 specialist groups, 4 museums, a miniature railway and a narrow-gauge railway. The Princess Royal Class Locomotive Trust is based at Butterley, also home to their 'Coronation' Class 4-6-2 No 6233 *Duchess of Sutherland*. Either on static display in the Matthew Kirtley Museum or being restored, other steam locomotives include MR '156' Class 2-4-0 No 158A, LMS 'Princess Royal' Class 4-6-2 No 46203 *Princess Margaret Rose*, 2 LMS Class '3F' 0-6-0Ts Nos 47327 and 47564, BR Standard Class '5' 4-6-0 No 73129 along with examples of 7 industrial tank locomotives. The large and varied collection of diesels are represented by industrial types along with examples of BR Classes 02, 03, 08, 11, 20, 25, 31, 40, 44 (D4 *Great Gable*), 45, 46, 47, 52 along with Class 77 (EM2) electric loco No 27000 *Electra*.

Over 100 items of historic rolling stock are also based here. The standard-gauge operating line is authentically signalled and boasts 3 fully restored and operational Midland Railway signal boxes, originally from Kettering, Ais Gill and Kilby Bridge. The dual-gauge (3½in. and 5in.) Butterley Park Miniature Railway operates on Sundays and Bank holidays from Easter to September. The 2ft-gauge Golden Valley Light Railway runs every weekend from mid-March to late October.

NOW
BR Class 40 diesel-electric D212 (40012) Aureol *recreates the 'Irish Mail' train at the Midland Railway – Butterley. Built at Vulcan Foundry by English Electric in 1959 this loco was withdrawn in 1984. Named after a ship of the Elder Dempster Lines, the loco received its name in 1960.*

Following closure of the remaining part of the Great Central mainline in 1969 (see page 110) a short section from Nottingham southwards to an MOD ordnance depot at Ruddington was kept open until the early 1980s. On closure of the depot the railway was reopened by a group of enthusiasts as Nottingham Transport Heritage Centre and now operates passenger trains between Ruddington and East Leake on most weekends during the year – trains are normally operated by diesel multiple units although the railway is also home to a large number of mainline diesels and a collection of mainly industrial steam locomotives, many of them in storage or being overhauled. Diesels based at Ruddington include examples of BR Classes 03, 08, 20, 37 46, 47, 31, 56 along with Class 108, 116, and 144 diesel multiple units.

NHR trains operate from Ruddington to Rushcliffe Halt and East Leake but there are currently no facilities to leave or join the train at East Leake. Freight trains carrying gypsum still use this line between Loughborough (via a spur from the Midland Main Line) and East Leake, making the NHR one of the only British heritage lines to support freight traffic. A long-term goal is to reconnect the two Great Central heritage railways by reinstating a bridge at Loughborough to enable trains to run between Leicester North and the outskirts of Nottingham once more.

Ruddington Fields Station,
Mere Way, Ruddington,
Nottingham NG11 6JS

0115 9405705
www.gcrn.co.uk

LENGTH
10 miles

GAUGE
Standard

OPEN
Most weekends & Bank Holiday Mondays, April to October; Santa Specials in December (see website)

NOW

Preserved Stanier Class '8F' 2-8-0 No 8274 stands outside the workshop at the Nottingham Heritage Railway on 10 June 2017. This loco had an interesting life being built by the North British Locomotive Company for the War Department in 1940 before being sent to Turkey where it worked until 1983. It was purchased by the Churchill 8F Locomotive Company in 1989 and returned to the UK for preservation.

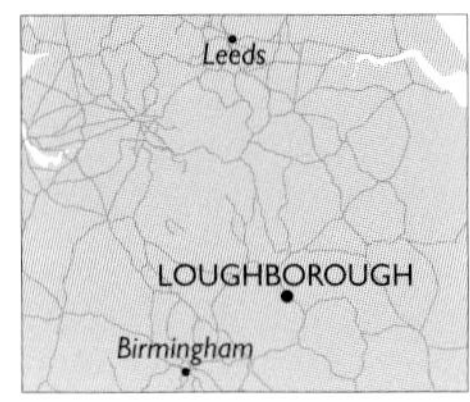

LOUGHBOROUGH

LOUGHBOROUGH CENTRAL
QUORN & WOODHOUSE
ROTHLEY
LEICESTER NORTH

Great Central Station,
Great Central Road,
Loughborough,
Leicestershire LE11 1RW

01509 632323
www.gcrailway.co.uk

LENGTH
8 miles

GAUGE
Standard

OPEN
Weekends throughout the year; selected weekdays & special events (see website)

Seen as part of a major trunk route linking the North of England and the East Midlands with London and the Continent, the Great Central Railway's (GCR) 88¾-mile London Extension from Nottingham (Victoria) to Aylesbury opened in 1899. To the north of Nottingham the GCR had already opened a loop line from Sheffield via Chesterfield while to the south of Quainton Road in Buckinghamshire the new railway was jointly owned with the existing Metropolitan Railway to Marylebone. Built to the Continental loading gauge and with no level crossings, the new double-track railway was designed for fast freight and passenger traffic although the extension south from London through a planned Channel Tunnel to northern France never materialised.

An 8¼-mile line linking the London Extension at Culworth Junction (south of Woodford Halse) with the Great Western Railway at Banbury was opened in 1900 – this was by far the busiest section of the Great Central with vast amounts of freight including coal and iron ore and through cross-country passenger trains passing over it day and night until the early 1960s.

Competing with the parallel Midland Railway route out of St Pancras and the Great Northern route out of King's Cross, the Great Central never lived up to its promoters' expectations as an important high-speed passenger railway – freight traffic was far more lucrative although 2 named trains, the 'Master Cutler' (to Sheffield until 1958) and the 'South Yorkshireman' (to Bradford until 1960), operated out of Marylebone until the whole route was transferred from the Eastern Region of British Railways to the London Midland Region in 1960. From that date passenger services were restricted to around 4 stopping trains a day between Marylebone and Nottingham along with 1 overnight train to Manchester – the through coach carried on this train to and from Liverpool (Central) was withdrawn on 5 March 1962. The 2 inter-regional trains using the route ran between York and Bournemouth in the daytime and between York and Swindon overnight. With economies and rationalisation looming throughout the British Railways' network, the writing was on the wall for the Great Central – its duplication of other routes being its final downfall. Listed for closure in the 'Beeching Report' (BR had estimated this would save £900,000 per year), the line lost its through freight trains in 1965 and the Marylebone to Nottingham steam-hauled passenger service on 5 September 1966. The last scheduled steam services – the 5.15 p.m. Nottingham (Victoria) to Marylebone and the 10.45 p.m. return – ran on Saturday 3 September and were hauled by Stanier Class '5' 4-6-0 No 44984. The Great Central had indeed Gone Completely although the 43¼-mile section from Rugby Central to Nottingham Victoria continued to be served by a DMU service until 5 May 1969.

Following closure of the Great Central, the section from Loughborough to Quorn & Woodhouse was re-opened by the Main Line Steam Trust in 1973, to Rothley in 1976 and finally to a new station at Leicester North in 1991. Uniquely among heritage lines, it is double-track from Loughborough to Rothley so that the railway can operate with the appearance of a mainline. A very large collection of impressive mainline preserved steam and diesel locomotives is based on the Great Central Railway to provide a variety of train operations, and visiting locomotives can frequently be seen in action. The impressive collection of steam locomotives, either operational or being overhauled, based at Loughborough include the following: GWR 'Modified Hall' Class 4-6-0 No 6990 *Witherslack Hall*, BR Standard Class '9F' 2-10-0 No 92214, LMS Ivatt Class '2' 2-6-0 No 46521, BR Standard Class '2' 2-6-0s Nos 78018 and 78019, LMS Class '5' 4-6-0s No 45305 and 45491, BR Standard Class '5' 4-6-0 No 73156, LMS Class '8F' 2-8-0s Nos 48305 and 48624, BR Standard Class '7' 4-6-2 No 70013 *Oliver Cromwell*, GCR '8k' Class 2-8-0 No 63601, SR 'N15' Class 4-6-0 No 777 *Sir Lamiel* and SR 'West Country' Class 4-6-2 No 34039 *Boscastle*. BR diesels are represented by examples from Classes 08, 10, 20, 25, 27, 31, 33, 37, 45, 47 and 50.

A restored Travelling Post Office train complete with mail bag exchanger is occasionally demonstrated on the railway. Stations have been restored to different periods in the railway's history – Loughborough is typical of the 1960s, Quorn & Woodhouse recreates the 1940s and Rothley captures the Edwardian era. Passengers are conveyed in traditional mainline style through delightful Leicestershire hunting countryside. The 1-mile former industrial branch line serving granite quarries from Swithland Sidings to Mountsorrel was reopened in 2013.

NOW
Preserved BR-built Class 'K1' 2-6-0 No 62005 heads through Quorn & Woodhouse station on the Great Central Railway with a demonstration goods train, 13 January 2020. This loco was built by the North British Locomotive Company in 1949 and withdrawn from Sunderland shed at the end of 1967. It regularly performs on the Fort William to Mallaig 'The Jacobite' train in the summer months (see pages 198–9).

CHURNET VALLEY RAILWAY

LEEKBROOK
CHEDDLETON
CONSALL
KINGSLEY & FROGHALL

Kingsley & Froghall Station,
Froghall,
Staffordshire ST10 2HA

01538 360522
www.churnetvalleyrailway.co.uk

LENGTH
5¼ miles

GAUGE
Standard

OPEN
Sundays, March to early October; weekends & Bank Holidays, Easter to end September; Wednesdays in August; for special events see website

By the late 18th century the region centred on Stoke-on-Trent was at the heart of the Industrial Revolution. Rich in coal, ironstone and limestone deposits, the area was a heavy mix of mines, quarries, blast furnaces and ironworks. All of these industries depended on a transport network to move raw materials and finished goods – the main artery being the 93½-mile Trent & Mersey Canal which, as its name implies, linked two of Britain's major rivers through the industrial heartland of Staffordshire. Completed in 1777, its construction included the building of 70 locks and 5 tunnels. An 18-mile branch, known as the Caldon Canal, was opened between Etruria and Froghall via the Churnet Valley in 1779 – with branches to Leek and Uttoxeter it was linked to limestone quarries at Cauldon [sic] by a horse-drawn tramway.

However, the canals' monopoly was short-lived with the opening of the North Staffordshire Railway (NSR) from Macclesfield southwards to a junction with the Grand Junction Railway at Norton Bridge in 1845. By 1852, with its headquarters in Stoke, the railway, nicknamed the 'Knotty' after the company's Staffordshire Knot trademark, owned over 200 miles of railway and the Trent & Mersey Canal – all serving the growing industries in this area.

Despite its industrial heartland, the highly profitable NSR also owned several routes that were later widely promoted for their scenic beauty. One of these, opened in 1849, was the 27¾-mile double-track line along the scenic Churnet Valley from North Rode, south of Macclesfield, to Uttoxeter on the company's line from Crewe to Derby. Paralleling the Caldon Canal from Leek to Froghall, the railway was built over the course of the Uttoxeter branch of the canal south of here. With its ornate stations and usefulness as an alternative route for through goods trains avoiding congested Stoke, the line also carried locally-generated agricultural and livestock traffic, daytrippers from the industrial Potteries to scenic delights along the line and racegoers to Uttoxeter racecourse.

The Churnet Valley line ended as a through route in 1960 with the closure of the section north of Leek. The remainder of the line from Leek to Uttoxeter struggled on with a few workmen's trains until they were withdrawn in 1965. All that remained were industrial sand trains from Oakamoor northwards to Leekbrook Junction and thence to Stoke, which ceased in 1988.

In the meantime, the Cheddleton Railway Centre had opened its doors to the public at Cheddleton station in the 1970s. The purchase of 7 miles of the mothballed line between Oakamoor and Leekbrook Junction followed in 1994 and public services commenced a few years later. The railway trackbed south of Oakamoor through Alton Towers station is now a footpath and cycleway forming part of National Cycle Network 54. North of Leekbrook Junction the railway awaits reopening through Birchall Tunnel to the town of Leek.

Operated almost entirely by a large band of volunteers, the scenic Churnet Valley Railway operates both steam and diesel trains between Kingsley & Froghall and Cheddleton stations. In 2010 certain train journeys from the Churnet Valley Railway were extended to Cauldon Low via Leekbrook Junction and the Moorland & City Railway. In 2015 this steeply-graded line as far as Ipstones Loop was purchased by the Churnet Valley Railway which now operates occasional extended services from Cheddleton. Trains no longer operate to Cauldon Low and there are no passenger facilities currently at Ipstones.

Steam locomotives, both operational, being restored or stored, at the CVR include some foreigners: Polish 'TKh' 0-6-0Ts Nos 2871 and 2944 *Hotspur*, USATC Class 'S160' 2-8-0s Nos 5197 and 6046 and LMS Class '8F' 2-8-0 No 48173. Diesels are represented by examples of BR Classes 08, 20, 25 and 33.

NOW

A night-time scene at Cheddleton station on the Churnet Valley Railway on 2 February 2008. On the left is preserved BR Standard Class '4' 2-6-4T No 80098 with a demonstration goods train while on the right is a Derby Lightweight diesel railcar.

APEDALE VALLEY LIGHT RAILWAY

SILVERDALE
APEDALE ROAD
BURLEY SHALES
MIRY QUARRY

Apedale Community Park, Loomer Road, Chesterton, Newcastle-under-Lyme, Staffordshire ST5 7LB

0845 0941953
www.avlr.org.uk

LENGTH
¼ mile

GAUGE
2ft

OPEN
See website for details

The Moseley Heritage Trust owns a major collection of industrial narrow-gauge locomotives and other equipment and the Apedale Valley Light Railway is its working arm. The Trust was formed in 1967 by pupils at the Moseley Hall Grammar School (later to become a comprehensive) and by the 1990s there was ½-mile of 2ft-gauge track running round the school grounds with about 15 locomotives. However the Trust were evicted from the school in 1998 and the search for a suitable alternative site eventually led them to the Apedale Country Park, formerly a colliery, near Stoke-on-Trent where they plan to develop a 1-mile-long railway on which they can operate and display their collection of 60+ locomotives. Once owned by the Reverend 'Teddy' Boston, the narrow-gauge equipment from the Cadeby Light Railway (closed 2005) now forms part of the collection.

The Trust moved to Apedale in 2006 and started to convert former colliery buildings as a new home for their collection. A new locomotive storage building opened in 2008 and the ¼-mile running line 2 years later. Silverdale station was opened in 2011 and a demonstration light railway, 'Tracks to the Trenches', was opened in 2014 to commemorate the start of the First World War. The railway currently ends at Apedale Road but plans are in hand to extend it to Burley Shales and Miry Quarry, giving a total operating length of 1 mile.

NOW
Restored Henschel locomotive No 15968 and Kerr Stuart No 3014 at work on the Apedale Valley Light Railway during the 100th anniversary of the start of World War I, 7 September 2014.

Operating on an old colliery railway that opened in 1893 to serve the Cheadle Coalfield, the Foxfield Railway is situated very close to Blythe Bridge station on the main Stoke-on-Trent to Derby railway line. After closure in 1965 a preservation group took over and passengers were first carried in 1967, with Caverswall station being opened in 1982. Small and powerful industrial steam and diesel locomotives haul trains up gradients as steep as 1-in-19 to a summit 705 ft above sea level. The large collection of industrial locomotives, of which 4 steam are operational, includes 23 steam and 12 diesel including a BR Class 142 'Pacer' 2-car unit. The operational steam locomotives include 1879-built Beyer, Peacock 0-4-0ST No 1827, 1901-built Dübs 0-4-0 crane tank No 4101 Dübs, 1950-built Hunslet Austerity 0-6-0ST No 3694 *Whiston* and 1956-built Hunslet Austerity 0-6-0ST No 3839 *Wimblebury*. Future plans include opening both ends of the railway to passenger operation, including the 1-in-19 Dilhorne Bank, and developing a mining museum at the old colliery.

The North Staffordshire Railway Rolling Stock Restoration Trust has a collection of historically important NSR coaches and wagons, some of which are operational or being restored. Some of these vehicles were discovered in recent years in woodland alongside Rudyard Lake, with one that was being used as a barn.

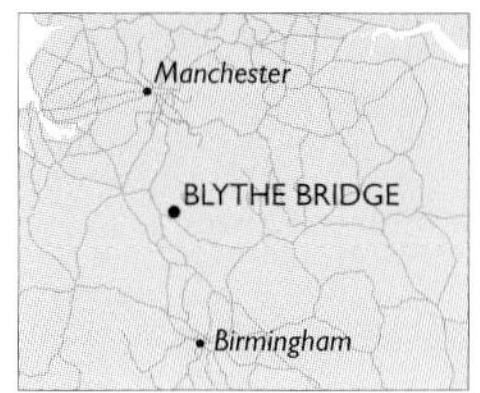

BLYTHE BRIDGE
CAVERSWALL ROAD
DILHORNE PARK
FOXFIELD COLLIERY

Caverswall Road Station,
Blythe Bridge, Stoke-on-Trent,
Staffordshire ST11 9BG

01782 396210
www.foxfieldrailway.co.uk

LENGTH
2¾ miles

GAUGE
Standard

OPEN
Weekends and Bank Holiday Mondays, April to October and December; Wednesdays, mid-July–end August

NOW
Former National Coal Board Andrew Barclay 0-4-0ST No 22 shunting at Dilhorne Colliery on the Foxfield Railway, 22 July 2007.

BARROW HILL ROUNDHOUSE

BARROW HILL ROUNDHOUSE □

Campbell Drive, Barrow Hill, Staveley, Chesterfield, Derbyshire S43 2PR

01246 475554
www.barrowhill.org

GAUGE
Standard

OPEN
Weekends throughout the year; for special events see website

Opened by the Midland Railway in 1870 to serve the local Staveley Iron Works, Barrow Hill is the last surviving operational roundhouse engine shed in Britain. The shed comprised 24 roads, each between 60 ft and 80 ft long, served by a central turntable. At its peak in the 1920s around 90 locos were based there. It closed to steam on 4 October 1965 when there were about 30 locomotives allocated to the shed (41E) but continued to be used by diesel shunters until complete closure in February 1991.

In the same year the Barrow Hill Engine Shed Society persuaded the local council to give the building a Grade 2 Listed Building Status to prevent demolition. Following years of neglect and vandalism the historic building was eventually purchased by Chesterfield Borough Council from the British Rail Property Board in 1996. Since then the building has been completely restored, opening its doors to the public for the first time in 1998. With physical links to the national rail network, the Roundhouse is now home to a wide range of preserved steam, diesel and electric locomotives and is frequently visited by mainline railtours and heritage steam locomotives. Steam and diesel trains also operate within the site. The Deltic Preservation Society (www.thedps.co.uk) has recently built a maintenance depot and museum next to the Roundhouse.

Steam locos currently based at Barrow Hill include 1919-built GCR Class '11F' (LNER Class 'D11') 4-4-0 No 506 *Butler Henderson*, 1902-built MR Compound 4-4-0 No 1000, 1878-built MR '1F' 0-6-0T No 41708, 1930-built GWR Class '5101' 2-6-2T No 5164 and several examples of early-20th-century industrial 0-4-0STs. Diesels are represented by examples of BR Classes 02, 03, 07, 10, 23 (new-build 'Baby Deltic'), 26, 27, 33, 40, 45 and 55.

NOW
An LMS Scammell 3-ton mechanical horse of the 1930s patiently waits for ex-Midland Railway Class '1F' half-cab 0-6-0T No 41708 to depart from the short demonstration line at Barrow Hill Roundhouse. The veteran loco was built at Derby Works in 1880 and worked at Staveley Ironworks until withdrawal in 1965.

Originally seen as part of an independent railway route to the north, the branch line from Duffield (a junction on the Midland Railway's mainline north of Derby) to Wirksworth was opened by the Midland Railway in 1867. Bridges on the line were built to accommodate double track but, in the event, this never materialised. Following the Second World War increasing competition from buses and a national coal shortage led to the suspension of passenger services in 1947 – they were never reinstated. Despite the loss of passenger services the branch occasionally witnessed 'ghost trains' consisting of brand new lightweight diesel multiple units from Derby Works being tested in the early 1950s. The line remained open for limestone traffic from Middlepeak Quarry until 1989, thereafter the trackbed and rusting rails were overtaken by nature.

In 1996 the community-owned and locally-managed company Wyvern Rail was awarded a Light Railway Order for the entire line. Trains started operating over the short distance from Wirksworth to Gorsey Bank in 2004 with the steeply-graded mineral line to Ravenstor opening a year later. In 2005 Wyvern Rail purchased the entire railway and adopted Duffield station, the junction with the national rail network. With intermediate stations at Shottle and Idridgehay, the entire line was reopened in 2010 and now tourist passenger services along the scenic branch are operated by restored diesel multiple units. Steam haulage features on special event days. The steeply-graded (1-in-27) line from Wirksworth to Ravenstor (for the High Peak Trail, National Stone Centre and the Steeple Grange Light Railway) is worked separately from the 'mainline'.

The EVR has also provided the location for various TV films and adverts including Hellman's Mayonnaise, *Casualty* and *Five Days II*.

Wirksworth Station,
Coldwell Street, Wirksworth,
Derbyshire DE4 4FB

01629 823 076
www.e-v-r.com

LENGTH
9½ miles

GAUGE
Standard

OPEN
Weekends, April to October; Wednesdays, end July to end August

NOW
Preserved Class 33 diesel-electric No 33035 (formerly D6553) built by the Birmingham Railway Carriage & Wagon Company in 1961 departs from Wirksworth station on 29 September 2012 with a train for Duffield. On the right is a Derby Lightweight diesel railcar for the service to Ravenstor.

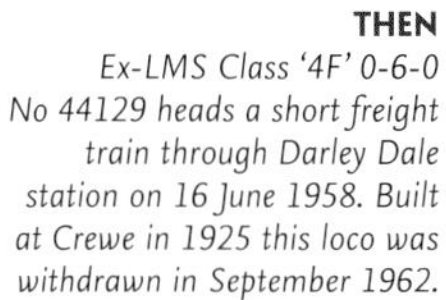

The first section of this scenic route through the Peak District was opened by the Manchester, Buxton, Matlock & Midlands Junction Railway (MBM&MJR) from Ambergate to Rowsley in 1849. The high cost of building numerous tunnels and bridges through the limestone hills soon put a halt to further construction and Rowsley remained at the end of a branch line for the next 14 years. Leased jointly by the LNWR and the MR, the MBM&MJR eventually completed its heavily engineered line to Buxton in 1863 and from Miller's Dale to Chinley in 1867 – this was all despite strong opposition from wealthy local landowners and the poet John Ruskin. The LNWR let go of its lease in 1871 and the MBM&MJR was then taken over by the MR.

Now owning a through route from London St Pancras to Manchester, the MR heavily promoted the line for its scenic beauty – in publicity material describing it as 'Little Switzerland'. Daily through trains ran between London, Buxton and Manchester and the line was also heavily used for through freight traffic. The diesel 'Midland Pullman' was introduced in 1960 but withdrawn in 1967 on the completion of electrification on the competing West Coast Main Line. In the same year many intermediate stations were closed and on 1 July 1968 the section from Matlock to Chinley was closed to through passenger trains – sacrificed in favour of the once-threatened Hope Valley route to the north. While Matlock to Miller's Dale Junction closed completely, the northern section through Dove Holes Tunnel (1 mile 1,224 yds) remains open for stone, limestone and cement traffic. Matlock is now the end of a branch line from Ambergate again, served by trains from Derby and Nottingham.

Today, the scenic section of the line from Rowsley to Miller's Dale is a footpath and cycleway known as the Monsal Trail while the line from

THEN

Ex-LMS Class '4F' 0-6-0 No 44129 heads a short freight train through Darley Dale station on 16 June 1958. Built at Crewe in 1925 this loco was withdrawn in September 1962.

Matlock to Rowsley South has been reopened as a heritage railway by Peak Rail.

It was 1975 before Peak Rail took over the trackbed of this picturesque line between Matlock and Rowsley through the heart of the Peak District National Park. Initially work was commenced at both Buxton and Matlock but this was later confined to the latter end, where the railway now makes an end-on connection with the national rail network. Steam and diesel passenger trains started running again to Darley Dale in 1992, with the extension to Rowsley South opening in 1997. A 60-ft turntable, originally from Mold Junction shed, became operational in 2010 and the railway was finally extended from Matlock Riverside station to the national rail network station at Matlock in 2011. An extension to the site of Rowsley station followed by an extension through the closed Haddon Tunnel to Bakewell are planned for the future.

There are several added attractions at Rowsley South: owned by members of the Heritage Shunters Trust (www.heritageshunters.co.uk), a large collection of diesel shunter locomotives is now housed in a new shed here; 2 Class 50 mainline diesels, No 50029 *Renown* and No 50030 *Repulse*, are owned by a restoration group. Other organisations based here are the LMS Carriage Association, Ashover Light Railway Society, North Notts Locomotive Group and the Waterman Railway Heritage Trust. The latter's collection at Rowsley South includes GWR '4575' Class 2-6-2T No 5553, GWR '5205' Class 2-8-0T No 5224, GWR '5600' Class 0-6-2T No 6634 and examples of BR diesel Classes 08, 25 and 46.

Matlock Station, Matlock,
Derbyshire DE4 3NA

01629 580381
www.peakrail.co.uk

LENGTH
3½ miles

GAUGE
Standard

OPEN
Weekends, April to October; some weekdays during summer, see website for details

NOW
Peak Rail is the home base for many preserved diesel locomotives. Here is Class 44 'Peak' 1Co-Co1 diesel-electric D8 Penyghent *in immaculate condition. This loco was built at Derby Works in 1959 and withdrawn in 1980.*

WALES

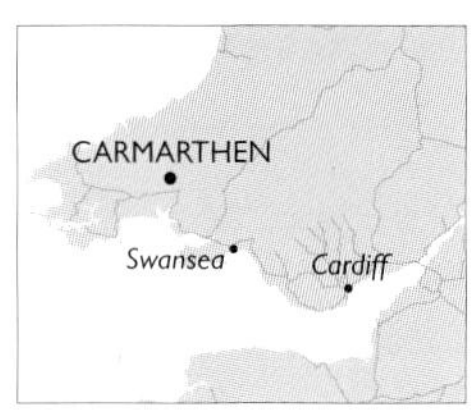

DANYCOED HALT
LLWYFAN CERRIG
BRONWYDD ARMS
ABERGWILI JUNCTION

The 56¼-mile single-track railway from Carmarthen to Aberystwyth started life at its southern end when the impoverished broad-gauge Carmarthen & Cardigan Railway (C&CR) opened to Conwil in 1860. This 6½-mile line was worked by the South Wales Railway with Great Western Railway (GWR) locomotives. Unable to pay its way, the C&CR closed at the end of that year but reopened in August 1861. The railway was extended to Pencader and Llandyssul in 1864 but within a few months an Official Receiver had been called in. However, the line kept operating until it was taken over by the GWR in 1881 – the latter company eventually extended the line to Newcastle Emlyn in 1895 but there it stopped, its hoped for goal of Cardigan never being achieved.

From the north, the Manchester & Milford Railway (M&MR) had aspirations to link the important port of Milford Haven with Manchester. Their plan was to build an independent line from Llanidloes (on the Mid-Wales Railway) and through the mountains to link with the C&CR at Pencader and thence use running powers to Milford Haven via Carmarthen. Despite making a start on the new line at Llanidloes this was soon abandoned. Instead, the M&MR chose a cheaper option by opening a new railway between Pencader and Aberystwyth – this opened in stages: to Lampeter and Strata Florida in 1866 and throughout in 1867. Never financially successful, the railway was leased to the GWR in 1906 before being absorbed by that company in 1911.

Both passenger and goods traffic was never heavy and the railway failed miserably as a through route between the North of England and Milford Haven. Trains were slow and by the late-1950s the end was nigh for passenger services – the 3 weekday trains then operating each way between Aberystwyth and Carmarthen took up to 2½ hours to complete the 56¼-mile journey.

Listed for closure in the 'Beeching Report', the end came prematurely for the section from Aberystwyth to Lampeter when floods effectively severed the northern part of the line on 14 December 1964. From that

THEN
Two trains pass at Strata Florida station on 9 June 1960. On the right is ex-GWR '4300' Class 2-6-0 No 6310 of Neyland shed.

date passenger services from Carmarthen terminated at Lampeter until they, too, ceased on 22 February 1965. However this was not quite the end for this delightful country railway as goods and milk traffic continued to run from a large creamery at Felin Fach (on the Aberayron branch) and from Newcastle Emlyn and Lampeter until road transport won the day on 1 October 1973.

In 1978 a preservation group had starting running services over a short length of track at Bronwydd Arms station 3 miles north of Carmarthen. By 1987 the line was extended to Llwyfan Cerrig, where there is a picnic site and the 7¼in.-gauge Llwyfan Cerrig Miniature Railway. The line has since been extended northwards to Danycoed (reached in 2001) with plans to extend to Llanpumpsaint where the station has already been purchased by the railway. Aided by material and equipment from the former Swansea Vale Railway project, the railway has also been extended southwards from Bronwydd Arms to Abergwili Junction (reached in 2017) on the northern outskirts of Carmarthen. The railway owns a large collection of mainly industrial steam and diesel locomotives and a wide variety of passenger and goods rolling stock, including an award-winning Taff Vale Railway coach, dating from 1891, which was fully restored after being found in a field in Herefordshire. Bronwydd Arms signal box originally stood at Llandybie on the Central Wales Line and was bought in 1985 for use on the Gwili Railway. Dating from 1885, the 21-lever box is now fully restored and operates signals in the station area.

Steam locomotives found on the Gwili Railway include GWR '5700' Class 0-6-0PT No 5786 (later London Transport L92), 2 Robert Stephenson & Hawthorns locos, 0-6-0ST No 7849 *Moorbarrow* and 0-4-0ST No 7058 *Olwen*, Peckett 0-4-0ST No 1345 *Mond Nickel No. 1*, Hunslet Austerity 0-6-0 No 3879 *Haulwen*, Taff Vale Railway 0-6-2T No 28 (on loan from the National Railway Museum in York) and Hunslet 0-6-0ST No 3829. Diesels are represented by a rare 1959-built Peckett, a BR Class 03 shunter and a diesel multiple unit.

Bronwydd Arms Station,
Carmarthen SA33 6HT

01267 238213
www.gwili-railway.co.uk

LENGTH
4½ miles

GAUGE
Standard

OPEN
Daily (except Mondays & Fridays), Easter to September; selected days, October to December (see website)

NOW
Preserved ex-GWR '4575' Class 2-6-2T No 5541 (masquerading as No 5549) hauls a mixed train on the Gwili Railway.

BRECON MOUNTAIN RAILWAY

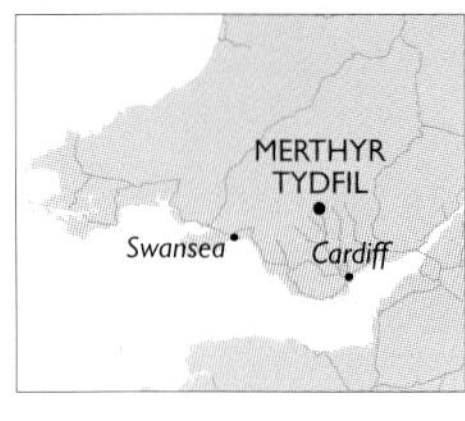

TORPANTAU
PONTSTICILL
PANT

Pant Station, Dowlais,
Merthyr Tydfil,
Mid-Glamorgan CF48 2DD

01685 722988
www.bmr.wales

LENGTH
5 miles

GAUGE
1ft 11¾in.

OPEN
Weekends, January to March; more frequent service April to October (daily, June to August); Santa Specials in December

The Brecon & Merthy Tydfil Junction Railway (B&MTJR) was opened between Brecon and Talybont in 1863. From Brecon to Talyllyn Junction (for the Mid-Wales Railway) the railway followed the course of a 3ft-6in.-gauge horse-drawn tramway (the Hay Railway) opened in 1816. The railway was extended southwards through Torpantau Tunnel – at 1,312 ft above sea level the highest in Britain – to Merthyr in 1868 and to Dowlais (the latter jointly with the London & North Western Railway) in 1869. Also wishing to reach Newport, the B&MTJR bought the Rumney Tramroad in 1868 – this had originally opened as a horse-drawn tramway from Rhymney Ironworks to Bassaleg Junction (west of Newport) in 1825. The company remained independent until becoming part of the Great Western Railway in 1922. While the southern half of the railway remained fairly busy, especially with coal traffic, the section north of Merthyr was quieter although trains, often double-headed, had to cope with gradients as steep as 1-in-37 up to Torpantau Tunnel.

As with all the railways to Brecon, the line from Newport was already living on borrowed time by the late 1950s. In 1958 there were 3 return through services (plus an extra on Saturdays) along the 47-mile route – journey time was a leisurely 2½ hours! Along with the other loss-making railways to Brecon the line from Newport lost its passenger service on 31 December 1962. Coal traffic continued to use the section down the Rhymney Valley from Bedwas until 1985 but all that remains open today is the 4¾ miles from Bassaleg Junction to a limestone quarry at Machen.

North of Merthyr the 1ft-11¾in.-gauge steam-hauled Brecon Mountain Railway today follows part of the trackbed of the B&MTJR between Pant and Torpantau. In 1972 a scheme to build a narrow-gauge railway along part of the disused trackbed was put forward. Construction of the line from Pant to Pontsticill, in the Brecon Beacons National Park, began in 1978 and the first public train ran in 1980. A further ¼-mile extension along the side of Taf Fechan Reservoir to a terminus at Dolygaer was opened in 1995. The present terminus at Torpantau, near the southern entrance to Torpantau Tunnel and 5 miles from Pant, was opened in 2014.

Motive power is mainly steam and includes examples from Wales, Germany and South Africa including the most powerful locomotive built for this gauge, a 2-6-2+2-6-2 Garratt No 77. In recent years the mainstay has been 0-6-2WTT *Graf Schwerin-Löwitz*, built by Arnold Jung of Germany in 1908. Other steam locos on the BMR include 1897-built Baldwin 2-6-2 No 1 and 1930-built Baldwin 4-6-2 No 2 originally built for the Eastern Province Cement Company in South Africa. Replicas are also being built in the workshops of 2 more Baldwin locos, a 1913 2-6-2 and a 1916 2-4-4T.

Continental-style rolling stock, with end balconies, and a North American caboose have all been built in the company's well-equipped workshop at Pant which is open for public viewing.

THEN
Boy scouts off to their summer camp at Torpantau station on 9 June 1962. On the right is ex-GWR '8750' Class No 3661 which has just arrived from Brecon with a train for Newport.

NOW
Brecon Mountain Railway loco No 2 takes on water at Pant station prior to hauling its train to Torpantau. This loco was built in 1930 by US manufacturer Baldwin for the Eastern Province Cement Company in South Africa.

PONTYPOOL & BLAENAVON RAILWAY

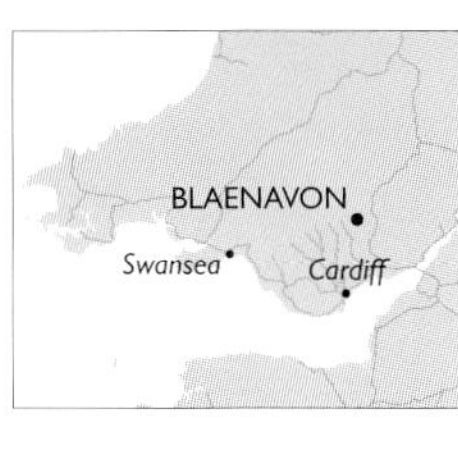

WAENAVON

WHISTLE INN HALT

FURNACE SIDINGS

BIG PIT HALT

BLAENAVON HIGH LEVEL

Furnace Sidings Station,
Garn Yr Erw, Blaenavon,
Gwent NP4 9SF

www.bhrailway.co.uk

LENGTH
3½ miles

GAUGE
Standard

OPEN
Most weekends, April to October (see website)

The former London & North Western Railway's branch between Brynmawr and Blaenavon was completed in 1869 to transport coal to the Midlands via the Heads of the Valley Line and Abergavenny. Passenger services commenced in 1870 and in 1878 the line was extended southwards to Abersychan & Talywain, where it met the Great Western Railway, and then onto Pontypool Crane Street and Newport. The line primarily served collieries at Waun Nantyglo, Clydach, Milfraen and Big Pit but these were successively closed from 1938 onwards until only the latter was left operating. The passenger service ceased in 1941 and the decline in the coal industry continued through the 1950s. The track was singled in 1965 and the closure of the final mine at Big Pit Colliery came in 1980 when the line finally closed.

Partial reopening by a preservation society in 1983 as the Pontypool & Blaenavon Railway (between Furnace Sidings and Whistle Inn) was centred around the Big Pit Mining Museum. It was another 27 years before an extension was opened to Blaenavon High Level in 2010. The railway is set in the heart of a World Heritage Site and runs by a newly-established country park that has been developed from ex-colliery waste sites – part of the line currently operated reaches 1,307 ft above sea level at Whistle Inn Halt. A branch line to serve the Big Pit Mining Museum (http://museum.wales/bigpit) opened in late 2011. The mainline is currently being extended in stages southwards to Abersychan over a number of new bridges and northwards to Brynmawr, a total distance of 8 miles. When the railway reaches Waenavon it will re-open the station that, at 1,400 ft above sea level, is the highest standard-gauge station in England and Wales. The preservation society has acquired a station building from the site of Pontypool Crane Street station, deconstructing it for eventual reconstruction along the line. Now known as 'Blaenavon's Heritage Railway', the line is home to a wide variety of industrial steam and mainline diesel locomotives, many of them currently awaiting restoration. Steam locos include 1914-built Andrew Barclay 0-4-0ST *Rosyth No. 1*, 1944-built Hunslet 0-6-0ST *Mech Navvies Ltd.* and 1954-built Bagnall 0-6-0ST *Empress*. Diesels include examples of BR Classes 31, 37 and a Class 117 diesel multiple unit.

THEN
A Class 120 diesel multiple unit with an enthusiasts' special visiting derelict Blaenavon High level station on 26 September 1964.

NOW
Built by W. Bagnall in 1954, 0-6-0ST Empress *hauls a demonstration train of empty mineral wagons on the Pontypool & Blaenavon railway on a cold 13 January 2019.*

WELSHPOOL & LLANFAIR LIGHT RAILWAY

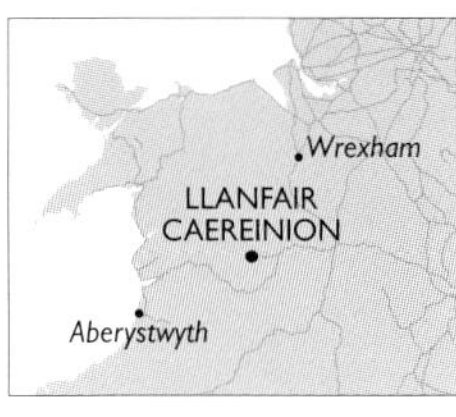

WELSHPOOL
WELSHPOOL RAVEN SQUARE
SYLFAEN
CASTLE CAEREINION
CYFRONYDD
HENIART
LLANFAIR CAEREINION

The Station, Llanfair Caereinion, Welshpool, Powys SY21 0SF

01938 810441
www.wllr.org.uk

LENGTH
8½ miles

GAUGE
2ft 6in.

OPEN
Weekends & selected days, April & May; daily except certain Fridays, June & July; daily, August; weekends & selected days, September–October; two weekends in December

With some of the steepest gradients in Britain, the 2ft-6in.-gauge Welshpool & Llanfair Light Railway (W&LLR) opened along the Banwy Valley between Llanfair Caereinion and the border town of Welshpool in 1903. Built to link the farms and villages along the valley with the market at Welshpool, it was worked by the Cambrian Railways from the outset until that company was absorbed by the Great Western Railway (GWR) in 1922. Until closure, trains ran through the back lanes of Welshpool to reach the interchange station where it met the standard-gauge Cambrian Railways' mainline. Passenger trains ceased in 1931 but the unprofitable railway struggled on through Nationalisation in 1948 before complete closure in 1956. A preservation group started to run trains again in 1963 and services from Llanfair Caereinion now terminate at Raven Square on the outskirts of Welshpool.

Train services are still operated by the 2 original 1902-built 'Swindonised' Beyer, Peacock 0-6-0T locomotives, No 1 *The Earl* and No 2 *Countess*, along with some foreign interlopers from Austria, Finland, Sierra Leone and Antigua and balconied coaches. The small collection of industrial diesels include No 7 *Chattenden* which once worked on the Admiralty's Chattenden & Upnor Railway in Kent and No 11 *Ferret* which once worked at the Royal Naval Armament Deport at Broughton Moor in Cumbria.

Trains along this delightful 8½-mile line start their journey at Raven Square terminus in Welshpool, close to the grounds of Powis Castle. Opened in 1981 the station used buildings from the 1863 Eardisley station. First climbing the notorious 1-in-24 Golfa Bank to the 600-ft summit of the line, the railway follows the contours round sharp curves, crossing country lanes on 4 level crossings, before reaching Cyfronydd. Here the line joins the fast-flowing River Banwy, crossing it near Heniarth and hugging the north bank to end at the little terminus at Llanfair Caereinion.

THEN
Welshpool & Llanfair Light Railway's Beyer, Peacock 0-6-0T No 823 at the trans-shipment sidings adjacent to Welshpool's standard-gauge station on 26 June 1954.

NOW
Preserved Welshpool & Llanfair Light Railway No 823 Countess *hauls a mixed train of original restored W&LLR coaches and wagons just west of Sylfaen station on 29 April 2014.*

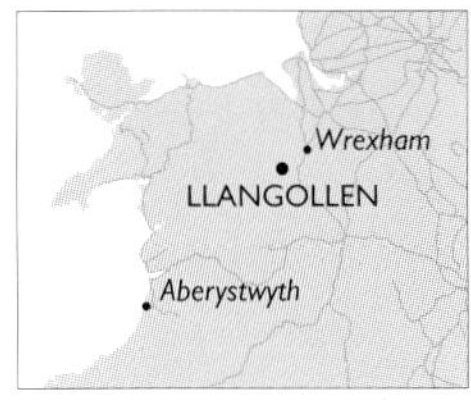

LLANGOLLEN
BERWYN
GLYNDYFRDWY
CARROG
CORWEN EAST
CORWEN

For the full story of the Ruabon to Barmouth Junction via Llangollen railway see Bala Lake Railway, pages 132–3. Llangollen station was closed to passengers on 18 January 1965 and to goods services on 1 April 1968.

Founded in 1972, the Flint & Deeside Railway Preservation Society moved into Llangollen, its station attractively situated on the north bank of the River Dee, in 1975 with the ultimate goal of reopening the line as far as Corwen. Since then much progress has been made, with Berwyn being reached in 1985, Deeside Halt in 1990, Glyndyfrdwy in 1992, Carrog in 1996 and Corwen East in 2014. Here a new station will eventually be built in the town centre. The two major engineering features of the line are the bridge over the River Dee to the west of Llangollen and the 689-yd single-bore tunnel near Berwyn.

A journey along the line, the only preserved standard-gauge example in North Wales, gives passengers wonderful views of the Dee Valley as the train climbs high above the river and parallels the A5 trunk road. Berwyn station, now a holiday cottage, with its black and white timbered building and tea room is located in a magnificent position

THEN
Ex-LMS Ivatt Class '2MT' 2-6-0 No 46508 restarts its train from Berwyn Halt on 28 November 1964, a month before premature closure after floods permanently cut the line at Carrog.

overlooking the River Dee. A large collection of steam, including many ex-GWR examples, and diesel locomotives maintain passenger services on the line, which is also a frequent host to visiting mainline engines from other heritage railways. GWR steam locomotives based at Llangollen include '5101' Class 2-6-2T No 5199, '6400' Class 0-6-0PT No 6430 and '3800' Class 2-8-0 No 3802 while 'Hall' Class 4-6-0 No 5952 *Cogan Hall* is awaiting restoration. BR diesels include a Class 08 diesel shunter and a Class 26 along with representatives of Classes 104, 108 and 109 multiple units.

A new locomotive shed was opened at Llangollen in November 1995 and this provides accommodation for up to 10 locomotives and a carriage restoration section. The locomotive works at Llangollen is famous for its new-build steam locomotives which include the GWR steam railmotor completed in 2011 and two current projects, GWR '4700' Class 2-8-0 No 4709 *Night Owl* and LNER 'B17' Class 4-6-0 No 61673 *Spirit of Sandringham*. The 'Berwyn Belle' Wine & Dine train operates on some Saturday evenings and Sunday lunchtimes.

Llangollen Station,
Abbey Road, Llangollen,
Denbighshire LL20 8SN

01978 860979
www.llangollen-railway.co.uk

LENGTH
10 miles

GAUGE
Standard

OPEN
Selected Sundays in January; weekends & school holidays, February; daily early April to early October; weekends & school holidays, October; selected days, November–December (see website for operating days and special events)

NOW
The headquarters of the Llangollen Railway at Llangollen station occupies a highly scenic position on the north bank of the River Dee.

BALA LAKE RAILWAY

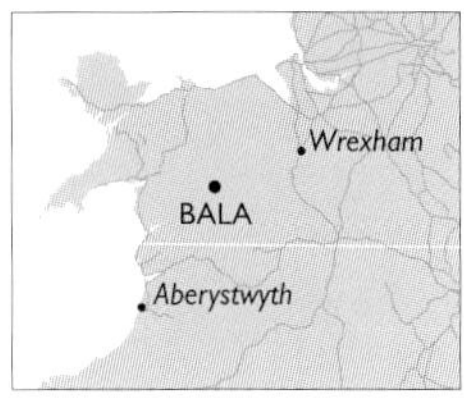

LLANUWCHLLYN
PENTREPIOD HALT
GLAN LYN HALT
LLANGOWER
BALA (PENYBONT)
BALA

Although the mainly single-track 53-mile railway between Ruabon, on the Great Western Railway's (GWR) mainline between Chester and Shrewsbury, and Barmouth Junction was built by five different railway companies, on its completion it formed an important cross-country route for the GWR. From east to west, the first railway to be built was the Vale of Llangollen Railway which opened along the Dee Valley from Ruabon to the small town of Llangollen in 1862. It was worked from the outset by the GWR and absorbed by that company in 1896.

The second railway to be built along the Dee Valley was the Llangollen & Corwen Railway which opened in 1865. The third railway was the Corwen & Bala Railway which opened throughout in 1868. Both railways were also worked from the outset by the GWR and absorbed in 1896. Next to be built and worked by the GWR was the Bala & Dolgelly Railway (B&DR) which opened in 1868 – it was absorbed by the GWR in 1877. From that date the town of Bala was served by a shuttle service to and from the isolated Bala Junction station. At the western end, the Cambrian Railways had already opened a branch line from Barmouth Junction alongside the Mawddach Estuary to Penmaenpool in 1865. The intervening 2¼-mile gap between Dolgellau and Penmaenpool was opened by the B&DR in 1870. Worked throughout by the GWR, the entire route was now open for through traffic from the GWR system to North Wales.

Although only serving small towns, villages and farming communities along its route, the Ruabon to Barmouth line was kept busy during the summer months with holiday traffic from Birmingham destined for the seaside resort of Barmouth. Feeder traffic from the GWR branch from Blaenau Ffestiniog to Bala and the LNWR line from Rhyl and Denbigh also kept the line alive until their closures in 1960 and 1953 respectively.

With increasing competition from road transport and little intermediate traffic, the line's future was in doubt by the early 1960s – to the south it was duplicated by the Cambrian mainline from Shrewsbury to Machynlleth on to which all through freight trains were soon diverted.

THEN

An engine changeover at Bala station with 2 pannier tanks on 30 March 1959. On the left is '7400' Class 0-6-0PT No 7428, still with GWR on the side of its tanks, which has brought a single coach train from Blaenau Ffestiniog. Class '5700' 0-6-0PT No 8727 is waiting to take over the train down to Bala Junction.

Listed for closure in the 'Beeching Report', the end came earlier than the planned 18 January 1965 when floods cut the line at Carrog on the night of 10/11 December 1964. From that date the short Bala Junction to Bala line also closed and only the eastern (Ruabon to Llangollen) and western (Corwen to Barmouth Junction) sections (linked by a temporary bus service) continued to operate a passenger service until complete closure on the planned date. Goods traffic continued between Ruabon and Llangollen until 1 April 1968.

Since closure several sections of this railway have seen a renaissance: the Llangollen Railway (see pages 130–1) operates a standard-gauge heritage line between Llangollen and Corwen; the narrow-gauge Bala Lake Railway runs alongside Lake Bala from near Bala to Llanuwchllyn; the 8-mile section from Barmouth Junction (now renamed Morfa Mawddach) to the outskirts of Dolgellau is now a footpath and cycleway known as the Mawddach Trail.

The Bala Lake Railway skirts the eastern shore of Lake Bala, at 1,084 acres the largest natural lake in Wales, and was opened in stages between 1972 and 1976. Passenger trains were initially diesel-hauled but steam services commenced in 1975. Trains are normally operated by 5 Hunslet 0-4-0 saddle tanks, 1885-built *Winifred*, 1898-built *George B*, 1899-built *Nesta*, 1902-built *Holy War* and *Alice* and 1904-built *Maid Marian* along with Peckett 1911-built 0-6-0ST *Triassic*, all originally from the Dinorwic Slate Quarry or Penrhyn Slate Quarries, and 2 industrial narrow-gauge diesels. The railway now has the largest collection of narrow-gauge slate quarry locomotives built by Hunslet of Leeds. Passengers are carried in purpose-built covered carriages. Llanuwchllyn station, the headquarters of the railway, is a finely preserved example of an original Bala & Dolgelly Railway building. Also at Llanuwchllyn are the railway's engine sheds and an original GWR signal box. Llangower station has a passing loop and signal box. Future plans include extending the line ¾-mile eastwards to a new terminus in the town of Bala.

The Station, Llanuwchllyn,
Bala, Gwynedd LL23 7DD

01678 540666
www.bala-lake-railway.co.uk

LENGTH
4½ miles

GAUGE
1ft 11⅝in.

OPEN
Daily except Mondays & Fridays, early April to end June & September; Bank Holidays, April to end August; daily, July & August

NOW
Built by Kerr Stuart in 1917 0-4-0T Diana hauls a train of slate wagons near Llanuchilly Crossing on the Bala Lake Railway on 16 May 2016.

VALE OF RHEIDOL RAILWAY

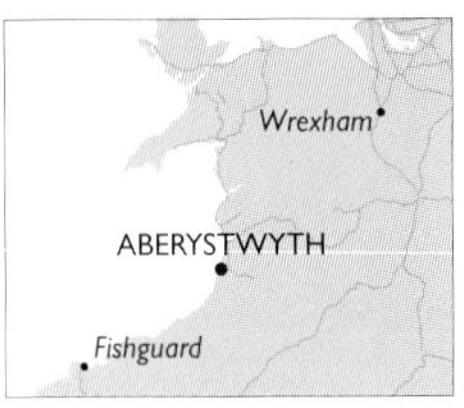

ABERYSTWYTH
LLANBADARN
GLANYRAFON
CAPEL BANGOR
NANTYRONEN
ABERFFRWD
RHEIDOL FALLS
RHIWFRON
DEVIL'S BRIDGE

The 1ft-11¾in.-gauge Vale of Rheidol Light Railway was opened between the seaside resort of Aberystwyth and Devil's Bridge in 1902. Climbing high up into the Rheidol Valley the railway was built to serve lead mines and carry tourists to the beauty spot of Devil's Bridge. The railway was taken over by the Cambrian Railways in 1913 before becoming part of the Great Western Railway in 1922. The GWR then virtually rebuilt the line, scrapped two of the original locomotives, rebuilt one (built originally by Davies & Metcalfe) and built two new ones, 'Swindonising' them at the same time. These three 2-6-2T locomotives, No 7 *Owain Glyndwr*, No 8 *Llywelyn* and No 9 *Prince of Wales* are still working on the line today. Goods traffic ceased in 1920, winter passenger services in 1931, the Aberystwyth Harbour branch was closed in 1933 and from then on the railway had to earn its living purely from tourism. Following closure for 6 years during the Second World War the railway was reopened in June 1946. It was nationalised as part of the new British Railways in 1948 along with two other Welsh narrow-gauge lines, the Welshpool & Llanfair Light Railway (see pages 128–9) and the Corris Railway (see page 138). The end of steam haulage on

THEN

In the days of British Railways ownership Vale of Rheidol Railway 2-6-2T No 8 Llywelyn, *built at Swindon works in 1923, gets ready for a day's work at the old engine shed in Aberystwyth on 14 August 1965.*

British Railways' standard-gauge lines in 1968 left the VoR the only nationalised steam-operated line in Britain. In 1989 BR controversially sold the whole operation to Peter Rampton and Tony Hills, the late owner and General Manager of the Brecon Mountain Railway. In 1996 the partnership was split, with the VoR being sold to the Phyllis Rampton Narrow Gauge Railway Trust.

Departing from Aberystwyth's terminus, the railway initially runs beside the standard-gauge line before crossing the Afon Rheidol and heading up the southern slopes of the valley. Following the contours on sharp curves, the railway climbs continuously, hugging the wooded slopes along a ledge through Nantyronen, Aberffrwd and Rheidol Falls with the meandering Rheidol far below. The final dramatic approach on a 1-in-50 gradient to Devil's Bridge passes through a narrow rock cutting. From here, deep in the Cambrian Mountains, 11¾ miles from Aberystwyth and 639 ft above sea level, there are walks to nearby beauty spots such as Jacob's Ladder, the Devil's Punchbowl and Mynach Falls.

Park Avenue, Aberystwyth, Ceredigion SY23 1PG

01970 625819
www.rheidolrailway.co.uk

LENGTH
11¾ miles

GAUGE
1ft 11¾in.

OPEN
Daily, June to early September; daily (except selected Mondays, Fridays & Sundays) & Bank Holiday weekends, April, May, September & October

NOW
Built at Swindon Works in 1924 Vale of Rheidol 2-6-2T No 1213 (No 9 Prince of Wales*) receives attention from the driver at Devil's Bridge terminus before returning with its train to Aberystwyth.*

TALYLLYN RAILWAY

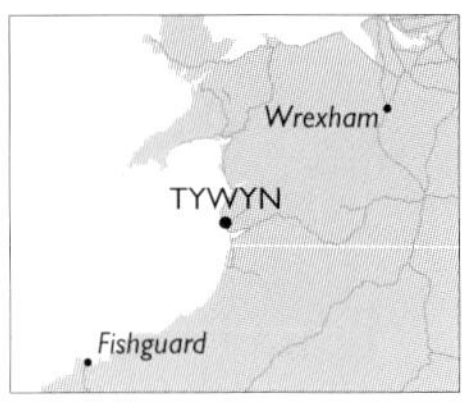

TYWYN
TYWYN WHARF
PENDRE
HENDY HALT
FACH GOCH HALT
CYNFAL HALT
RHYDYRONEN
TYNLLWYNHEN HALT
BRYNGAS
DOLGOCH
QUARRY SIDING HALT
ABERGYNOLWYN
NANT GWERNOL

Wharf Station, Tywyn, Gwynedd LL36 9EY

01654 710472
www.talyllyn.co.uk

LENGTH
7½ miles

GAUGE
2ft 3in.

OPEN
February half term & Sundays in March; daily, April to end October; selected days in November & December (see website)

Opened in 1866 to carry slate from the quarries above Nant Gwernol to Tywyn this scenic 2ft-3in.-gauge railway has never actually closed. When the slate quarry closed in 1946 the owner, Sir Henry Haydn Jones, managed to keep the railway running, but with little or no maintenance the line was in a very run-down state by the time of his death in 1950. However, a group of volunteers led by the author Tom Rolt amongst others, saved it from imminent closure by taking over the running of the line to Abergynolwyn, thus making it the world's first successful railway preservation project.

In 1976 the Preservation Society reopened the ¼-mile section of mineral line from Abergynolwyn to Nant Gwernol at the foot of the first incline that led to the quarry. Trains are still hauled by some of the original and beautifully restored Talyllyn Railway and ex-Corris Railway (see page 138) locomotives. Four-wheeled coaches are used as well as more recent additions with one from the Corris Railway. Locomotives, including 3 diesels, are numbered 1 to 9 and are named *Talyllyn* (0-4-2 saddle tank built 1865), *Dolgoch* (0-4-0 well tank built 1866), *Sir Haydn* (0-4-2 saddle tank built 1878 for the Corris Railway), *Edward Thomas* (0-4-2 saddle tank built 1921 for the Corris Railway), *Midlander* (diesel mechanical built 1940), *Douglas* (0-4-0 well tank built 1918), *Tom Rolt* (0-4-2 tank built 1949), *Merseysider* (diesel-hydraulic built 1964) and *Alf* (diesel-mechanical built 1950). The fascinating Narrow Gauge Railway Museum is located at Tywyn Wharf station.

Leaving Tywyn Wharf station, the railway climbs up through the town, passing the railway's workshops at Pendre before heading off up the tranquil Afon Fathew valley. Clinging to contours on the southern side of the lush valley, the railway passes small farms nestling in the shadows of the Cambrian Mountains. Threading through oak woodland the railway reaches Dolgoch where locomotives take water fed from a mountain stream – passengers can alight here to enjoy a walk to the nearby beauty spot of Dolgoch Falls. Still climbing steadily up the side of the valley the railway reaches Abergynolwyn station, the passenger terminus until 1976 when the line was extended along the route of a mineral line to the Nant Gwernol ravine. While the station here has no road access, walkers can explore tracks and footpaths in the surrounding forest and to the incline of the old slate workings at Bryn Eglwys.

THEN
A photo from the early preservation era showing a Talyllyn Railway Preservation Society special train hauled by 0-4-0WT No 6 Douglas at Dolgoch station in September 1957.

NOW
Talyllyn Railway 0-4-0WT No 2 Dolgoch, built by Fletcher Jennings in 1866, and vintage train crosses Dolgoch viaduct on 16 May 2011, the 60th anniversary of the railway's rebirth.

CORRIS RAILWAY & MUSEUM

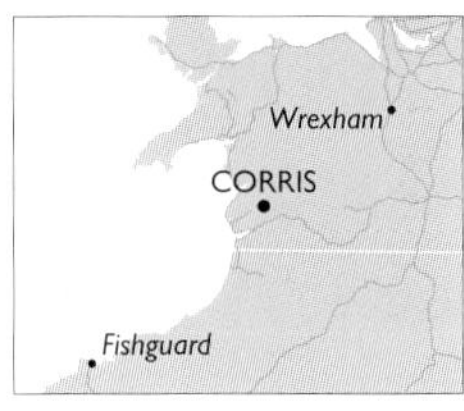

CORRIS
MAESPOETH JUNCTION
TAN-Y-COED

Station Yard,
Corris, Machynlleth,
Powys SY20 9SH

01654 761303
www.corris.co.uk

LENGTH
2 miles

GAUGE
2ft 3in.

OPEN
Selected Saturdays, Bank Holidays & every Sunday, Easter to September; daily, Easter week; Mondays & most Tuesdays, August (see website)

Opened in 1859 to transport slate from the quarries around Corris to the mainline at Machynlleth, this narrow-gauge line was originally worked as a horse-tramway running from quays on the River Dyfi at Morben and Derwenlas, skirting Machynlleth and then following the Dulas Valley northwards to Corris and Aberllefenni. Steam locomotives and passenger trains were introduced in 1879 and in 1930 the railway was taken over and worked by the GWR. Passenger traffic ceased at the beginning of 1931 and goods traffic in 1948, when flooding severed the line north of Machynlleth only 8 months after the railway had become nationalised as part of the new British Railways.

Short of locomotives, the fledgling Talyllyn Railway preservation society purchased from British Railways in 1951 the 2 redundant Corris Railway locomotives and some goods wagons and a brake van. These 2 locomotives are 1878-built Falcon Works 0-4-2ST No 3 (*Sir Haydn*) and 1921-built Kerr Stuart 0-4-2ST No 4 (*Edward Thomas*). They are still working on the Talyllyn Railway (see pages 136–7) and have also visited the current Corris Railway.

Formed in 1996, the Corris Railway Society has reopened the line from Corris to Maespoeth and planning permission has been obtained for a further 2 miles southwards through the beautiful Esgairgeiliog Gorge. The original engine shed at Maespoeth, built in 1878, has been restored and adapted to meet the current-day needs of the railway. Hauled by replica Corris Railway locomotive No 7, steam-operated trains run on most weekends between May and September. Housed in the former Corris Railway buildings at Corris, the museum was opened in 1970 and is devoted to many exhibits and photographs from the railway. Future plans include recreating the overall roofed station at Corris and extending the line south to Tan-y-Coed, increasing the railway's mileage to 2½ miles.

THEN
One of the 3 Hughes Falcon Works 0-4-2STs built for the Corris Railway in 1878 is seen here hauling a mixed train up the valley towards Corris, c.1920. One of these locos was saved from the scrapyard and can be seen at work as No 3 Sir Haydn *on the nearby Talyllyn Railway (see pages 136–7).*

The Welsh Highland Heritage Railway has been operating passenger services over a ¾-mile stretch of track from their own station at Porthmadog, literally just across the road from the national rail network station, for 40 years. The company's initial aim was to reopen the entire Welsh Highland Railway but a High Court action in 1995 decided that the Ffestiniog Railway could rebuild and operate it from Caernarfon to Porthmadog Harbour. The heritage railway currently owns and operates several steam locomotives, notably 2-6-2T *Russell* built by Hunslet in 1906 for the North Wales Narrow Gauge Railway and 1953-built Bagnall 0-4-2T *Gelert*. The railway also owns a First World War Baldwin Class '10-12-D' 4-6-0T which was found in India and is now being restored to working condition at the Vale of Rheidol Railway (see pages 134–5). In addition there is a fleet of 9 industrial narrow-gauge diesels including examples from Poland, Pilkingtons Glass and one that was used in the construction of the Jubilee Line in London. All of these along with the steam locos, are housed in the railway's workshop at Gelert's Farm. Special trains occasionally venture onto the Welsh Highland Railway's mainline via a connection at Pen-y-Mount. On normal operating days visitors are given a ride on the railway, which parallels the standard-gauge Cambrian Line, as far as Pen-y-Mount Junction with a visit to the museum in Gelert's Farm Works and a ride on a 7¼in.-gauge miniature railway.

NOW
Built by Hunslet of Leeds for the original Welsh Highland Railway in 1906, preserved 2-6-2T Russell *is one of the star attractions at the Welsh Highland Heritage Railway in Porthmadog.*

PORTHMADOG

- PORTHMADOG
- GELERTS FARM HALT
- PEN-Y-MOUNT JUNCTION

Tremadog Road, Porthmadog, Gwynedd LL49 9DY

01766 513402
www.whr.co.uk

LENGTH
¾ mile

GAUGE
1ft 11½in.

OPEN
Daily, March to end September; daily except Mondays in October

The 1ft-11½in.-gauge Ffestiniog Railway (FR) opened as a horse-drawn tramway between slate quarries at Blaenau Ffestiniog and the harbour town of Porthmadog in 1836. Enormous tonnages of slate were transported down the 13½-mile railway by gravity to Porthmadog for onward shipment around the coast of Britain – the loaded trains were controlled by brakemen who rode precariously on the wagons while the empties were hauled back to Blaenau by horse.

Horse power was replaced by steam in 1865 and 4 years later the FR introduced the first of its powerful double-ended locomotives. Designed by Robert Fairlie, they were in effect 2 steam locomotives attached back to back with the cab in the centre and supported on 2 swivelling powered bogies. The first, *Little Wonder*, was such a success that Fairlie went on to stage a series of demonstrations on the railway in 1870 – witnessed by railway engineers from around the world, the trials led to many export orders for his unique locomotives. The FR eventually owned 6 and 3 are still in service on the line today. Passenger services were introduced at the same time as steam power, and the FR went on to order the first iron-framed (as opposed to wooden) bogie coaches in Britain.

Slate traffic peaked in 1897, with 139,000 tons being carried, but by 1939, when passenger services were withdrawn, this had dropped to 30,000 tons. Independent to the end, the FR struggled through the ▶

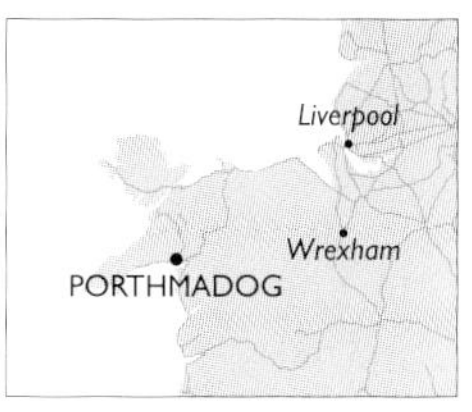

PORTHMADOG
- PORTHMADOG HARBOUR
- BOSTON LODGE HALT
- **MINFFORDD**
- PENRHYN
- PLAS HALT
- TAN-Y-BWLCH
- DDUALLT
- TANYGRISIAU
- BLAENAU FFESTINIOG JUNCTION

BLAENAU FFESTINIOG

NOW
Ffestiniog Railway 0-4-0ST+T Palmerston *hauls a train of vintage coaching stock towards Dduallt at Campbell's Platform, 4 November 2013. This loco was built by George England & Co in 1864, making it 158 years old at the time of publication.*

THEN
End of the line for the Ffestiniog Railway – hundreds of redundant slate wagons parked at closed Porthmadog Harbour station in 1950.

Harbour Station, Porthmadog, Gwynedd LL49 9NF

01766 516000
www.festrail.co.uk

LENGTH
13½ miles

GAUGE
1ft 11½in.

OPEN
Daily, end March to end October; Wednesdays & Thursdays, March & November; selected days in December (see website)

Second World War only to close completely in 1946. However, spurred on by the success of the world's first railway preservation scheme further down the coast at Tywyn (see page 136), a group of early preservationists set about reopening the railway – the first trains ran across the Cob (a man-made embankment) from Porthmadog Harbour station to Boston Lodge in 1955, and since then the railway has re-opened in stages, finally reaching Blaenau Ffestiniog in 1982. Here a new station was built alongside the standard-gauge Conwy Valley Line's terminus. Meanwhile, a reservoir for a new hydro-electric scheme near Tanygrisiau had already flooded part of the line necessitating the building of a spiral to gain height at Dduallt and through a new tunnel on a higher route along the valley.

Many historic steam locomotives currently operate on the railway including Double Fairlies *Merddin Emrys* (built 1879) and *David Lloyd George* (built 1992), 0-4-0STT *Palmerston* (built in 1864), *Hunslet* 2-4-0STT *Blanche* and 0-4-0 tender *Linda* (both built in 1893) and the replica of a Lynton & Barnstaple Railway 2-6-2T, named *Lyd*. The oldest surviving FR locomotive, 0-4-0STT *Prince*, has also been returned to service.

Since 2011, the Ffestiniog Railway has been physically connected to the newly-opened Welsh Highland Railway (see pages 143–5) at Porthmadog Harbour station – it is now possible to travel once again by narrow-gauge railway the 38½ miles from Caernarfon to Blaenau Ffestiniog.

NOW
Ffestiniog Railway 0-4-4-0T Merddin Emrys *comes off the Cob with a train of empty slate wagons past the entrance to Boston Lodge Works, 4 November 2013.*

The 1ft-11½in.-gauge North Wales Narrow Gauge Railways Company (NWNGR) was originally seen as an ambitious narrow-gauge system in North Wales but it ended up as a much smaller operation with a 4¼-mile line from Dinas Junction, on the LNWR's Caernarfon to Afon Wen standard-gauge line, to slate quarries at Bryngwyn opening in 1877. A branch from Tryfan Junction to Rhyd-Ddu, on the lower slopes of Snowdon, was opened in 1881. An extension southwards to Beddgelert never materialised and the company, facing mounting losses due to a recession in the slate industry, went into receivership. Meanwhile a completely separate company, the Portmadoc, Beddgelert & South Snowdon Railway (PB&SSR), had plans to reach Beddgelert from the south using part of the route of the horse-drawn Croeser Tramway. This was all to no avail and by 1916 the NWNGR had suspended passenger services and work had stopped on building the PB&SSR.

Both railways were saved from extinction in 1921 – with the financial support of the Government and local government they were reformed as the Welsh Highland Railway (WHR). Construction work recommenced and by 1923 trains were able to run for the first time between Dinas Junction and Porthmadog. Although operated on a shoestring by the indomitable Colonel H. F. Stephens, the WHR lurched from one financial crisis to another, only being saved from closure when it was leased by the neighbouring Ffestiniog Railway in 1934. Despite some improvements and the injection of FR motive power and carriages, services were painfully slow with passengers having to change trains at Beddgelert. The end came in 1936 when passenger services ceased and by the following year the railway had closed completely. ▶

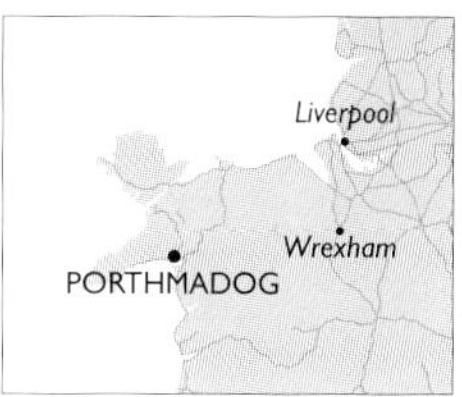

- CAERNARFON
- BONTNEWYDD
- DINAS
- TRYFAN JUNCTION
- WAUNFAWR
- PLAS-Y-NANT
- SNOWDON RANGER
- RHYD DDU
- MEILLIONEN
- BEDDGELERT
- NANTMOR
- PONT CROESOR
- PORTHMADOG HARBOUR
- **PORTHMADOG**

Harbour Station, Porthmadog, Gwynedd LL49 9NF

01766 516000
www.festrail.co.uk

THEN
Welsh Highland Railway 0-6-4T Moel Tryfan *with a short train at Beddgelert station, c.1927. This Single Fairlie loco was originally built for the North Wales Narrow Gauge Railway by Vulcan Foundry in 1875 and transferred to the new Welsh Highland Railway in 1922. It was later scrapped by the Ffestiniog Railway in 1954.*

LENGTH
25 miles

GAUGE
1ft 11½in.

OPEN
Selected days in March, November and December; most days, April to June & October; daily, July to September

Six decades later, after years of legal wrangling with a competing preservation group, the Ffestiniog Railway once again came to the rescue. With substantial funding provided by the Millennium Commission, the Welsh Assembly Government and regional authorities, a new Welsh Highland Railway rose like a phoenix from the ashes when the FR purchased the old narrow-gauge trackbed – the northerly section from Caernarfon to Dinas Junction follows the trackbed of the former standard-gauge line to Afon Wen, which closed in 1964.

One of the most ambitious railway preservation schemes in the world, the reborn WHR was opened in stages between 1997 and 2011 when for the first time in 75 years narrow-gauge trains, this time hauled by restored ex-South African Railways Garratt articulated steam locomotives, once again ran through the streets of Porthmadog.

From south to north intermediate stations are provided at Pont Croesor, Nantmor, Beddgelert, Meillionen, Rhyd Ddu, Snowdon Ranger, Plas-y-nant, Waunfawr, Tryfan Junction, Dinas, and Bontnewydd. The railway owns six 2-6-2+2-6-2 articulated Beyer, Peacock locos, some of which are undergoing overhaul or awaiting restoration. Other steam locos include Beyer, Peacock 0-4-0+0-4-0 No K1 which was built in 1909 for Tasmanian Government Railways and 2 ex-South African Railways 'NG15' Class 2-8-2s. Locomotives from the Ffestiniog Railway (see pages 140–2) are also regular performers on the railway.

NOW
Welsh Highland Railway 2-6-2+2-6-2 Garratt locos No 87 and No 138 double-head a long demonstration goods train at Ynys-Fach on 3 November 2013. No 87 was built by Cockerill in 1937 and No 138 by Beyer, Peacock in 1958, both for South African Railways where they operated as Class NGG16 Garratt.

LLANBERIS LAKE RAILWAY

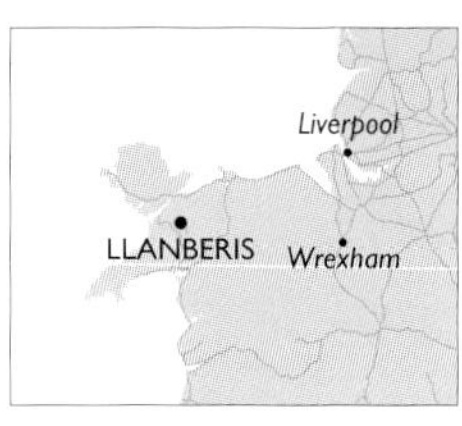

LLANBERIS
GILFACH DDU
CEI LLYDAN
PENLLYN

Gilfach Ddu, Llanberis,
Gwynedd LL55 4TY

01286 870549
www.lake-railway.co.uk

LENGTH
2½ miles

GAUGE
1ft 11½in.

OPEN
Selected days in February, March, November & December; most days, April to September (see website)

The 4ft-gauge Padarn Railway was opened in 1843 to transport slate from the quarries at Llanberis to Port Dinorwic along the north shore of Llyn Padarn. Both the port and the railway were owned by the Dinorwic Quarry Company, which also operated a network of 1-ft-10¾-in. lines within their quarries. Initially the line was a horse-worked tramway but steam power was soon introduced in 1848. An unusual feature of the railway were flat transporter wagons each of which accommodated 4 narrow-gauge slate wagons. After years of workmen riding unofficially on slate wagons, workmen's trains were finally introduced in the 1890s with the delivery of 19 4-wheel coaches from the Gloucester Railway Carriage & Wagon Company. Stations were also opened for the workmen and were in use until 1947 when the service was withdrawn. Of the railway's 5 steam locomotives only the oldest, 0-4-0 *Fire Queen* built in 1848, survives and is now preserved at the National Trust's Penrhyn Castle Railway Museum.

The decline in the slate industry eventually caused the closure of the line in 1961 but in 1970 work began on building a narrow-gauge tourist railway along part of the trackbed. By 1971 the route from Gilfach Ddu to Pen Llyn was complete and open to passengers. In 2003 the railway was extended from Gilfach Ddu to Llanberis with a new station across the road from the Snowdon Mountain Railway (see pages 148–9). Trains are operated by 3 historic Hunslet 0-4-0ST steam locomotives that originally worked in the nearby Dinorwic quarries: 1889-built No 1 *Elidir*, 1904-built No 2 *Thomas Bach*, 1922-built No 3 *Dolbadarn*. Four Ruston & Hornsby diesels complete the motive power line-up. Passengers are carried in both open and closed carriages which were all built in the railway's workshop. A journey along the line gives good views across the lake to Snowdon and the massive pumped storage hydro-electric plant that is located deep inside the nearby mountain on the same side of the lake as the railway. The railway's workshops and loco shed are located in the National Slate Museum at Gilfach Ddu.

THEN
The 4ft-gauge Padarn Railway's 0-6-0T Amalthæa *at Llanberis in the late 1950s. This loco was built by Hunslet in 1886 when it was named* Pandora *before being renamed in 1909. The line closed in 1961 and the loco was scrapped in 1963.*

NOW
Built by Hunslet in 1889, Llanberis Lake Railway's 0-4-0ST No 1 Elidir *on arrival at Llanberis station with a train from Penllyn. This loco carried various names when it originally worked at Dinorwic slate quarry, first being named* Enid *then later* Red Damsel.

SNOWDON MOUNTAIN RAILWAY

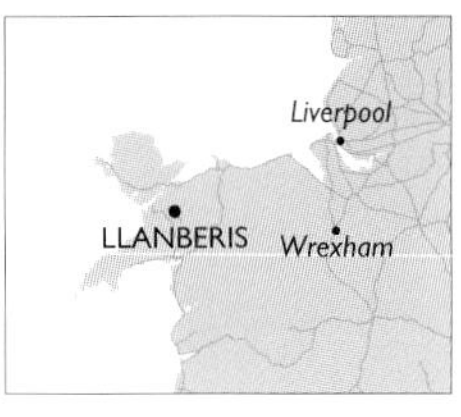

LLANBERIS
HEBRON
HALFWAY
ROCKY VALLEY HALT
CLOGWYN
SUMMIT

Invented by Swiss locomotive engineer Roman Abt, the Abt rack system allows steam trains to ascend mountain railways on gradients (up to 1-in-4) that are too steep for adhesion locomotives. In effect a rack-and-pinion system, locomotives are fitted with cogs placed between the driving wheels that mesh with a double rack laid between the rails. First used on the Harzbahn in Germany in 1885, the Abt system was chosen for Britain's first and only tourist steam mountain railway, which opened from Llanberis to the summit of Snowdon in 1896.

Employing 0-4-2 tank locomotives with sloping boilers, this 2ft-7½in.-gauge railway climbs for 4¾ miles on gradients as steep as 1-in-5 to the 3,560-ft summit of the mountain – from here, on clear days, tourists are treated to a magnificent view over Snowdonia and the Irish Sea. Apart from a tragic accident on the railway's opening day when a locomotive became derailed and a passenger killed, the railway has been operating without incident for 125 years. Trains are restricted to a speed limit of 5 mph on the line where gradients as

THEN
An early photograph, c.1899, of a Snowdon Mountain Tramroad & Hotels Company train. The loco is 0-4-2RT No 4 Snowdon built by the Swiss Locomotive & Machine Works of Winterthur in 1896.

severe as 1-in-5 can be encountered. Four Hunslet-built diesel hydraulic locomotives were introduced in 1986 as an economy measure but many of the seven 0-4-2T (the continental nomenclature would be 0-2-IT) steam locos, 4 of which are now 125 years old, are still in use. Built by the Swiss Locomotive & Machine Works of Winterthur these are numbered 2 to 8 (No 1 being involved in the accident on the opening day) and are named *Enid*, *Yr Wyddfa*, *Snowdon*, *Moel Siabod*, *Padarn*, *Ralph* and *Eryri*.

Subject to weather conditions, trains on the Snowdon Mountain Railway depart daily from Llanberis from late March to the end of October. From March to early May trains will normally terminate at either Clogwyn or Rocky Valley. Trains may be operated by steam or diesel traction. The spectacular new station and visitor centre on the summit were opened in 2009. Passengers are advised that train services can be restricted by bad weather conditions, especially at the beginning and end of the operating season.

Llanberis,
Gwynedd LL55 4TT

01286 870223
www.snowdonrailway.co.uk

LENGTH
4¾ miles

GAUGE
2ft 7½in.

OPEN
To Clogwyn, daily between late March & May; to the Summit, daily from May to end October (services can be restricted or cancelled by bad weather conditions; see website for details)

NOW
Clogwyn station with two ascending trains. At 2,556 ft above sea level the station is on an exposed ridge overlooking Llanberis Pass. Snowdon Summit station is another 937 ft higher.

NORTHERN ENGLAND

EAST LANCASHIRE RAILWAY

HEYWOOD
BURY BOLTON STREET
BURRS COUNTRY PARK
SUMMERSEAT
RAMSBOTTOM
IRWELL VALE
RAWTENSTALL

Bolton Street Station, Bury, Lancashire BL9 0EY

0333 320 2830
www.eastlancsrailway.org.uk

LENGTH
12 miles

GAUGE
Standard

OPEN
Weekends, January to March & October to November; daily (except Mondays & Tuesdays) & Bank Holidays, April to September; Santa Specials in December (see website)

THEN
There are few customers about on Rawtenstall station on 8 August 1964. The line from here to Bacup closed to passengers on 3 December 1966 with Bury to Rawtenstall passenger services ending on 3 June 1972.

NOW
BR Standard Class '2' 2-6-0 No 78018 crosses Brooksbottom Viaduct with a train on the East Lancashire Railway on 12 March 2019. Built at Darlington in 1954 this loco was withdrawn in November 1966 before being bought for preservation.

The 8¼-mile line from Bury (Bolton Street) to Rawtenstall was opened by the original East Lancashire Railway in 1846. Serving the important cotton spinning and weaving mills of the Rossendale valley, the ELR extended the line to Newchurch in 1848. A further extension to the town of Bacup was opened in 1852. The railway was absorbed by the Lancashire & Yorkshire Railway (L&YR) in 1859.

Although an increased frequency of new diesel multiple units was introduced on the Bury to Bacup service as early as 1956, the route, along with the line to Accrington, was listed for closure in the 'Beeching Report'. While the section from Bury to Rawtenstall was reprieved until 1972, the steeply-graded 4 miles of line east from Rawtenstall to Bacup closed completely on 5 December 1966. Rawtenstall continued to be served by a diesel multiple unit service from Bury until 3 June 1972 when the line closed to passengers. Coal trains continued to serve Rawtenstall until 1980 when the line closed completely.

Prior to closure a preservation group had already moved into Bury and subsequently opened a transport museum in 1969. After financial assistance, exceeding £1 million, from the local councils and county council, the newly-formed East Lancashire Railway started running public trains between Bury and Ramsbottom in 1987, with Rawtenstall being reached in 1991. Opened in 2003, the steeply-graded eastward link from Bury to Heywood connects with the Calder Valley Line of the national rail system. Trains are operated along the picturesque Irwell Valley with its several viaducts, via the intermediate stations of Burrs Country Park, Summerset, Ramsbottom and Irwell Vale, by a variety of preserved mainline steam and diesel locomotives. Steam locomotives on the ELR, either operational or being overhauled, include L&YR 0-6-0 No 52322, LMS 'Crab' 2-6-0 No 42765, SR 'West Country' Class 4-6-2 No 34092 *City of Wells*, BR Standard Class '4' 2-6-4Ts Nos 80080 and 80097 and GWR '7200' Class 2-8-2T No 7229.

Visiting locomotives from other railways can frequently be seen in action and the ELR has built up a reputation for its varied collection of preserved diesels which can be seen in action on several diesel weekends. Preserved mainline diesels include examples from BR Classes 01, 05, 08, 20, 24, 33, 37, 40, 50 and 55.

Close to the ELR Bury Bolton Street station is the Bury Transport Museum with its varied transport collection.

Castlecroft Goods Warehouse, Castlecroft Road, Bury BL9 0LN
0161 763 7949
www.burytransportmuseum.org.uk

CLAYTON WEST
CUCKOOS NEST
SKELMANTHORPE
SHELLEY

Park Mill Way,
Clayton West, Huddersfield,
West Yorkshire HD8 9XJ

01484 865727
www.whistlestopvalley.co.uk

LENGTH
3 miles

GAUGE
15in.

OPEN
Weekends & Bank Holidays throughout year; daily during school holidays; Santa Specials prior to Christmas (see website)

A curious survivor of the 'Beeching Axe', the 4-mile branch line from Shepley, on the Huddersfield to Penistone line, to Clayton West was opened by the Lancashire & Yorkshire Railway in 1879. Although built as a single-track railway, all bridges and the 511-yd Shelley Woodhouse Tunnel were designed to accommodate double track. The branch was served by through trains to and from Huddersfield with diesel multiple units being introduced in 1959. In 1961, 6 return trains on weekdays plus a late night service on Saturdays sufficed to serve the few customers that used the line. Needless to say this loss-making branch line along with the Huddersfield to Penistone service were both listed for closure in the 'Beeching Report' but, despite poor patronage, it survived another 20 years before closure on 24 January 1983. The Huddersfield to Penistone (for Barnsley) line was reprieved and is open today.

The Clayton West branch line came back to life in 1991 when the 15in.-gauge miniature Kirklees Light Railway was opened along the trackbed from the terminus to Cuckoo's Nest. The railway was the brainchild of Brian Taylor who was also involved in the building of a 10¼in.-gauge miniature steam railway at Shibden Park, Halifax. After several years of searching for a suitable site, work started on the present line in 1990. The first train ran to Cuckoo's Nest in 1991, to Skelmanthorpe in late 1992 and Shelley via Shelley Woodhouse Tunnel in 1997. Locomotives operating on the line include Hunslet-type 2-6-2 tank *Fox*, articulated 0-4+4-0s *Hawk* and *Owl* and 0-6-4 saddle tank *Badger*. Rolling stock consists of 20-seat carriages, the fully enclosed examples being heated. All locomotives and rolling stock were built for the railway by Brian Taylor who has built and continues to supply equipment for other railways. The Kirklees Light Railway was rebranded as 'Whistlestop Valley' in 2021.

NOW
Two locos named Katie *side by side at Clayton West shed on 14 September 2019. The miniature loco on the far left is a 15in.-gauge 4-4-0 'Cagney' from Rhyl Miniature Railway.*

Founded by Act of Parliament in 1758, the Middleton Railway is the world's oldest continuously working railway. It was originally built as a wooden waggonway to a gauge of 4ft 1in. to carry coal from collieries on Charles Branding's Middleton Estate to the city of Leeds. Initially using horsepower, in 1812 it became the first commercial railway in the world to successfully employ steam locomotives. Designed by John Blenkinsop, 4 2-cylinder steam locomotives were built using a rack-and-pinion system with cogs on the driving wheels meshing with an outer toothed rail. The first 2 locomotives were built by Matthew Murray of Holbeck in 1812 and proved an immediate success, staying in service until 1835 when horse power was reintroduced. Steam haulage returned in 1866 and the railway was converted to standard gauge in 1881. The Middleton Estate became part of the nationalised National Coal Board in 1947.

In 1960, the Middleton Railway became the first standard-gauge line to be run by volunteers, mainly Leeds University undergraduates, and continued to operate freight services until 1983. Home to a large number of preserved industrial steam and diesel locomotives built in Leeds by companies such as Hunslet, Manning Wardle and Hudswell Clarke, the railway also owns an interesting collection of rolling stock which is used on the line or exhibited in the museum. Operating steam locomotives include North Eastern Railway Class 'Y7' 0-4-0T No 1310, built in 1891, and 0-6-0ST No 2387 *Brookes No. 1*. Of more recent interest is the only tunnel on the railway, 263-ft-long, that carries the line under the M621. Future plans include extending the line from Park Halt into Middleton Park, site of former waggonways and collieries.

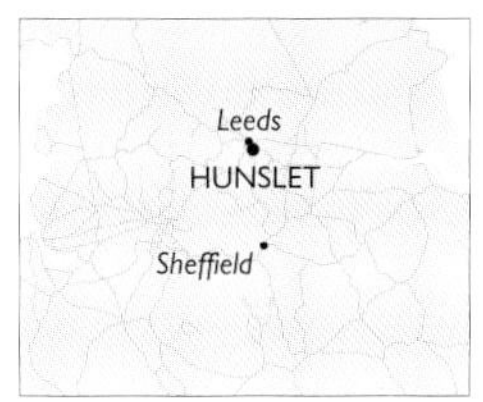

MOOR ROAD
PARK HALT

The Station, Moor Road, Hunslet, Leeds LS10 2JQ

0845 680 1758
www.middletonrailway.org.uk

LENGTH
1 mile

GAUGE
Standard

OPEN
Diesel service every Saturday afternoon; steam service every Sunday & Bank Holiday

NOW
Preserved departmental 0-4-0VBT locomotive No 54 (BR No 68153) heads a short train on the Middleton Railway. Built by the Sentinel Waggon Works in 1933 as LNER Class 'Y1' this loco was withdrawn from service in 1961.

EMBSAY & BOLTON ABBEY STEAM RAILWAY

EMBSAY
HOLYWELL HALT
BOLTON ABBEY

Bolton Abbey Station,
Bolton Abbey, Skipton,
North Yorkshire BD23 6AF

01756 710614
www.embsayboltonabbeyrailway.org.uk

LENGTH
4 miles

GAUGE
Standard

OPEN
Daily during school summer holiday & Bank Holidays; weekends, April to June, September & October; Sundays in November; weekends in December (excluding 25th & 26th); see website for special event days

The first railway to reach Ilkley was the North Eastern Railway (NER) and Midland Railway's (MR) joint line from Otley (the then terminus of the NER's branch line from Arthington Junction, on the Leeds to Harrogate line) in 1865. From the west, the MR's 11½-mile line from Skipton to Ilkley opened in 1888 – part of this line ran through the Duke of Devonshire's estate at Bolton Hall and required considerable landscaping to hide it from his view. A popular destination for excursion trains, Bolton Abbey station was also frequented by royalty when visiting the Duke in his country mansion. So popular was it with daytrippers that even as late as the summer of 1961 it was still served by 7 trains from Leeds and further afield on Sundays.

While diesel multiple units were introduced in 1959, all railways serving Ilkley were subsequently listed for closure in the 'Beeching Report'. The services from Leeds via Apperley Junction and from Shipley via Esholt Junction were reprieved and have since been electrified. The line from Skipton via Otley was not so lucky and closed to passengers on 22 March 1965. Goods services ceased 4 months later.

In 1979 the Yorkshire Dales Railway obtained a Light Railway Order for part of the line and since then has re-opened 4 miles from Embsay, with its original Midland Railway buildings, to a new award-winning terminus at Bolton Abbey via Holywell Halt. The railway owns and operates a very large collection of finely restored industrial steam locomotives, vintage carriages and diesels. Among the latter are Class 14 diesel-hydraulic D9513 and Class 37 No 37294. A Class 31, D5600, is currently being overhauled while Class 47 D1524 is in storage. Of particular interest is a 1903 North Eastern Railway petrol-electric autocar and trailer that have been restored to operational condition. Operational steam locomotives include Hunslet 0-6-0ST *Beatrice* and Hudswell Clarke *Illingworth* while there are 10 others either under overhaul, restoration or stored.

Future plans include a physical link at the site of Embsay Junction with the main railway network to Skipton station via the freight-only line from Swinden Quarry on the former Grassington branch. In the other direction it is a long-term aim for the railway to be extended to Addingham, doubling its current length, but this would be a huge task.

THEN
Two years after closure, dereliction and decay is setting in at Embsay station in October 1967.

NOW
Seen here at Bolton Abbey station 0-6-0ST Beatrice *was built by Hunslet in 1945 and is a former National Coal Board loco that once worked at Ackton Hall Colliery in Pontefract.*

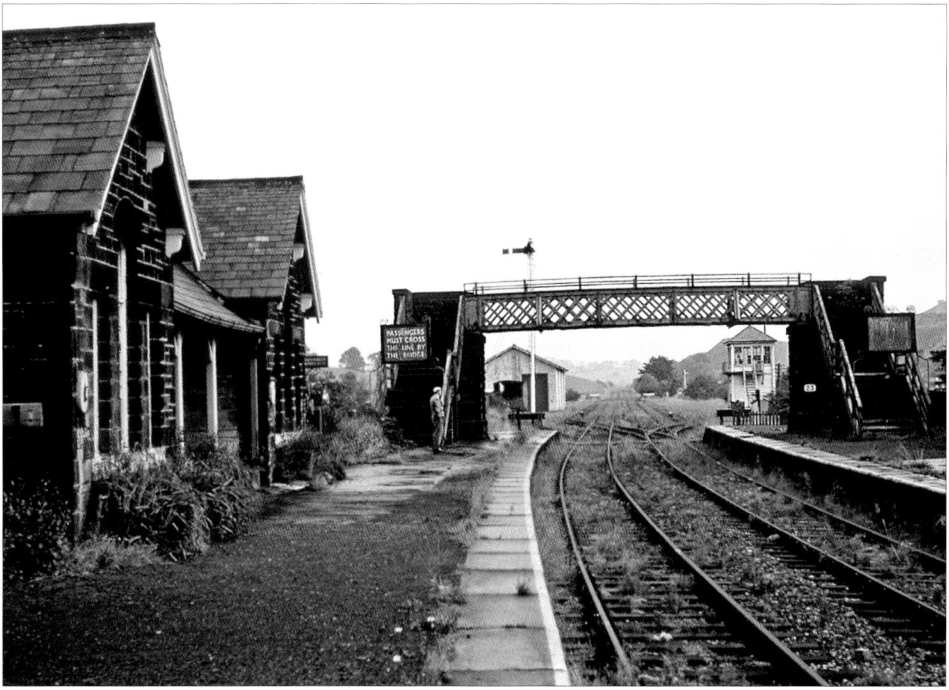
PASSENGERS
MUST CROSS
THE LINE BY
THE BRIDGE
23

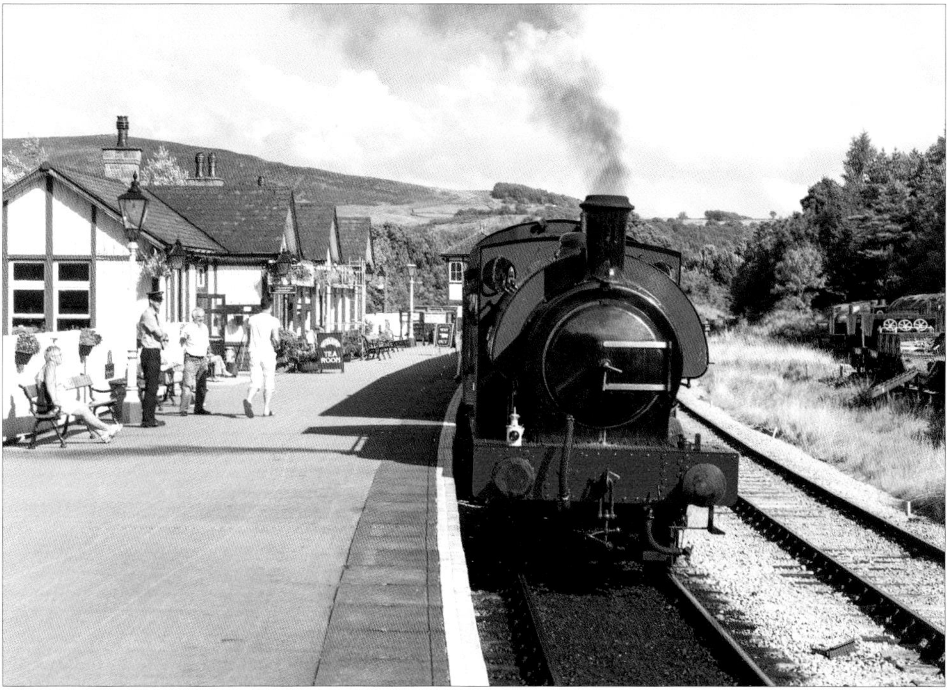
TEA
ROOM

61264

This was one of the earliest preserved standard-gauge railways in Britain, re-opened by a preservation society in 1968. The single-track railway still serves the community of the Worth Valley as originally intended. The former Midland Railway branch from Keighley, on the main Leeds to Skipton line, to Oxenhope opened in 1867 to serve 3 small towns and the 15 mills along the valley. In 1892 the deviation through Mytholmes Tunnel, between Haworth and Oakworth, was opened and the old route across a large wooden viaduct closed.

The branch line was closed by British Railways on 30 December 1961 although goods traffic continued until 18 June 1962. A last train from Bradford organised by the fledgling Keighley & Worth Valley Preservation Society was run to Oxenhope on 23 June after which the railway closed completely between there and Ingrow Junction. The society purchased the line from British Railways and reopened it on 29 June 1968 – the very first train on that date was the only one to operate in Britain due to a national rail strike.

The line, although short, offers much to the visitor together with its associations with the Brontës at Haworth and the filming of E. Nesbit's *The Railway Children* at Oakworth. It has also starred in many films and TV series, including *Last of the Summer Wine*, *Pink Floyd – The Wall*, *Peaky Blinders* and *Swallows and Amazons*. A collection of 20 steam locos, 10 diesel locomotives and 6 diesel railcars has been built up over the years and the railway is also home to 2 museums, The Vintage ▶

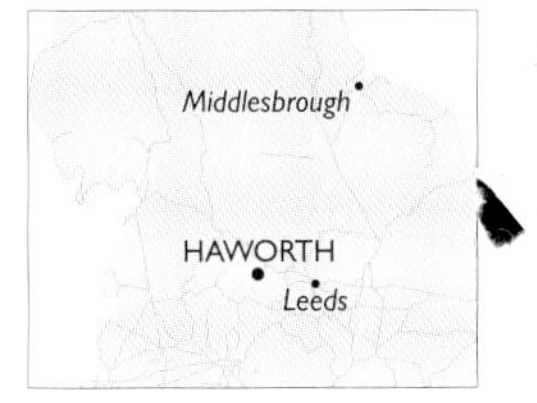

- **KEIGHLEY**
- INGROW (WEST)
- DAMEMS
- OAKWORTH
- HAWORTH
- OXENHOPE

NOW
Reflections in Mytholmes Tunnel on 9 March 2017 as ex-LNER Class 'B1' 4-6-0 No 61264 approaches with a freight train.

THEN
A Class 108 diesel multiple unit heading for Oxenhope pauses at Haworth station on 13 May 1961. The line closed at the end of that year.

The Railway Station, Haworth,
West Yorkshire BD22 8NJ

01535 645214
www.kwvr.co.uk

LENGTH
5 miles

GAUGE
Standard

OPEN
Weekends all year; daily, Easter week, Spring Bank Holiday, July, August, October half term & Boxing Day to New Year's Day

NOW
Preserved ex-LNER Class 'B1' 4-6-0 No 61264 makes a fine sight as it heads up the Worth Valley near Damems on 9 March 2017. Built by the North British Locomotive Company in 1947 this loco was withdrawn in November 1965.

Carriage Trust at Ingrow (see page 206) and the Railway Museum at Oxenhope, along with extensive workshop facilities. Locomotives on the KWVR include 1874-built Haydock Foundry 0-6-0WT *Bellerophon*, Taff Vale Railway 'O2' Class 0-6-2T No 85, L&YR 0-6-0 No 52044, L&YR 0-4-0ST No 51218, LMS '4F' 0-6-0 No 43924, LMS Ivatt 2-6-2T No 41241, LMS '5MT' 4-6-0 No 45212, double-chimney LMS 'Jubilee' Class 4-6-0 No 45596 *Bahamas* built in 1935, BR Standard Class '2' 2-6-0 No 78022 and BR Standard Class '4' 4-6-0 No 75078. National Trust-owned LNWR 0-6-2 'Coal Tank' No 1054 is on display at Oxenhope Exhibition Shed. Diesels are represented by BR Classes 08, 20, 25, 37, several industrial examples, the prototype English Electric shunter D0226, Class 101 and 108 diesel multiple units and 2 Waggon & Maschinenbau railbuses.

Steam trains operate most of the services along this picturesque route calling at carefully restored award-winning gas-lit stations. Early morning services at weekends are usually operated by a diesel multiple unit or railbus. Tiny Damems station is reputably the smallest in Britain.

Linking the docks at Victoria Quay on the River Ribble to Preston's mainline station, the Preston Dock Branch Line opened in 1845. The network of lines, at its peak extending to 27 miles around both sides of Albert Edward Basin, was initially operated by the North Union Railway until 1889 when Preston Corporation took over operations. The corporation employed 8 steam tank engines until 1968 when they were replaced by 3 Sentinel diesels. They remain in service today with Ribble Rail working bitumen trains.

The Ribble Steam Railway opened in 2005 and runs steam-hauled trains along part of the standard-gauge Preston Dock Branch Line, crossing Preston Marina on a swing bridge, during summer months. The adjoining museum includes a very large collection of nearly 50 industrial steam and diesel locomotives, many from the now defunct Southport Railway Museum. The 1863-built Furness Railway 0-4-0 tender locomotive No 20 is currently being overhauled in the workshops while GWR 'Hall' Class 4-6-0 No 4979 *Wootton Hall* is awaiting restoration. One little-known fact about the railway is that it is one of a small handful of heritage railways in the UK to operate regular revenue-earning freight trains – bitumen trains once again operate three times a week between the Total oil refinery at Lindsey in Lincolnshire to a bitumen plant served by the railway.

NOW

Former Vulcan Foundry works shunter 0-4-0ST Vulcan, *built in 1918, moves off shed at the Ribble Steam Railway to take up its duties on the first passenger service train of the day on 13 September 2014. On the right, Aspinall L&YR Class '27' 0-6-0, LMS No 12322 (BR No 52322), built in 1896, also prepares to leave the shed during one of the railway's regular gala events.*

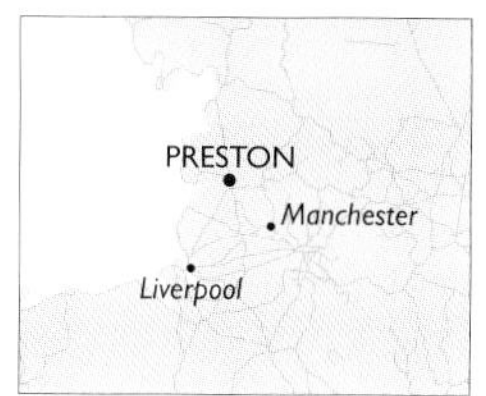

PRESTON RIVERSIDE

Chain Caul Road, Preston, Lancashire PR2 2PD

01772 728 800
www.ribblesteam.org.uk

LENGTH
1½ miles

GAUGE
Standard

OPEN
Every weekend & Bank Holiday, May to October; Wednesdays in August; during Easter & on Sundays in April; Santa Specials in December

EDEN VALLEY RAILWAY

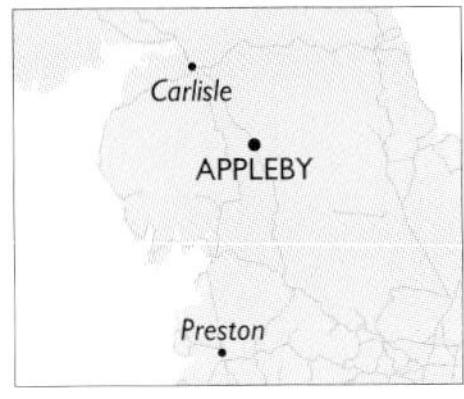

Warcop Station, Warcop, Appleby, Cumbria CA16 6PR

017683 42309
www.evr-cumbria.org.uk

LENGTH
2¼ miles

GAUGE
Standard

OPEN
Bank Holiday Mondays & most Sundays, March to September (see website)

The Eden Valley Railway opened between Kirkby Stephen and Clifton, south of Penrith, in 1862. Carrying freight was the primary role for this railway, notably iron ore from Cumberland and Lancashire to steel works in the North East via Barnard Castle and coal and coke in the other direction. The railway soon amalgamated with the Stockton & Darlington Railway before becoming part of the North Eastern Railway in 1863. In more recent times 2-car diesel multiple units were introduced in 1958 for the sparse passenger service. This was to no avail and this service was withdrawn on 22 January 1962. However the Appleby to Warcop section was left open for military trains to an army training centre but these ceased in 1989 when the track was mothballed.

The Eden Valley Railway Society was formed in 1995 with the aim of restoring the 6-mile line between Appleby East and Flitholme, near Warcop. In 2004 the Eden Valley Railway Trust was given permission to reopen the railway. Since 2006 trains have been running again but at present only along the short section between Warcop and Sandford. A large collection of mainly industrial diesel locomotives along with diesel and electric multiple units is based at Warcop. Mainline diesels Class 37 37042 and Class 47 47799 *Prince Henry* (in Royal Train livery) are currently being restored. A model railway operates in the exhibition coach.

NOW
On 2 February 2012, the Eden Valley Railway was undertaking track maintenance work in preparation for the 2012 operating season, and their 1962-built 0-6-0 diesel-hydraulic locomotive Darlington *is seen soon after leaving Warcop station propelling a Shark brake van and Lowmac wagon.*

Connected to York via the Foss Islands branch line, the original Derwent Valley Light Railway, an independent company, opened in 1913 and ran for 16 miles from Layerthorpe in York to Cliffe Common, just outside Selby. Trains originally ran as mixed traffic but passenger services ceased in 1926. Closure of the line to goods traffic was in stages – to Elvington in 1968, to Dunnington in 1973 with final closure of the remainder in 1982. Once serving Rowntree's chocolate factory and Layerthorpe, the Foss Islands branch line was closed in 1989. The ½-mile section of the DVLR that remains today runs from Murton Lane to the Osbaldwick road. During the Second World War the railway was heavily used by the War Department as a supply route to the airfields at Elvington, Skipwith and the depot at Wheldrake. The railway was nicknamed 'The Blackberry Line' from the days when it transported the fruit to markets in Yorkshire and London.

The railway has been run since 1993 by the Great Yorkshire Railway Preservation Society and is based on a site at the former DVLR station at Murton Lane which also houses the Yorkshire Museum of Farming and a reconstructed Viking village. Diesel shunter locomotives on the DVLR include 1956-built BR 0-6-0 D2245, 1960-built BR Class 03 No 03079 and industrial examples from builders such as Ruston & Hornsby and Fowler. Rolling stock includes 2 BR Mk 1 coaches, a replica NER 4-wheel coach, an observation car, BR goods wagons and guards van, a Wickham trolley and a restored original DVLR pump trolley.

The award-winning restored former North Eastern Railway signal box is also open to visitors. Wheldrake station is one of three surviving original DVR timber station buildings and was dismantled piece by piece from its former site and reconstructed at Murton. To the west, the trackbed of the line from Layerthorpe to Osbaldwick is now a footpath and cycleway, part of National Cycle Network Route 66.

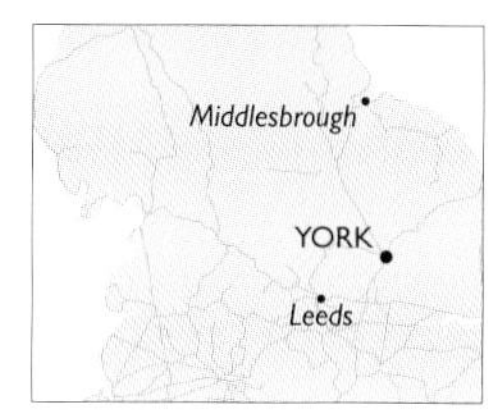

YORKSHIRE MUSEUM OF FARMING

Yorkshire Museum of Farming, Murton Park, Murton, York YO19 5UF

01904 489966
www.dvlr.org.uk

LENGTH
½ mile

GAUGE
Standard

OPEN
Sundays & Bank Holidays, Easter to end September

THEN
Ex-NER Class 'J25' 0-6-0 No 65714 pauses at York Layerthorpe station with a freight train for the Derwent Valley Light Railway, c.1959. This veteran loco was built at Darlington in 1900 and withdrawn from York shed in January 1961.

Nº 29

The 35¼-mile line between Malton and Whitby was opened by the Whitby & Pickering Railway (W&PR) in 1836. One of the earliest railways in Britain, it was initially horse-drawn and included the rope-worked 1-in-15 Beck Hole Incline. The W&PR was taken over by George Hudson's York & North Midland Railway in 1845 – the same year that he had opened the railway between York and Scarborough. The Malton to Whitby line was then rebuilt for steam haulage but the Beck Hole Incline still impeded progress until after the North Eastern Railway (NER) had taken over in 1854. Bypassing the incline, a new deviation with a gradient of 1-in-49 was opened between Goathland and Grosmont in 1865.

By the 20th century the line's scenic qualities through Newtondale Gorge and across the moors were being heavily promoted by the NER and its successor, the London & North Eastern Railway. During the summer months through trains from York and Leeds were running over the line to Whitby. These continued to run after the Second World War although by the late 1950s new diesel multiple units had taken over some of these duties. Even as late as the summer of 1961 there were 4 through trains from York (one included a through carriage from King's Cross) and 1 from Leeds on Saturdays – the journey time from Malton to Whitby being around 1 hr 10 mins. There were also 2 trains from Whitby that terminated at Goathland. The 3 Sunday services included through trains from Selby and Leeds. ▶

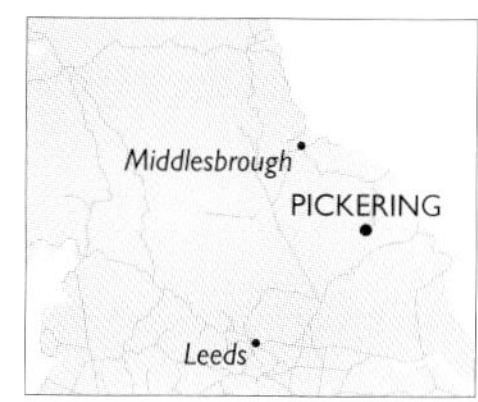

WHITBY
RUSWARP
SLEIGHTS
GROSMONT
GOATHLAND
NEWTON DALE HALT
LEVISHAM
PICKERING

Pickering Station, Pickering, North Yorkshire YO18 7AJ

01751 472508
www.nymr.co.uk

NOW
Built for Lambton Collieries by Kitson of Leeds in 1904, preserved 0-6-2T No 29 retired from hauling coal trains at Philadelphia in Wearside in 1969. The loco is seen hauling a short goods train at Beck Hole on 26 September 2019.

THEN
BR Standard Class '2' 2-6-2T No 82029 and 3-coach train departs from Levisham station on 13 October 1961. Built at Swindon Works in 1954 this loco was later transferred to Nine Elms shed in southwest London from where it was withdrawn in July 1967.

LENGTH
18 miles

GAUGE
Standard

OPEN
Daily, end March to end October; Santa Specials at Christmas; for numerous special events see website

Listed for closure in the 'Beeching Report', the 29 miles between Malton and Grosmont (for the Esk Valley Line) closed on 8 March 1965 – on that day Whitby also lost its train service from Scarborough. Goods trains continued to run from Malton to Pickering until the following year.

The North Yorkshire Moors Railway Preservation Society took over part of the line in 1967 and in 1973 trains started running again on what is now the second-longest preserved standard-gauge railway in the UK. A workshop and engine sheds have been established at Grosmont and trains are operated by a large collection of powerful mainline steam and diesel locomotives. Locomotives include SR 'Schools' Class 4-4-0 No 30926 *Repton*, LMS Class '5' 4-6-0 No 5428 *Eric Treacy*, SR Class 'S15' 4-6-0 No 30825, Lambton Collieries 0-6-2T No 29, LNER Class 'Q7' 0-8-0 No 63395, Class 'B1' 4-6-0 No 1264 and BR Standard Class '9F' 2-10-0 No 92134 as well as several ex-BR mainline diesels (Classes 04, 08, 11, 24, 25, 26, 37) and diesel multiple units (Class 101). A large and varied collection of rolling stock includes a Pullman set. NYMR trains connect with the main network at Grosmont, on the scenic Whitby to Middlesbrough Esk Valley Line. Certain NYMR steam-hauled trains continue their journey for 6 miles along the Esk Valley from Grosmont to the historic harbour town of Whitby. A journey on the railway, one of the most visited in Britain, across the wild grandeur of the North Yorkshire Moors National Park to Pickering involves a steep climb to Goathland, known to TV addicts as 'Aidensfield' in *Heartbeat*, before entering the picturesque Newtondale Gorge. In addition to Heartbeat the railway has featured in many film and TV productions including *Harry Potter*, *Dad's Army*, *Downton Abbey*, *Casualty*, *Poirot*, and *Sherlock Holmes*.

NOW
Preserved BR Standard Class '4' 2-6-0s No 76038 and No 76084 disturb the peace and tranquility of Newtondale as they double-head a passenger train on the North Yorkshire Moors Railway on 3 November 2016.

This delightful single-track rural line through the Yorkshire Dales was opened by the North Eastern Railway between Northallerton and Hawes in 1878. It was extended westward from Hawes to Garsdale by the Midland Railway in 1878. Passenger traffic between Northallerton and Hawes ceased in 1954 and from Hawes to Garsdale, by then consisting of 1 train each way a day, in 1959. The remaining branch from Northallerton was cut back to Redmire in 1964 but the line remained open for stone trains from Redmire Quarry until 1992.

Since then the Wensleydale Railway Association (formed in 1990), with financial help from the MOD who use the line to transport military vehicles to and from Catterick Garrison, have reintroduced in stages passenger trains between Northallerton and Redmire, making it one of longest heritage railways in Britain. From east to west there are now intermediate stations at Scruton, Leeming Bar, Bedale, Finghall and Leyburn. Trains are normally operated by diesel multiple units or are diesel-hauled but steam can also be seen in action on certain weekends during the summer.

Two steam locomotives are awaiting overhaul and preservation: North Eastern Railway Class 'J72' 0-6-0 No 69023 *Joem* and BR Standard Class '9F' 2-10-0 No 92219. A large number of BR mainline diesels are based on the railway, either operational or awaiting restoration/overhaul. They include examples of Classes 20, 25, 31, 37, 47 and 60.

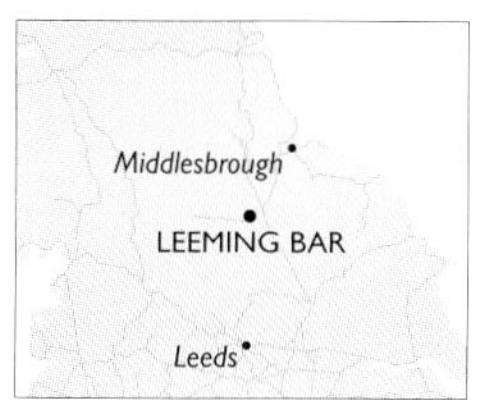

- NORTHALLERTON
- NORTHALLERTON WEST
- SCRUTON
- LEEMING BAR
- BEDALE
- FINGHALL
- LEYBURN
- REDMIRE

Leeming Bar Station,
Leases Road, Leeming Bar,
Northallerton,
North Yorkshire DL7 9AR

01677 425805
www.wensleydale-railway.co.uk

LENGTH
22 miles

GAUGE
Standard

OPEN
Tuesdays, Fridays, weekends & Bank Holidays, April to November; daily, mid June to September

NOW
Built at Darlington in 1923 preserved ex-LNER Class 'J27' No 65894 hauls a passenger train near the village of Wensley on the Wensleydale Railway on 25 August 2018. This long-lived loco was withdrawn by British Railways in September 1967.

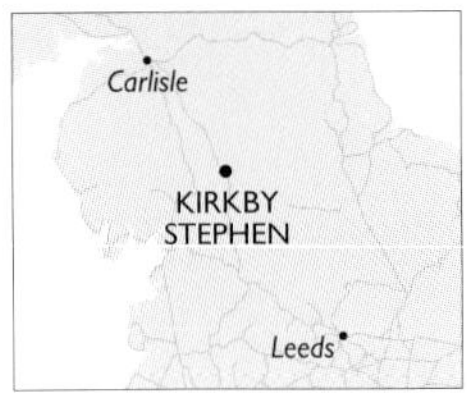

KIRKBY STEPHEN

KIRKBY STEPHEN EAST

Built to transport iron ore from Cumberland to the northeast and coke to blast furnaces in Workington and Barrow-in-Furness, the South Durham & Lancashire Union Railway (SD&LUR) opened between Barnard Castle and Tebay in 1861. It was worked from opening by the Stockton & Darlington Railway (S&DR)

Trains heading for the ironworks of West Cumberland were soon able to travel via the single-track line from Kirkby Stephen to Clifton, south of Penrith, which opened in 1862. Known as the Eden Valley Railway it was also worked from the outset by the S&DR and, along with the SD&LUR, was taken over by that company a year later. The S&DR was itself merged with the larger North Eastern Railway (NER) in July 1863. A spur south of Penrith linked the Eden Valley Railway to the Cockermouth, Keswick & Penrith Railway when that railway opened in 1864, enabling coke trains to travel across the Lake District to the Workington ironworks.

Trains were usually double-headed over the line's Stainmore Summit (1,370 ft above sea level) and across Belah Viaduct – at 196 ft high and with a span of 1,040 ft it was the tallest railway bridge in England. The railway was so successful that the single line was doubled by the NER in 1870 but working heavy trains up the steeply-graded line to Stainmore Summit from both directions necessitated double heading and/or banking in the rear right through to the British Railways era. The line was also at the mercy of winter weather with snowdrifts often blocking the line near Stainmore.

The Kirkby Stephen to Tebay line closed to passengers in 1952 but it was still used by the summer-Saturday trains from the northeast to

THEN
BR Standard Class '3' 2-6-0 No 77003 and Class '4' 2-6-0 76049 about to depart from Kirkby Stephen East station with the Railway Correspondence & Travel Society's 'Stainmore Ltd' special on the last day of services on the line from Barnard Castle to Penrith, 20 January 1962.

Blackpool until 1961. On the mainline over Stainmore summit diesel multiple units replaced steam passenger services in 1959 but this was all to no avail. First to go were the freight trains, which were diverted via Hexham and Carlisle, then the few remaining passenger services were withdrawn on 22 January 1962 when the line closed completely between Barnard Castle and Penrith.

The line from Appleby East to the army depot at Warcop (see Eden Valley Railway, page 162) remained open until 1989 but by then Kirkby Stephen East station had become a mill. By 1992 the mill had closed and the station site had become derelict. In 1997 the site was bought for use as the eastern terminus of a proposed preserved railway by the Stainmore Railway Company. Since then a group of volunteers have been restoring the station and laying track within the 6½-acre site with the long-term aim of opening a Heritage Centre and a working railway. First reopened to the public in 2009, the station saw working steam locomotives once again in August 2011 in celebration of the 150th anniversary of the opening of the Stainmore line. In 2017 the railway received lottery funding to restore to working condition 19th-century North Eastern Railway Class 'J21' 0-6-0 No 65033. Other steam locomotives based here include 1875-built NER 2-4-0 No 910 (on loan from the National Collection), a 1954-built Hunslet ex-NCB 0-6-0 No 68009 and two 1948-built Peckett 0-4-0STs, *F. C. Tingey* and *Lytham St. Annes*. Five LNER Gresley teak carriages are also being restored at the railway.

Kirkby Stephen East Station,
South Road, Kirkby Stephen,
Cumbria CA17 4LA

017683 71700
www.kirkbystepheneast.co.uk

LENGTH
⅓ mile

GAUGE
Standard

OPEN
Weekends throughout the year; for details of special events see website

NOW
During one of its occasional operating days, Stainmore Railway's Frank Hibberd 'Planet' 4-wheel diesel-hydraulic, built in 1961, pilots 'OY1 Special' Class Peckett 0-4-0ST F.C. Tingey, built in 1948, originally working in industry for Courtaulds at Holywell Junction.

HAVERTHWAITE
NEWBY BRIDGE
LAKESIDE

Haverthwaite Station, Ulverston, Cumbria LA12 8AL

015395 31594
www.lakesiderailway.co.uk

LENGTH
3½ miles

GAUGE
Standard

OPEN
Weekends, April to Christmas week; daily early April to end October; see website for special events

The 9½-mile branch line from Ulverston, on the mainline between Carnforth and Barrow-in-Furness, to Windermere Lake Side, at the southern tip of Lake Windermere, was opened in 1869 by the Furness Railway (FR). It was connected to the mainline by a triangular junction at Plumpton to the east of Ulverston. At Lakeside, trains connected directly with steamers operated by the Windermere United Steam Yacht Company, which plied up and down Lake Windermere – the FR bought this company in 1875. The stations at each end of the line were magnificent affairs – a grand Italianate building had been opened at Ulverston in 1872 while the pier station at Lakeside was fitted out in an opulent style complete with a Palm Court restaurant and orchestra.

The branch remained popular with tourists until the Second World War but a rapid decline in passenger numbers had set in by the 1950s. Despite this, the branch was still served by through trains/carriages to and from Morecambe, Blackpool, Preston and Barrow during the summer months until the early 1960s. Listed for closure in the 'Beeching Report', the line closed to passengers on 5 September 1965. The Windermere steamers, by then owned by British Railways, were also sold off. Goods traffic continued to serve ironworks at Haverthwaite until 24 April 1967 when the line closed completely. It was subsequently severed by 'road improvements' at Haverthwaite.

A preservation group took over the steeply-graded section from Haverthwaite to Lakeside and steam trains started running again in 1973 when the line was opened by the then Bishop of Wakefield (also a famous railway photographer) the Rt Rev. Eric Treacy. The short but highly scenic journey can be taken in conjunction with a 10½-mile trip along Lake Windermere to Ambleside as trains connect with steamers at Lakeside terminus. A collection of 5 restored industrial and 2 ex-BR steam and diesel locomotives are used on the line with the main motive power being 2 LMS designed and BR-built Fairburn 2-6-4 tank engines, Nos 42073 and 42085, dating from 1950 and 1951 respectively. Diesel locomotives include examples from BR Classes 03, 11, 20 and 33 along with a Class 110 diesel multiple unit.

THEN
Ex-LMS 'Jubilee' Class 4-6-0 No 45574 India *runs round its train at Lake Side after arriving from Blackpool on 6 July 1964. Built by the North British Locomotive Company in 1934 this loco was withdrawn in 1966.*

NOW
BR-built Fairburn Class '4' 2-6-4T No 42073 makes a fine sight in the late autumn sunshine as it heads through Great Hagg Wood en route to Lakeside on 11 November 2016. This loco was built at Brighton Works in 1950 and withdrawn in October 1967.

RAVENGLASS

- RAVENGLASS
- MUNCASTER MILL
- MITESIDE HALT
- MURTHWAITE HALT
- IRTON ROAD
- THE GREEN
- FISHERGROUND
- BECKFOOT
- DALEGARTH FOR BOOT

Opened on 24 May 1875, the original Ravenglass & Eskdale Railway (R&ER) was built as a 3-ft narrow-gauge mineral line designed to carry haematite iron ore from three mines near the village of Boot to Furness Railway transhipment sidings at Ravenglass. Following calls from local people a passenger service was introduced in November 1876 but the cost of upgrading the line forced the railway company into bankruptcy the following year. However, trains continued to be run under the control of official receivers. To make matters worse all the mines had closed by 1885 and although the R&ER became popular with daytrippers in the summer months the end for the little line was nigh. The line was in such a poor state that it was declared unsafe for passengers in 1908 with goods trains struggling on until April 1913 when it closed completely.

However, Wenman Joseph Bassett-Lowke, the famous manufacturer of model and miniature railways, came to the rescue and rebuilt the line to 15in.-gauge. The first locomotive was 'Atlantic' 4-4-2 *Sans Pareil* and in 1915 trains ran again on what was billed as the 'World's Smallest Public Railway'. A daily train service operated and an additional locomotive, 0-8-0 *Muriel* (later to become *River Irt* and converted to 0-8-2), was purchased from Sir Arthur Heywood's privately-owned Duffield Bank line in Derbyshire. The line flourished with the growth of new granite traffic and a new locomotive, 2-8-2 *River Esk*, was built. In 1925 the R&ER was purchased by Sir Aubrey Brocklebank, a wealthy shipping owner, who enlarged the quarry and stone crushing plant. Following the end of the Second World War the R&ER was purchased by the Keswick Granite Company in 1948. The granite quarry closed in 1953 although passenger trains continued to operate in the summer months until 1960 when the owners announced that the railway would be closed and sold off at auction as 60 separate lots.

THEN
Passenger train on the 15in.-gauge Ravenglass & Eskdale Railway, c.1927. The train is hauled by 2-8-2 River Esk *which was built by Davey Paxman in 1923 and is still in service today. The track is still laid on the old 3ft-gauge sleepers of the previous narrow-gauge railway that closed in 1913.*

However, a last minute rescue operation was mounted by railway enthusiasts and the line was saved again when they bought the entire operation at the auction held in September. In 1967 another locomotive, 2-8-2 *River Mite*, entered service and with improved revenues the railway has been progressively restored. The railway workshops at Ravenglass constructed 2-6-2 *Northern Rock* in 1976 and have also built new diesel and steam locomotives for other 15in.-gauge lines. The R&ER also pioneered the use of radio for operation of their trains, a safety system that is now widely used by the mainline railways. The headquarters of the line at Ravenglass, also home to the railway-owned 'Ratty Arms' public house and an interesting railway museum, is situated adjacent to the national rail network station on the Cumbrian Coast Line between Barrow-in-Furness and Carlisle. Nine steam and 8 internal combustion locomotives now operate on the line, and coaching stock consists of a mixture of open, semi-open and closed saloons. The eastern terminus at Dalegarth is ideally located as a starting point for hill walkers to the Roman fort at Hardknott Pass.

Railway Station, Ravenglass, Cumbria CA18 1SW

01229 717171
www.ravenglass-railway.co.uk

LENGTH
7 miles

GAUGE
15in.

OPEN
Weekends & half term, early February & March; daily, April to end October; first two weekends, November; weekends, December (except 25th and 26th); daily, Boxing Day to early January

NOW
Built by Davey Paxman in 1927, the Romney Hythe & Dymchurch Railway's visiting 4-8-2 'Mountain' Class Hercules *is turned on the turntable at Dalegarth terminus, 27 May 2014.*

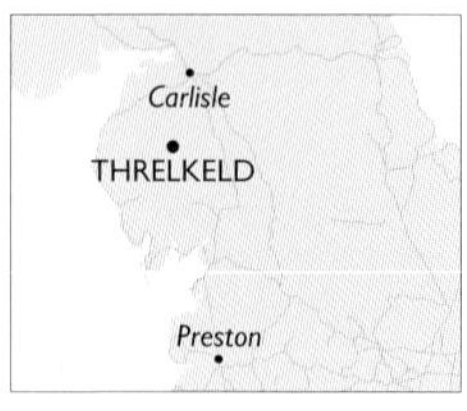

THRELKELD QUARRY & MINING MUSEUM

Threlkeld Quarry, Threlkeld, Cumbria CA12 4TT

01768 779747
www.threlkeldquarryandminingmuseum.co.uk

LENGTH
½ mile

GAUGE
2ft

OPEN
Tuesday to Saturday from Easter until end October; for details of vintage excavator working weekends see website

Threlkeld Quarry was opened in 1870 to supply railway ballast to the Penrith to Keswick railway line. By 1894 the quarry's output had risen to 80,000 tons per year with the stone being used by the Manchester Corporation Waterworks for their Thirlmere scheme, for railway ballast for the West Coast Main Line, for roadstone and for facing buildings with dressed stone. In 1936 the Threlkeld Granite Company merged with the Cumberland Granite Company to form the Keswick Granite Company but a year later Threlkeld Quarry was closed. It reopened in 1949 after undergoing modernisation.

A 2ft-4in.-gauge railway also operated within the quarry to transport the rock to crushers. As the quarry expanded so did the railway with 3 steam locomotives (2 Bagnalls and a Barclay) working there in the 1930s. Threlkeld Quarry closed in 1982 and is now the site for a mining museum, 2ft-gauge working quarry railway and a unique collection of working vintage excavators. Locomotives include 1925-built Bagnall 0-4-0ST *Sir Tom*, a 1945-built ex-NCB 0-4-0 Hunslet diesel and a 1947-built Ruston 0-4-0 diesel that once worked at the Royal Navy Armaments Depot near Cockermouth.

NOW
Against the stunning backdrop of Blencathra (2,848 ft above sea level) on 22 June 2021, William Bagnall 0-4-0ST Sir Tom*, built in 1925, tackles the steep grade with a demonstration quarry train on Threlkeld's 2ft-gauge western extension quarry line.*

Coal had been mined on a small scale in east Cumberland since Roman times. By the 17th century the primary landowner, the Earl of Carlisle, started to develop collieries at Tindale Fell but transporting the coal by packhorse was a slow and tedious business. It is known that towards the end of the 18th century the then Earl had opened a wooden horse-drawn waggonway from the collieries to staithes at Brampton. The wooden rails on this 5½-mile railway were soon replaced by wrought iron rails and the network expanded to serve other collieries and limeworks. In 1838 the completion of the Newcastle & Carlisle Railway (N&CR) provided a much more efficient outlet for the Earl of Carlisle's coal with an interchange at Milton station – from here the Earl opened a short railway to the nearby town of Brampton, providing a passenger service operated by a horse-drawn coach.

The opening of the N&CR soon led to proposals for a railway to be built along the South Tyne Valley to serve collieries and lead mines around the town of Alston. Both the N&CR and the Stockton & Darlington Railway had their sights set on reaching Alston – the latter company was already progressing up the Wear Valley but only managed to reach Wearhead where work stopped due to the high cost of continuing. However, the NCR's proposal for a branch line from Haltwhistle, on that company's mainline between Carlisle and Newcastle, to Alston received parliamentary approval in 1846. Involving the construction of 9 viaducts, the steeply-graded line climbed over 500 ft over its 13-mile length – elegant 850-ft-long Lambley Viaduct was (and still is) the major feat of engineering with its 9 arches carrying the railway 105 ft above the South Tyne River. The Alston branch line was opened throughout on 17 November 1852 but later proposals to extend it to Middleton-in-Teesdale never materialised. ▶

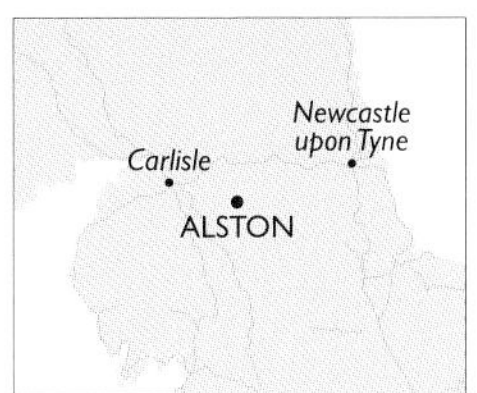

- ALSTON
- KIRKHAUGH
- LINTLEY HALT
- SLAGGYFORD

The Railway Station,
Station Road, Alston,
Cumbria CA9 3JB

01434 338214
www.south-tynedale-railway.org.uk

THEN
A 2-car Gloucester RC&W Co/Metro-Cammell diesel multiple unit calls at Lambley station with the 5.40 p.m. Haltwhistle to Alston train on 27 June 1968. The station building is now a private residence.

LENGTH
5 miles

GAUGE
2ft

OPEN
Weekends & Bank Holidays, Easter to end October; selected weekdays, April to mid July, September, October & December; daily, mid July to August; see website for full details

The Earl of Carlisle's Railway (also known as the Brampton Railway) was extended eastward to serve Lambley Colliery and link up with the newly-opened Alston branch at Lambley. Britain's coal industry was nationalised in 1947 and the Brampton Railway became part of the newly-formed National Coal Board. But by then coal mining in east Cumberland was in decline and this historic railway closed in March 1953.

Passenger train services on the Alston branch were never generous – in 1922 they amounted to only 4 trains each way on weekdays but by 1950 this figure had risen to 6 with an additional late evening service for pub-goers on Saturdays. The journey time for the 13-mile trip was 35 minutes. Economies were introduced in 1955 when the intermediate stations of Featherstone Park, Coanwood, Lambley and Slaggyford became unstaffed halts. Diesel multiple units replaced steam-hauled trains in 1959 and freight services had all been withdrawn by 1965. By then closure of the branch had been recommended in the 1963 'Beeching Report' but, due to the poor state of the roads in the area, the obligatory replacement bus service could not be operated. Eventually the roads were improved, the railway closed and the buses introduced – closure for the Alston branch came on 3 May 1976, one of the last railways in the country to become a victim of Dr Beeching's 'axe'.

Initially, preservation of this scenic branch in its standard-gauge form was planned but this scheme failed. A new proposal for a 2ft-gauge line was put forward and in 1983 a short length of narrow-gauge track was opened from Alston. Kirkhaugh station was reopened 1999 and

NOW
Built by Hunslet in 1952 this diesel mechanical loco formerly worked for the National Coal Board at Seaham in County Durham. It is seen here hauling a train on the South Tynedale Railway north of Alston. On the left is the South Tyne Trail cycle trail and footpath to Haltwhistle.

Slaggyford was reached in 2018. It is possible that one day in the future the railway may extend even further northwards towards Lambley, but in the meantime a footpath follows the route and crosses Knar Burn on the Grade II* listed railway viaduct.

Many of the steam and diesel locomotives used on the railway have been obtained from a wide variety of sources, both in the UK and abroad. Much of the equipment is secondhand, and many items have been rebuilt before being used on the railway. Included are 0-6-0 well tank No 3 *Sao Domingos*, built in Germany in 1928, 0-4-0 tank No 6 *Thomas Edmondson*, built in Germany in 1918, 0-6-0 tender engine No 10 *Naklo*, built in Poland in 1957, 0-4-2 tanks No 12 *Chaka's Kraal* and No 6 built by Hunslet in 1940 for a South African railway, as well as many industrial diesel locomotives. Many of the coaches were newly constructed at Alston in 1991 to a continental design. Comprehensive signalling equipment and a former North Eastern Railway signal box from Ainderby have been re-erected at Alston and all train movements are controlled from here. All journeys start at Alston's Grade II listed terminus, which stands 875 ft above sea level and makes this England's highest narrow-gauge railway. A journey along the line via Lintley Halt and Kirkhaugh gives passengers views of the beautiful South Tyne valley, crossing the river on a 3-arch viaduct north of Alston, and a viaduct between Gilderdale until the present terminus is reached at Slaggyford.

NOW

Carrying the old railway route across the South Tyne River, Lambley Viaduct can be accessed on foot from Slaggyford station at the northern end of the South Tynedale Railway.

WEARDALE RAILWAY

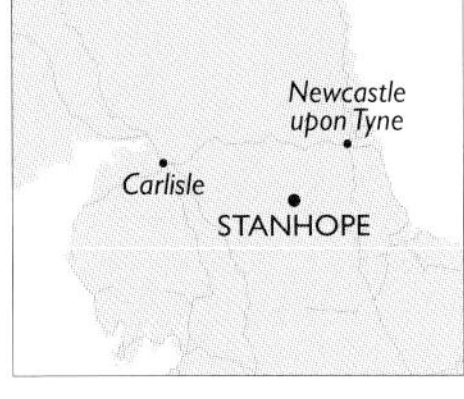

EASTGATE
STANHOPE
FROSTERLEY
WOLSINGHAM
WITTON-LE-WEAR
BISHOP AUCKLAND WEST
BISHOP AUCKLAND

Station Road, Stanhope, Bishop Auckland, Co. Durham DL13 2YS

01388 526203
www.weardale-railway.org.uk

LENGTH
16 miles

GAUGE
Standard

OPEN
Most weekends March to October & December, also selected weekdays (see website)

The Weardale Railway Preservation Society was formed in 1993 to assist with the campaign to re-open the mothballed 18-mile railway line from Bishop Auckland to Eastgate in the scenic Wear Valley. Originally opened in stages between 1843 and 1895 to serve the local limestone quarries, the passenger service ceased in 1953 with freight lingering on until 1961 when the line was cut back to St John's Chapel. The present terminus is at Eastgate where, until 1993, bulk cement trains operated from the Lafarge factory. Coal trains from an opencast site near Wolsingham to Scunthorpe and Nottinghamshire operated on a daily basis on the line between 2011 and 2013. The line was sold by Iowa-Pacific to Auckland Project, a charity, in 2020. Now operated by the Weardale Railway Trust, regular train services on this scenic line along the Wear Valley are normally catered for by a 2-car Class 141 railbus known as a 'Pacer' and a Class 122 'Bubble Car'. Several members of Class 31 diesels are also operational. Steam power in the form of National Coal Board 0-6-0T No 40 was purchased in 2006 and has recently been completely overhauled at the railway's Wolsingham workshop. With a mainline connection at Bishop Auckland the line's future appears secure.

NOW
Ex-Network Rail Class 31 diesel-electric locos Nos 31285 and 31465 double-head a train on the Weardale Railway at Engineman's Terrace Crossing near Witton-le-Wear on 11 April 2019.

Located on the site of the coal-carrying horse-drawn wooden-rail Tanfield Waggonway which opened in 1725, the Tanfield Railway features 3 miles of running track from Sunniside to East Tanfield and the world's oldest surviving railway bridge, Causey Arch, which opened in 1726 reached via a woodland walk from Causey station. The bridge was once crossed by over 900 horse-drawn wagons of coal each day. Once used by the Bowes Railway, the engine shed at Marley Hill dates from 1854 and was in use until the end of steam in 1970. Reopened in stages between 1981 and 1992, the modern Tanfield Railway has two intermediate stations, at Andrews House and Causey. Passengers are carried in restored 19th-century coaches hauled by a large collection of small, mainly steam, industrial locomotives, the oldest of which dates from 1873. In total the railway has 69 of these locos, many of which are being overhauled, restored or are in storage.

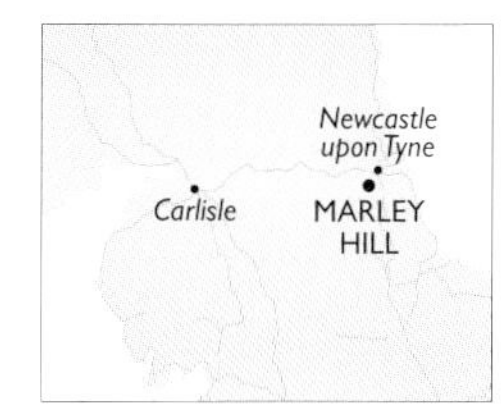

- SUNNISIDE
- ANDREWS HOUSE
- CAUSEY ARCH
- EAST TANFIELD

Marley Hill Engine Shed,
Old Marley Hill, Gateshead,
Tyne & Wear NE16 5ET

07508 092365
www.tanfield-railway.co.uk

LENGTH
3 miles

GAUGE
Standard

OPEN
Sundays & Bank Holidays; see website for special event days

NOW
Hauling a train of vintage carriages 0-6-0ST Renishaw Ironworks No. 6 *makes a good job of polluting the skies at East Tanfield on 8 September 2012. This loco was built by Hudswell Clarke in 1919 and worked at various steel works in Scunthorpe and Derbyshire before being saved for preservation.*

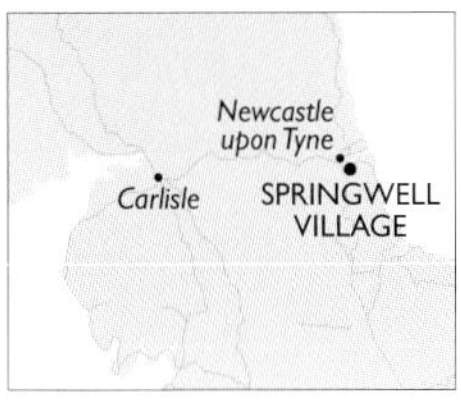

BOWES RAILWAY

Springwell Road, Springwell Village, Gateshead, Tyne & Wear NE9 7QJ

0191 4161847
http://bowesrailway.uk

From as early as the 17th century simple horse-drawn wooden waggonways were being used to transport coal from collieries in north Durham to staithes on the River Tyne. Here the coal was loaded onto barges for transfer to seagoing colliers. Before Acts of Parliament became the norm for railways to be built, the operators of waggonways required permission from landowners to cross their land – these financial agreements were known as wayleaves. By the 18th century there were a number of these waggonways operating in northeast England, notable among them being the Beamish, Chopwell, Garesfield, Tanfield, Washington, Lambton and Londonderry waggonways. Wooden waggonways were gradually replaced by plateways with the introduction of cast iron rails in the 1780s.

Built to connect Springwell and Mount Moor collieries in northwest Durham to staithes on the River Tyne at Jarrow, the Pontop & Jarrow Railway was one of the first railways in the world. The plan for the line was first put forward by a group of local colliery owners known as the 'Grand Allies' who soon handed the project over to up-and-coming local railway engineer George Stephenson. After refining the 'Grand Allies' plan, he went on to design an 11½-mile line using 3 inclined planes and a level locomotive-worked section. The railway opened across the Team Valley, climbing to a height of 567 ft before descending again, on 17 January 1826 and was extended to collieries at Kibblesworth in 1842, Marley Hill in 1853 and Dipton in 1855. This was the furthest extent of the railway, 15 miles, with 2 gravity-worked inclines, 4 powered inclines using stationary steam engines and locomotive-worked sections at each end – at its peak the railway carried over 1 million tons of coal a year.

THEN

Built by Robert Stephenson & Hawthorns, the National Coal Board's 0-6-0ST No 81 shunts coal wagons at Shop Pit on the Bowes Railway in July 1970.

Springwell Colliery closed in 1932 and the Pontop & Jarrow Railway was taken over by another group of colliery owners, notable among them being members of the Bowes-Lyon family, and renamed the Bowes Railway. The colliery buildings at Springwell became the workshops for the new railway. The nationalisation of Britain's coal industry in 1947 saw the railway becoming part of the newly-formed National Coal Board (NCB). Modernisation followed in 1950 with the stationary steam winding engines at the top of the inclines being replaced by electric power and, 5 years later, a new line was built to connect the Bowes Railway with the nearby Pelaw mainline. With the decline in coal mining and the closure of collieries the railway eventually succumbed to closure at the end of 1974, apart from a 1-mile section between Jarrow and Springwell Bankfoot which remained open to serve a coal washing plant until 1986.

Fortunately the 1½-mile section of the Bowes Railway between Springwell and Black Fell, including the workshops at Springwell and a number of coal wagons were purchased by Tyne & Wear Council and reopened as a working museum. The Bowes Railway site includes the Blackham's Hill East and Blackham's Hill West inclines which are worked by the 300 hp Blackham's Hill winding engine. At the western end of the line the engine shed at Marley Hill was also saved by preservationists and today forms part of the Tanfield Railway (see page 179). The Bowes Railway Path links Routes 7 and 14 of the National Cycle Network.

LENGTH
1 mile

GAUGE
Standard

OPEN
Mondays to Saturdays throughout the year; selected Sundays and special days (see website)

NOW
Rainfall is threatening as Andrew Barclay 0-4-0ST N.C.B. *No. 22, built in 1949, heads a demonstration freight on the Pelaw Curve near Blackham's Hill, Bowes Railway, on 31 August 1998.*

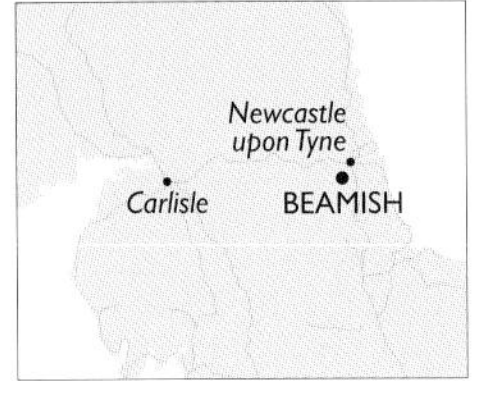

BEAMISH MUSEUM ☐

Beamish,
Co. Durham DH9 0RG

0191 3704000
www.beamish.org.uk

OPEN
Daily, April to end October; weekends, November to March (also open Tuesdays to Thursdays, end November to early January)

Opened in 1972, Beamish is a very large, 300-acre, open-air award-winning museum of late 19th-century life in Northern England. Exhibits include recreated houses, shops, a school, farm and colliery. There is much of railway interest including a range of typical North Eastern Railway buildings, including the 1867 Rowley station (reconstructed at Beamish after being moved from its site near Newcastle), goods shed and signal box and a short length of line. Locomotives on display include full-size working replicas of William Hedley's *Puffing Billy* and the famous Stockton & Darlington Railway *Locomotion No 1*. Resident locomotives include a 1871-built Head Wrightson 0-4-0 vertical boiler tank loco, 1877-built Stephen Lewin 0-4-0ST and 1895-built Sharp, Stewart 0-4-4T *Dunrobin*. Restored rolling stock includes historic examples from the Stockton & Darlington Railway, North London Railway, Highland Railway and North Eastern Railway.

The museum also owns 11 examples of vintage electric trams including one from British Railways' Grimsby & Immingham Electric Railway. These operate public services on a 1½-mile route around the museum site. Two trolleybuses, a collection of vintage motor buses and other road vehicles complete the collection of transport vehicles.

NOW
The Beamish Museum on 24 April 2006, with Andrew Barclay 0-4-0ST N.C.B. No. 22 *making a short-term visit from the Bowes Railway, enabling the recreation of a typical former Co. Durham colliery scene.*

The railway shares the same building with the Stephenson Railway Museum that was originally used as the Tyne & Wear Metro Test Centre. The museum displays the progress of railways with a collection of vintage and more modern steam, diesel and electric locomotives. Exhibits include Killingworth Colliery 0-4-0 *Billy* dating back to the early 19th century, Bo-Bo electric locomotive No E4 built by Siemens in 1909 and a 1904-built North Eastern Railway electric parcels' van. The 2-mile standard-gauge steam railway runs along the alignment of former horse-drawn coal waggonways dating back to 1755. The last British Railways line from Backworth to Percy Main closed in 1983. Opened in 1991 the railway connects the Tyne & Wear Metro station at Percy Main with the site on Sundays and Bank Holiday Mondays. Trains are normally hauled by either 1950-built Bagnall 0-6-0ST No 401, BR Class 08 0-6-0 No 08915 or Class 03 0-6-0 No 03078.

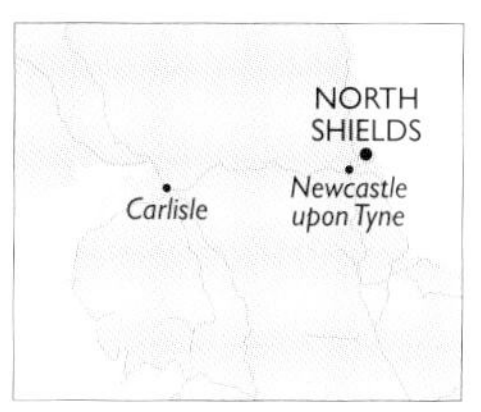

MIDDLE ENGINE LANE

PERCY MAIN

Middle Engine Lane,
West Chirton, North Shields,
Tyne & Wear NE29 8DX

0191 2777135
www.stephensonsteamrailway.org.uk

LENGTH
2 miles

GAUGE
Standard

OPEN
Weekends & Bank Holidays, mid April to end October; Santa Specials in December

NOW
All is revealed on the North Tyneside Steam Railway! Built by Peckett & Sons of Bristol in 1939, 0-6-0ST Ashington No. 5 *worked for the Ashington Coal Company until 1969 when it was sold by the National Coal Board for preservation.*

ALN VALLEY RAILWAY

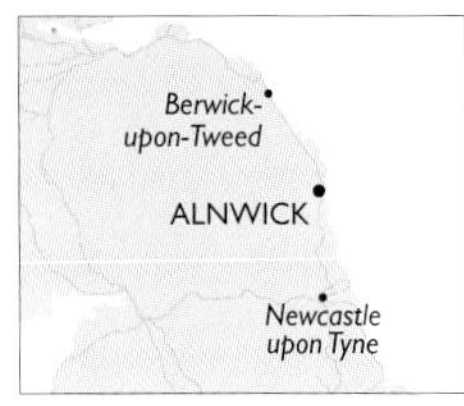

ALNWICK LIONHEART
GREENRIGG HALT
ALNMOUTH

Lionheart Station,
Lionheart Enterprise Park,
Alnwick,
Northumberland NE66 2EZ

0300 030 3311
www.alnvalleyrailway.co.uk

LENGTH
½ mile

GAUGE
Standard

OPEN
See website for details

The 3-mile branch line from Alnmouth, on the Newcastle to Berwick mainline, to the historic market town of Alnwick was opened by the Newcastle & Berwick Railway (N&BR) in 1850 – in 1854 the N&BR became part of the newly-formed North Eastern Railway (NER). Replacing the original station which was inconveniently situated on the town's outskirts, the NER opened a new overall-roofed terminus near the town centre on 5 September 1887. On the same day the 35½-mile railway to Coldstream was opened – serving only scattered farming communities in a sparsely populated region this line lost its passenger service as early as 1930. The Alnwick branch was served by a regular shuttle service from the East Coast Main Line at Alnmouth with some trains remaining steam-hauled until 1966 – BR Standard Class '9F' 2-10-0 No 92099 had the honour of hauling the last steam-hauled train on 18 June. Surprisingly, the branch was not listed for closure in the 'Beeching Report' but despite economies such as singling the line and much local opposition passenger services ceased on 30 January 1968. Goods trains continued to run until October.

Today, the impressive station building (home to a famous secondhand bookshop) at Alnwick and its overall roof survives. Britain's newest heritage railway the Aln Valley Railway is dedicated to reopening the branch line as a heritage railway from Alnmouth to Alnwick. A new station at Alnwick Lionheart was opened in 2013 and the railway currently has an operating line of ½-mile while work is ongoing to extend it in stages back to Alnmouth via Edenhill Bridge with a new intermediate station at Greenrigg Halt. Motive power currently is provided by 1917-vintage Hudswell Clarke 0-6-0T No 9 *Richboro* and several industrial diesel locomotives. A Class 144 'Pacer' diesel unit recently arrived on the railway.

THEN
BR Standard Class '9F' 2-10-0 No 92099 stands at Alnwick awaiting departure for Alnmouth on 18 June 1966, the last day of steam services on the branch line from Alnmouth.

NOW
Preserved ex-National Coal Board 0-6-0ST No 60 hauling a short train on the Aln Valley Railway. Built by Hunslet in 1948 this Austerity-type loco was fitted with a rounded cab enabling it to work down the narrow bore tunnel to Lambton coal staithes at Sunderland.

N. C. B.
60
Nº 60

SCOTLAND

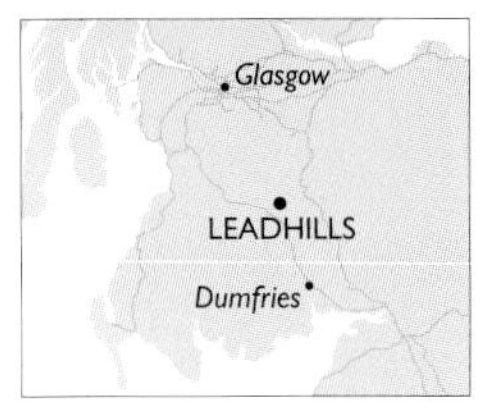

LEADHILLS
GLENGONNAR

For centuries lead, gold and silver had been mined in the remote Lowther Hills in the Scottish Southern Uplands and then carried on the difficult overland journey to the port of Leith, near Edinburgh. Railways first reached this sparsely populated region of Scotland in 1848 with the opening of Elvanfoot station on the Caledonian Railway's mainline between Carlisle and Glasgow. However, it wasn't until the end of the 19th century that serious thought was given to building a railway from Elvanfoot up to the mines in the Lowther Hills. Even in 1877 the Leadhills Silver-Lead Mining Company's request for a railway to serve their mines was turned down by the Caledonian Railway. Until 1896 the cost of building and operating such a line would have been prohibitive but in that year Parliament passed the Light Railways Act which allowed low-cost railways to be built in rural areas. Fencing, signalling, level crossings and station platforms were no longer required but the Act did limit weights to 12 tons per axle and imposed a speed restriction of 20 mph and 8 mph on bends. The fitting of cowcatchers on the locomotives was also mandatory. The scene was now set for 30 of these light railways to be built around Britain over the succeeding years.

One of the first of these railways to be built was the Leadhills & Wanlockhead Light Railway which was promoted by the Caledonian Railway to connect the mines in the Lowther Hills with their mainline at Elvanfoot. Engineered by Robert McAlpine ('Concrete Bob'), construction of the 7¾-mile line began in 1899 and involved the building of the 8-arch curving Rispin Cleuch Viaduct – a smaller version of Concrete Bob's famous Glenfinnan Viaduct on the Mallaig Extension. Unlike Glenfinnan, Rispin Cleuch Viaduct was faced with terracotta bricks to hide its concrete construction. The line, worked from the

THEN
Ex-Caledonian Railway McIntosh Class '2P' 0-4-4T No 15181 waits at Wanlockhead station with the 12.15 p.m. mixed train for Elvanfoot on 30 July 1931. The loco was built at St Rollox in 1907 and withdrawn in 1951. Behind the loco is a coach from the closed Garstang & Knott End Railway in Lancashire.

outset by the Caledonian, was opened to Leadhills on 1 October 1901 and to Wanlockhead a year later and with a summit of 1,498 ft was the highest standard-gauge railway in Great Britain. During particularly hard winters the exposed line was often closed due to heavy snowfall.

Mines and smelters at Leadhills and Wanlockhead were connected to the new railway by narrow-gauge feeder lines. The years following the opening of the railway were disappointing times for the local mining companies and the lead smelter at Wanlockhead closed in 1928. Closure of the mines came in 1931 but they were reopened for a short period in 1934, before permanently closing in this year.

Passenger services were also operated on the line by the Caledonian Railway and when the Garstang & Knott End Railway in Lancashire ceased running passenger trains in 1930 some of their coaches were moved to the Wanlockhead branch. With the closure of the mines the little railway's lifeblood had drained away and it closed on 2 January 1938. Elvanfoot station on the Carlisle to Glasgow mainline closed on 4 January 1965 and Rispin Cleuch Viaduct was demolished in 1991.

A preservation group was formed in 1983 to reopen part of the route as a narrow-gauge railway and work commenced in 1986. A limited diesel service was in operation in 1988/89 and in 1990 the railway borrowed a steam engine. An 0-4-0 Orenstein & Koppel, built in Berlin in 1913, and acquired from a Belgian museum is currently being restored at Leadhills. Passengers are carried in fully air-braked coaches with sprung axles. Although the line stops less than a mile short of the former terminus at Wanlockhead it is hoped that it will be extended for about 1 mile to the east of Leadhills in the near future.

Station Road,
Leadhills, Biggar,
South Lanarkshire ML12 6XP

01555 820778
www.leadhillsrailway.co.uk

LENGTH
1½ miles

GAUGE
2ft

OPEN
Weekends, May to September; Bank Holidays, Easter to August

NOW
Visiting W. Bagnall 'Woto', built in 1924 and on loan from a private Herefordshire railway, at Glengonnar station at the head of a demonstration stone train, waiting to return to Leadhills on 30 July 2016.

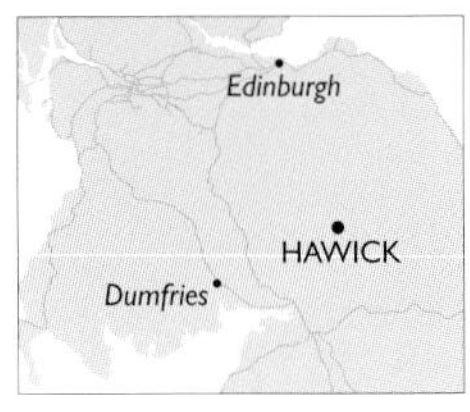

Known as the Waverley Route, the 98¼-mile railway from Edinburgh to Carlisle had its beginnings in the Edinburgh & Dalkeith Railway which opened in 1838 as a horse-drawn tramway between Leith Docks and collieries to the southeast of Edinburgh. Part of the route of this tramway was rebuilt by the Edinburgh & Hawick Railway (taken over by the North British Railway in 1845) that opened from South Esk to Hawick in 1849. With Carlisle now in its sights, the NBR-sponsored Border Union Railway was opened across sparsely-populated and desolate country from Hawick to Carlisle in 1862. Despite this achievement the NBR still had problems at Carlisle where disputes with the incumbent London & North Western Railway and Caledonian Railway continued for some years. The Waverley Route only made sense financially once the Midland Railway had reached Carlisle from Settle in 1876 and for the first time passengers between London and Scotland had a third choice for an Anglo-Scottish route.

Apart from locally generated livestock traffic, business from intermediate stations was never heavy. However, the double-track railway remained an important trunk route for Anglo-Scottish freight traffic until the 1960s. By 1964, passenger services consisted of 3 stopping trains between Carlisle and Edinburgh on weekdays plus 2 Edinburgh–Hawick all stations (plus an extra on Saturday) and 1 Carlisle–Hawick all stations. Two other through trains also operated – these were 'The Waverley' express and an overnight sleeper train, both between London St Pancras and Edinburgh. 'The Waverley' had its origins in the 1927 'Thames-Forth Express' and continued to run, apart from a break during the Second World War, until September 1968.

By the 1960s the steady closure of vital feeder lines had, inevitably, brought the Waverley Route to its knees and the entire route was listed for closure in the 'Beeching Report'. Despite strong objections from

THEN
Ex-LNER Class 'V2' 2-6-2 No 60813 emerges from Whitrope Tunnel with a freight train bound for Carlisle on 22 April 1965. This loco was built at Darlington in 1937 and withdrawn in September 1966.

local MPs (including Borders Liberal MP David Steel) and the public, closure was set for 15 July 1968. This date came and went due to the difficulties in arranging alternative bus services but finally the dreaded day came on 5 January 1969. That weekend special enthusiasts' trains were run and the local services were (unusually) filled to bursting with people witnessing the last rites. Famously, the final train to traverse the route, the 21.55 Edinburgh to St Pancras sleeper service headed by D60 *Lytham St Annes*, was halted in its tracks at Newcastleton by protestors blocking the level crossing gates. Tempers were high, police were called in and David Steel got out of the train to address the assembled throng. Finally peace was restored and the train got going again but not before the clock had ticked past the appointed closing time of midnight.

With nearly all of its infrastructure still intact the northern section from Edinburgh to Galashiels and Tweedbank was reopened as the Borders Railway in 2015. South of Hawick the impressive curving 15-arch viaduct at Shankend still stands in all its glory while at Whitrope Sidings – 11 miles south of Hawick and close to the summit of the line at 1,006 ft above sea level – the Waverley Route Heritage Association is bringing the line back to life again. Its long-term aims are to open a heritage railway from the Whitrope centre southwards to Riccarton Junction. In the meantime the group is busy reconstructing Whitrope signal box, erecting signs, benches and tourist information along the 5 miles of trackbed as far as Steele Road and surveying Whitrope Tunnel for its possible reuse. At Whitrope Sidings a short platform has already been built and about 1 mile of track has been laid from the tunnel southwards. Rolling stock comprises the prototype BRE-Leyland railbus RB004, a Ruston & Hornsby diesel shunter and BR Class 26 diesel D5340 (currently stored).

The 1,208-yd-long Whitrope Tunnel is fenced off and currently out of bounds to walkers due to a roof collapse in 2008.

Whitrope Sidings, Hawick, Roxburghshire TD9 9TY

www.wrha.org.uk

LENGTH
1 mile

GAUGE
Standard

OPEN
See website for details of Open Days

NOW
One of the star attractions at Whitrope is preserved Prototype BRE-Leyland Railbus No RB004, built at Derby in 1984, seen here south of the station on 18 October 2015.

BO'NESS & KINNEIL RAILWAY

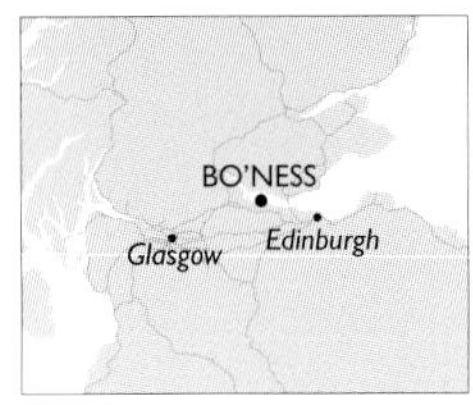

BO'NESS
KINNEIL HALT
BIRKHILL
MANUEL

Bo'ness Station,
Union Street, Bo'ness,
West Lothian EH51 9AQ

01506 822298
www.srps.org.uk

LENGTH
5 miles

GAUGE
Standard

OPEN
Weekends, school & Bank Holidays, April to June & September to October; daily, July (except Mondays) & August; for special events & Santa Specials see website

This former colliery line along the foreshore of the Firth of Forth was originally opened in August 1851 as the Slamannan & Borrowstouness Railway, part of the Monkland Railway that was formed of local colliery lines merging 3 years earlier. It was originally intended that the line to Bo'ness would only carry goods and minerals but there was demand for a passenger service which was eventually provided in June 1856. A station was sited at Bo'ness Junction (later renamed Manuel) which was connected by a footpath to the nearby station on the Edinburgh & Glasgow Railway.

The Monkland Railway was absorbed by the Edinburgh & Glasgow Railway on 31 July 1865, which in turn was absorbed by the North British Railway on the very next day. Passenger services ended on 7 May 1956 but the line remained open for freight and the storage of withdrawn BR steam locomotives in the early 1960s. It was finally closed to all traffic by British Rail in 1980.

By then, the Scottish Railway Preservation Society had already set up a base at Bo'ness and reopened the line in stages, from Bo'ness to Kinneil in 1984, to Birkhill in 1989 and to Manuel (with a physical link to the Edinburgh to Glasgow mainline) in 2010. Bo'ness station now has an eclectic mix of railway structures collected from around Scotland by the SRPS – the station building was originally at Wormit, at the southern end of the Tay Bridge, the 1842 train shed was originally at Haymarket station in Edinburgh, the signal box came from Garnqueen South Junction and the footbridge from Murthly.

The SRPS collection of locomotives and rolling stock, formerly based at Falkirk, were moved to Bo'ness in 1988. Visitors to the railway can also visit the clay mine near Birkhill station. A large collection of finely restored steam and diesel locomotives are based at Bo'ness, including such historic items as LNER Class 'D49' 4-4-0 No 246 *Morayshire*, built in 1928, North British Railway Class 'J36' 0-6-0 *Maude*, built in 1891, Caledonian Railway 0-4-4T No 419, built in 1907 and BR Standard Class '4' 2-6-4T No 80105. Diesels are represented by BR Classes 08, 20, 25, 27, 37 and 47. The Museum of Scottish Railways (see page 207) is situated adjacent to Bo'ness station.

THEN
Ex-North British Railway Class 'C16' 4-4-2T No 67494 waits to depart from Bo'ness station with the 5.20 p.m. train for Falkirk on 7 September 1955. The loco was built at Cowlairs Works in 1916 and withdrawn early in 1961.

NOW
Preserved ex-LNER Class 'D49/1' 4-4-0 No 62712 Morayshire *gets ready to depart from Bo'ness station with a train for Manuel on 8 May 2014. This loco was designed by Nigel Gresley and built at Darlington in 1928. Withdrawal took place in 1961 when it became a stationary boiler at a laundry in Edinburgh until being saved for preservation.*

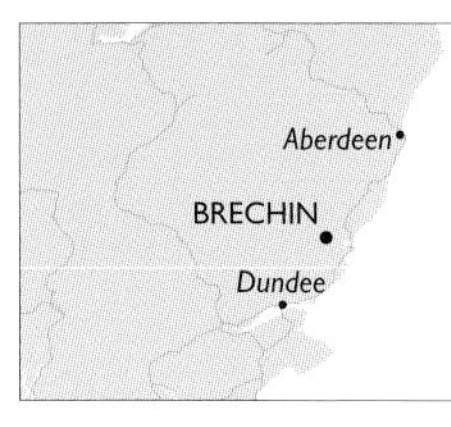

The Station, Park Road,
Brechin, Angus DD9 7AF

01356 622992
www.caledonianrailway.com

LENGTH
4 miles

GAUGE
Standard

OPEN
See website for details

The former Caledonian Railway line from Montrose to Brechin via Bridge of Dun was opened in 1848 by the Aberdeen Railway and was built as a branch line with its terminus at Brechin. The Aberdeen Railway merged with the Scottish Midland Railway in 1856 to form the Scottish North Eastern Railway. Ten years later this company was absorbed by the Caledonian Railway.

Two more lines were built from Brechin. Firstly the Forfar & Brechin Railway was opened by the Caledonian Railway in 1895. Low levels of passenger traffic saw it lose this service on 4 August 1952 with complete closure to Brechin coming on 17 March 1958. Secondly another line was opened to the up-and-coming holiday resort of Edzell in 1896 but passenger traffic did not live up to expectations either and this service was withdrawn by the LMS on 27 April 1931. Goods services continued until 7 September 1964 when the line finally closed.

Passenger services on the Brechin to Bridge of Dun section were also withdrawn on 4 August 1952, when many of the other lines in the county of Angus also lost their services. However the mainline through Bridge of Dun continued with a passenger service until 4 September 1967, when it closed and all Aberdeen to Glasgow trains via Forfar were re-routed via Dundee. A single-track line from Kinnaber Junction was retained for local freight and in 1979 the Brechin Railway Preservation Society took over the engine shed at Brechin. British Rail finally closed the freight-only line in 1981.

The trackbed to Bridge of Dun was purchased with the assistance of Angus District Council, Tayside Region and the Scottish Tourist Board. First trains ran to Bridge of Dun in 1992 and stock from the closed Lochty Railway in Fife also augmented the line's potential. Locomotive stock consists of ex-BR diesels (including examples of Classes 08, 11, 25, 26, 27 and 37) owned by the Caledonian Railway Diesel Group. Steam locos, operational, undergoing restoration or stored are represented by 8 industrial examples from Peckett, Barclay, Bagnall and Hunslet. In the future it is hoped that the railway will be extended a further 3½ miles in the direction of Montrose to Dubton.

THEN
Ex-LNER Class 'A4' 4-6-2 No 60034 Lord Faringdon *pauses at Bridge of Dun station with an Aberdeen to Glasgow express in May 1966, 4 months before the end of steam on this route. Designed by Nigel Gresley this loco was built at Doncaster Works in 1938 and originally named* Peregrine. *It was withdrawn from Aberdeen Ferryhill shed in August 1966 and scrapped.*

NOW
Built at Smethwick in 1958, preserved Birmingham Railway Carriage & Wagon Company Class '26/0' diesel-electric D5314 waits at Brechin station with a train for Bridge of Dun on 7 July 2004. On the left is Class 37 diesel-electric No 37097.

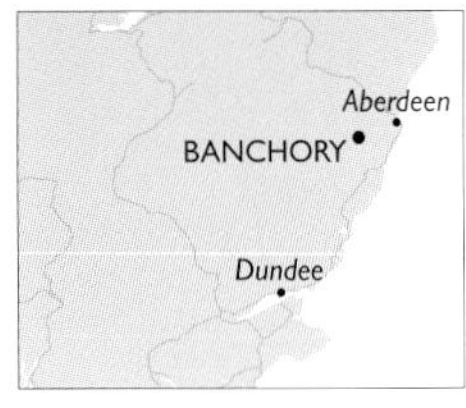

MILTON OF CRATHES
RIVERSIDE HALT

The 43½-mile railway up the Dee Valley from Aberdeen to Ballater was built in three stages. First on the scene was the Deeside Railway that opened from Guild Street station in Aberdeen to Banchory in 1853. The line included 12 intermediate stations and a private station for Crathes Castle. A westward extension up the valley to Aboyne was opened by the Deeside Extension Railway in 1859 – this line deviated away from the valley to serve Lumphanan. The two railways were leased by the Great North of Scotland Railway (GNoSR) in 1866. From 1867 trains for Aboyne left the new joint station which had opened at Aberdeen. The final push up the Dee Valley came in 1866 when the Aboyne & Braemar Railway opened as far as Ballater. Despite Braemar being the final goal, the section beyond Ballater was never completed (although the earthworks can still be seen) due to pressure from Queen Victoria who was not at all happy about hordes of daytrippers descending on her Balmoral estate. All three railways were absorbed by the GNoSR in 1875.

The section between Ferryhill and Culter was relaid as double-track in 1893 to allow a frequent service of suburban trains to run to and from Aberdeen and, in 1904, a connecting bus service was introduced from Ballater to Braemar. The line was also regularly used by royal trains bringing the royal family and their guests to Balmoral Castle. The first recorded royal train to visit Ballater was in 1866 and the last was on 15 October 1965, only a few months before closure of the line.

THEN

From April 1958 British Railways' experimental battery electric multiple units 79998 and 79999 replaced many steam locomotives on the Deeside route from Aberdeen to Ballater. It was withdrawn following closure of the line in 1966 but is now preserved on the Royal Deeside Railway.

By the 1950s competition from cars, buses and lorries had brought a steady decline in rail traffic along the Dee Valley. The introduction of the unique battery-electric twin railcar (known as the 'Sputnik') in April 1958 and the end of steam haulage in July of that year were sadly not enough to stem the rising losses and the line was listed for closure in the 'Beeching Report'. Despite its royal patronage and strong local protests the Ballater branch closed to passengers on 28 February 1966. Goods trains continued to serve Ballater until 18 July when the line was cut back to Culter. This last section from Ferryhill Junction continued to be served by goods trains until 2 January 1967.

Today, much of the trackbed is a footpath and cycleway known as the Deeside Way. Many of the stations along the line have found new uses but pride of place must surely go to the rebuilt station at Ballater which now houses a tourist information office and a café. The Royal Deeside Railway now runs trains for nearly 2 miles along relaid track between Milton of Crathes and Banchory. Trains are hauled by 1 of the railway's 2 Class '03' diesel shunters or recently restored 1897-built Andrew Barclay 0-4-0 saddle tank *Bon-Accord*. The railway also has the original 2-car battery electric twin railcar that ran on the line in the 1950s and early 1960s. These historic vehicles are presently hauled by one of the diesels.

Milton of Crathes, Banchory, Kincardineshire AB31 5QH

www.deeside-railway.co.uk

LENGTH
1¾ miles

GAUGE
Standard

OPEN
Most weekends & selected weekdays, April to September & December (see website)

NOW
One of the battery electric multiple units preserved on the Royal Deeside Railway at Milton of Crathes. Following closure of the Deeside line in 1966 it was used as test train 'Gemini' at Derby until withdrawal in 1984. There then followed a period at the West Yorkshire Transport Museum and on the East Lancashire Railway (see pages 152–3) until it arrived at Milton of Crathes in 2001.

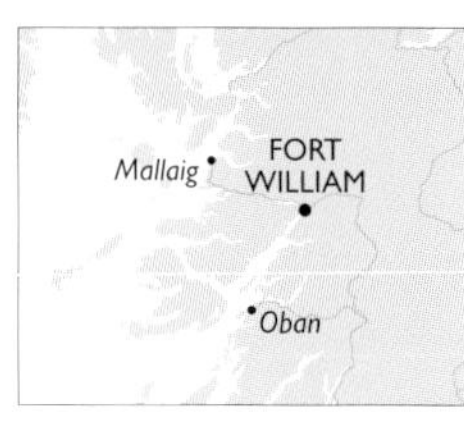

FORT WILLIAM
BANAVIE
CORPACH
LOCH EIL OUTWARD BOUND
LOCHEILSIDE
GLENFINNAN
LOCHAILORT
BEASDALE
ARISAIG (REQUEST STOP)
MORAR
MALLAIG

Postal address:
West Coast Railways,
Jesson Way,
Crag Bank, Carnforth,
Lancashire LA5 9UR

0333 996 6720
www.westcoastrailways.co.uk

LENGTH
42 miles

GAUGE
Standard

OPEN
Mid May to end October; advance booking is essential

'The Jacobite' is a very popular regular steam-operated tourist train that runs on the national rail network between Fort William and Mallaig between mid-May and the end of October each year. It was originally introduced by British Rail in 1984 when it was called the 'West Highlander' and later named 'The Lochaber'. Since privatisation of British Rail in 1995 the train, now named 'The Jacobite', has been operated by West Coast Railways. Motive power usually consists of preserved Peppercorn Class 'K1' 2-6-0 No 62005 or an LMS Stanier 'Black Five' 4-6-0 of which many have been preserved around the UK.

The train runs through stunning scenery along a route more recently made famous in the *Harry Potter* films. Overlooked by Ben Nevis, trains for Mallaig depart northwards from Fort Willam's 1970s-style terminus and strike off westwards at Mallaig Junction to Banavie station. Beyond Banavie, the railway first crosses the Caledonian Canal on a swing bridge before following the north shore of Loch Eil to the little-used stations at Loch Eil Outward Bound and Locheilside. Continuing westwards, the railway then makes a loop high over Glen Finnan on the iconic 21-arch curving viaduct that was built by 'Concrete Bob' McAlpine for the line's opening in 1901 – the views southward from here over the Glenfinnan Monument and along the length of Loch Shiel are truly awesome on a clear day. With gradients as steep as 1-in-40, numerous rock cuttings, viaducts and 11 tunnels, this heavily engineered route still demands the highest driving skills from the crew of the steam-operated service.

After slowly crossing the viaduct, trains reach Glenfinnan where the restored station building and signal box are now a railway museum. From here, the railway heads west alongside idyllic Loch Eilt to Lochailort station and then cuts across the Ardnish Peninsula through a series of tunnels and over Loch nan Uamh Viaduct to reach Beasdale. Beyond here, the railway continues westwards to reach the coast at Arisaig – the westernmost station in Britain – before turning northwards through Morar to terminate at Mallaig. This final coast-hugging part of the journey offers glorious views of the Sound of Sleat, the islands of Eigg and Rum and the White Sands of Morar (as featured in the film *Local Hero*).

THEN
Ex-LNER Class 'B1' 4-6-0 No 61140 about to depart from Mallaig Harbour with a train of fresh fish on 16 August 1960. Fish is no longer transported by rail from Mallaig (or anywhere else), progress indeed. The loco was built at Vulcan Foundry in 1947 and withdrawn at the end of 1966.

NOW
Ex-BR Class 'K1' No 62005 masquerading as No 62034 slowly crosses 'Concrete Bob' McAlpine's iconic Glenfinnan Viaduct with 'The Jacobite' train to Mallaig. Designed by Nigel Gresley and built by the North British Locomotive Company in 1949 this loco spent many years working on this route until withdrawal in 1963.

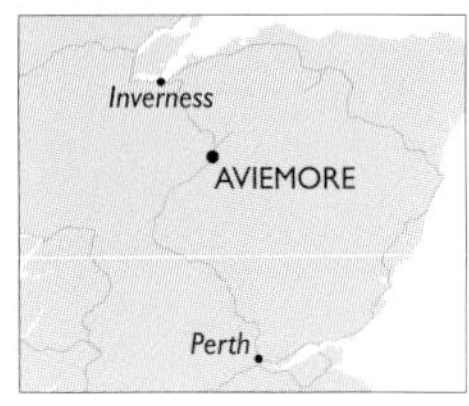

AVIEMORE
BOAT OF GARTEN
BROOMHILL

Aviemore Station, Dalfaber Road, Aviemore, Inverness-shire PH22 1PY

01479 810725
www.strathspeyrailway.co.uk

LENGTH
8¼ miles

GAUGE
Standard

OPEN
Selected Wednesdays, Thursdays & weekends in February & March; daily (excluding Mondays, Tuesdays, Fridays) & Bank Holidays in April, May & October; daily (except Mondays & Tuesdays) in June & September; daily, July–August; Santa Specials on selected days in December

The 36-mile railway between Aviemore and Forres was opened as part of the ambitious Inverness & Perth Junction Railway in 1863. The following year the company absorbed the Perth & Dunkeld Railway and in 1865 combined with the Inverness & Aberdeen Junction Railway to form the Highland Railway (HR). The section from Aviemore to Forres became a secondary route when the HR opened its more direct line from Aviemore to Inverness via Slochd Summit in 1898.

With intermediate stations at Boat of Garten, Broomhill, Grantown-on-Spey, Dava and Dunphail, the line from Aviemore to Forres was served on weekdays by through trains to and from Inverness. By 1964, when the line was already threatened with closure, there were 6 northbound services each weekday with 1 originating in Glasgow – southbound, there were only 4 including 1 that only ran on Saturdays. Curiously, in 1964, there were 2 through trains in each direction on Sundays, one a Glasgow/Edinburgh to Inverness service and the other an Inverness to London (Euston) sleeping car train. This all came to an end on 18 October 1965 when the line closed.

A preservation group started track relaying on the section to Boat of Garten in 1972 and trains started operating in 1978 with a further extension to Broomhill opening a few years later. Broomhill station was used as the location for 'Glen Bogle' in the BBC TV series *Monarch of the Glen*. Train services are operated by a variety of restored steam and diesel locomotives including former Caledonian Railway 0-6-0 No 828, built in 1899, BR Class '2MT' 2-6-0 No 46512, built at Swindon in 1952 and BR Class 31 diesel D5862. The railway has been used for location filming for several other TV programmes, including *Cloud Howe, Dr Finlay's Casebook* and *Strathblair*. Historic railway rolling stock is on display at Boat of Garten where there is also a museum housing railway artefacts. Work is now progressing on a 3¾-mile extension northwards from Broomhill to Grantown-on-Spey (West) – the 80-ft-span bridge over the River Dulnain is the major engineering feature on this section.

THEN
The sad remains of Grantown-on-Spey (West) station on 26 June 1975, nearly 10 years after closure. The Strathspey Railway aims to extend its line from Broomhill to Grantown where a new station will be built on the same site.

NOW
Former Caledonian Railway Class '812' 0-6-0 No 828 heads a passenger train on the Strathspey Railway. Built in 1899 at St Rollox this veteran loco was withdrawn as BR No 57566 in 1963.

C.R 828

KEITH & DUFFTOWN HERITAGE RAILWAY

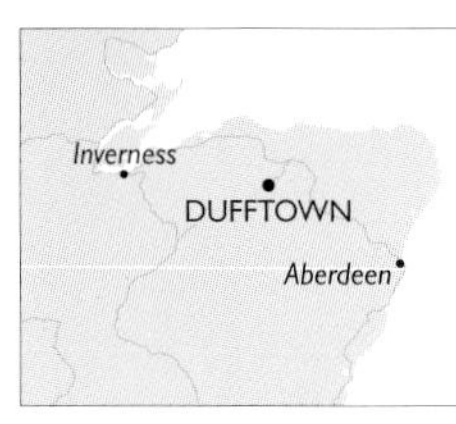

Dufftown Station,
Dufftown,
Banffshire AB55 4BA

01780 784444
http://keith-dufftown-railway.co.uk

LENGTH
11 miles

GAUGE
Standard

OPEN
Weekends & Bank Holidays, Easter to early October; Santa Specials on December weekends

The 14½-mile line from Keith to Craigellachie was built in two stages. Built to serve distilleries in the Spey Valley, the Keith & Dufftown Railway opened in 1862. The railway was extended northwards to Craigellachie and then down the Spey Valley to Abernethy by the Strathspey Railway in 1863 (see pages 200–201). Both railways were worked by the GNoSR and were taken over by that company in 1866. The line between Keith and Craigellachie was used as part of the GNoSR's secondary route for trains between Aberdeen and Elgin and these continued to operate through to British Railways' days when diesel multiple units were introduced. By 1964, with closure looming for most of the former GNoSR lines north of Aberdeen, the passenger service between Keith and Craigellachie was mainly handled by trains running from Cairnie Junction Exchange Platform (for the alternative coastal route to Elgin), east of Keith, through to Elgin. These were withdrawn on 6 May 1968, a black day for the railways in this region. The section from Dufftown and Craigellachie continued to see goods traffic for distilleries at Aberlour until 15 November 1971. The Glenfiddich Distillery at Dufftown remained rail-served for goods traffic and luxury charter trains until May 1985 when the line was mothballed.

Taken over by a group of volunteers in 2000, the 11-mile section between Keith Town and Dufftown was reopened as a heritage railway on 18 August 2001. Marketed as 'The Whisky Line', the Keith & Dufftown Railway is a fairly recent newcomer to the list of Britain's heritage railways. BR Class 108 diesel multiple unit services now operate along the scenic line between the beautifully restored station at Keith Town and Dufftown with an intermediate station at Drummuir. Sadly, the physical connection with the national rail network at Keith has been severed.

THEN
BR Standard Class '4' 2-6-0 No 76107 storms uphill towards Keith Town station with a train for Dufftown in June 1958. This loco was built at Doncaster Works in 1957 and withdrawn in 1965 after only 8 years of service.

NOW
The 'Spirit of Speyside' 2-car Class 108 diesel multiple unit (Nos 53628 and 54223) crosses Glenfiddich Viaduct on the Keith & Dufftown Railway. There are long-term plans to physically reconnect the heritage railway to the national rail network at Keith once again. This short connection was severed in 1998.

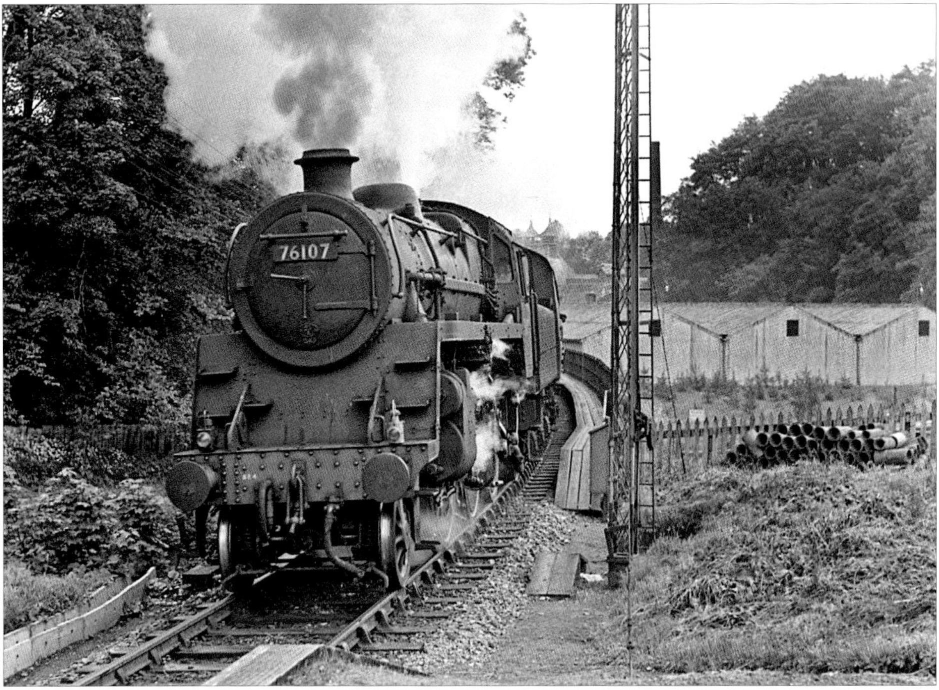
76107

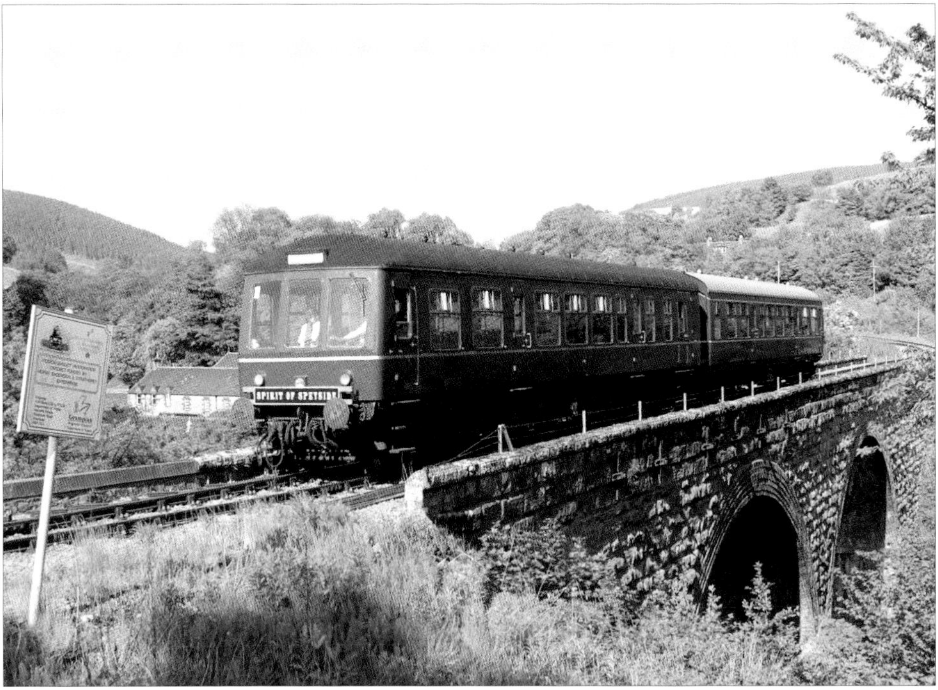
SPIRIT OF SPEYSIDE

SWINDON STEAM RAILWAY MUSEUM

Fire Fly Avenue, Swindon, Wiltshire SN2 2EY
01793 466646
www.steam-museum.org.uk

Open: Daily, except 24–26 December & 1 January

Located to the west of Swindon station in the fork between the Swindon to Gloucester and Swindon to Bristol mainlines, Swindon Works was the principal locomotive, carriage and wagon works for the Great Western Railway from 1843 and, from 1948, the Western Region of British Railways.

The Works were opened in 1843. The decision to build at Swindon was made in 1840 by 24-year-old Daniel Gooch, the first Superintendent for Locomotive Engines of the GWR. The Works transformed what was then just a rural village into a large railway town. Under the GWR's famous locomotive superintendents – Daniel Gooch, Joseph Armstrong, William Dean, G. J. Churchward, C. B. Collett and F. W. Hawksworth – the Works turned out firstly such broad-gauge giants as the single-wheeler 2-2-2 and 4-2-2 express locos followed by the famous standard-gauge 'City' and 'County' Class 4-4-0s, 'Star', 'Castle' and 'King' Class 4-6-0s and, at its peak in the 1930s, employed around 14,000 people. Following Nationalisation in 1948 Swindon turned its hand to building many of the BR Standard Class locos including 45 Class 3 2-6-2 tanks (Nos 82000–82044), 80 Class 4 4-6-0s, 20 Class 3 2-6-0s (Nos 77000–77019) and 53 Class 9F 2-10-0s including the last steam loco to be built for BR, No 92220 *Evening Star*. The ill-thought-out 'Modernisation Plan' of 1955 brought more work for Swindon including the building of 38 of the 'Warship' Class diesel-hydraulics (Class 42 D800–D832 and D866–D870) between 1958 and 1961, 35 'Western' Class diesel-hydraulics (Class 52 D1000–D1034) between 1961 and 1964 and 56 of the short-lived Type 1 diesel-hydraulics (Class 14 D9500–D9555) between 1964 and 1965 along with some of the more successful Class 03 0-6-0 diesel shunters and diesel multiple units – including some of the Inter-City, Cross-Country and Trans-Pennine units. Although building of locomotives ended in 1965, diesel locomotives continued to be repaired along with carriage and wagon work until March 1986 when the Works closed.

Today the Swindon Steam Railway Museum is housed in one of the Works' listed buildings and English Heritage have their headquarters in another. A large retail outfit is located in other buildings.

The museum opened in 2000 and contains many interesting exhibits including locomotives, rolling stock, a series of reconstructed work areas and an enormous collection of GWR archive material. Locomotives on display include replica broad-gauge loco 2-2-2 *North Star*, Dean Goods 0-6-0 No 2516, 'King' Class 4-6-0 No 6000 *King George V*, 'Castle' Class 4-6-0 No 4073 *Caerphilly Castle*, 'Manor' Class 4-6-0 No 7821 *Ditcheat Manor*, '2800' Class 2-8-0 No 2818 and streamlined diesel railcar (or 'Flying Banana') No 4.

LONDON TRANSPORT MUSEUM

Covent Garden Piazza, London WC2E 7BB
0343 222 5000
www.ltmuseum.co.uk

Open: Daily, except 24–26 December

A large collection of public transport road and rail vehicles used in London from Victorian times to the present day is housed in the former Flower Market at Covent Garden which dates back to 1870. The museum was extended during 2007 with increased display space and spectacular new mezzanine floors. Included on display are a 1866-built Metropolitan Railway 4-4-0 condensing tank No 23 and a 1922-built 1,200 horsepower Bo-Bo electric locomotive *John Hampden*, Wotton Tramway traction engine locomotive No 807 built in 1872, as well as examples of early underground electric trains such as the 1890-built City & South London Railway 'Padded Cell' car. Visitors to the museum can 'drive' an Underground train on a simulator.

Models, artefacts, posters and an audio-visual display are included. The museum has a large photographic and film archive section containing over 100,000 black and white photographs of London Transport and its predecessors.

The 6,000-sq-m London Transport Museum Depot at Acton houses the remainder of the Museum's vast collection of over 320,000 items including motor buses and underground trains. Also at the Depot is the London Transport Miniature Railway. The Depot is only open to the public for special events such as Open Weekends held three times a year and for pre-booked guided tours. It can be found at 2 Museum Way, 118–120 Gunnersbury Lane, Acton, London W3 9BQ.

CREWE HERITAGE CENTRE

Vernon Way, Crewe, Cheshire CW1 2DB
01270 212130
www.crewehc.co.uk

Open: Every weekend, Easter to October

Located on the site of the Old Railway Works adjacent to the West Coast Main Line near Crewe station and opened in 1987 as Crewe Railway Age, Crewe Heritage Centre houses a changing collection of mainly ex-BR mainline steam, diesel and electric locomotives. At any given time a varied selection of privately owned heritage steam locomotives can be seen at the Centre while awaiting repairs or restoration or being serviced in between mainline steam tours. The BR Class 370 Advanced Passenger Train Nos 370 003 and 006 are among the star attractions while examples of BR mainline diesel and electric locos include Classes 03, 37, 43 (HST), 47 and 87.

Passenger rides are given at weekends in steam-hauled brake vans over the 300-yd track within the site. Steam locomotives are also stabled here when working special trains to the North Wales coast. In addition there are 3 working signal boxes (Exeter West, Crewe Station A and Crewe North Junction), a collection of railway artefacts, model railways and a 600-yd passenger-carrying 7¼in.-gauge miniature railway. A West Coast Main Line viewing area with live-streaming cameras is located on the roof of North Junction Signal Box.

HEAD OF STEAM

North Road Station, Darlington, Co. Durham DL3 6ST
01325 405060
www.head-of-steam.co.uk

Open: Daily, except Mondays, April to September;
daily, except Mondays & Tuesdays, October to March

Formerly known as the Darlington Railway Centre and Museum, the 'Head of Steam' is located in the 1842-built Stockton & Darlington Railway's listed Grade II* North Road station, goods shed and the Hopetown Carriage Works in Darlington. Exhibits include the original Stockton & Darlington Railway 0-4-0 locomotive *Locomotion No. 1* that was built by George Stephenson in 1825, the 1845 Darlington-built 0-6-0 *Derwent*, 1885-built NER 2-4-0 No 1463, NER Class 'T3' (LNER 'Q7') 0-8-0 No 901 and historic rolling stock. The museum also houses the Ken Hoole Study Centre and the library collection of the North Eastern Railway Association. The historic station of North Road with its overall roof is still served by local trains on the Saltburn to Bishop Auckland Tees Valley Line.

NATIONAL RAILWAY MUSEUM

Leeman Road, York YO26 4XJ
0800 047 8124
www.railwaymuseum.org.uk

Open: Daily, except 24–26 December

The National Collection, formed from the Clapham Collection and the North Eastern Railway Museum Collection at York, opened in 1975 and is housed in two large halls, formerly part of York North engine shed, with the Great Hall opening in 1992.

York North engine shed was opened in 1878, close to the new station that had opened the previous year. The engine shed eventually contained 4 roundhouses, together with a 70-ft turntable and a mechanical coaling plant. The British Railways shed code for York North was 50A. It was rebuilt in 1954 with 2 of the earlier roundhouses (Nos 1 and 2) being replaced by a straight shed with a new 70-ft turntable being installed in roundhouse No 4. Of the 84 steam locomotives allocated to 50A in 1964 13 were Peppercorn Class 'A1' 4-6-2s, 11 Class 'B1' 4-6-0s, 26 Class 'V2 2-6-2' and 8 BR Standard Class '9F' 2-10-0s. The shed also had an allocation of 38 mainline diesels at that time. The 2 roundhouses were closed to steam in 1967 and the diesel depot closed in 1983.

Today the National Railway Museum has over 6,000 objects on display, including about 100 locomotives and pieces of rolling stock. Locomotives are displayed in the roundhouse around a central turntable in the Great Hall. Exhibits range from the very early days of rail transport to the present with British-built locomotives, steam, diesel and electric on view. Pride of place must go to Nigel Gresley's world speed record Class 'A4' 4-6-2 *Mallard*, the re-streamlined LMS 'Coronation' Class 4-6-2 *Duchess of Hamilton* and, the last mainline steam loco to be built by BR, Standard Class '9F' 2-10-0 No 92220 *Evening Star*. Often away on visits to heritage railways, operational steam locomotives include SR 'Schools' Class 4-4-0 No 925 *Cheltenham* and LNER Class 'A3' 4-6-2 No 60103 *Flying Scotsman*. The South Hall contains 130 exhibits that illustrate travel by train with both passenger and goods trains lined up at platforms. These range from Queen Adelaide's royal saloon, built in 1842, a Lynton & Barnstaple Railway coach, built in 1897 and a Wagons-Lits Night Ferry sleeping car, built in 1936, to numerous goods wagons dating from 1815 to 1970. In addition there is a hands-on children's centre, a superb model railway and an extensive library with poster, photograph and drawing collections. Numerous other locomotives, some in full working order, and rolling stock are on loan to other museums and heritage railways throughout Britain. The museum's conservation workshops now have a public viewing area where ongoing restoration work can be seen in action from a viewing platform.

The 7¼in.-gauge South Garden Miniature Railway operates on a 200-yd track in the South Yard of the museum. Trains are normally hauled by a petrol hydraulic locomotive and operate during weekends and school holidays.

NATIONAL RAILWAY MUSEUM 'LOCOMOTION'

Shildon, Co. Durham DL4 2RE
0800 047 8124
www.locomotion.org.uk

Open: Daily, except 24–26 December

Opened in 2004 and an offshoot of the National Railway Museum at York, Shildon has a rotating display of historic locos and rolling stock. The site includes the Welcome Building containing Timothy Hackworth's Rainhill Trials loco *Sans Pareil*, the Timothy Hackworth Museum, the Collection Building with its conservation workshop and a display of more than 70 railway heritage vehicles, the prototype 'Deltic' and APT-E, LNER 'V2' 2-6-2 *Green Arrow*, SR 'Battle of Britain' Class 4-6-2 No 34051 *Winston Churchill*, LSWR Class '0298' 2-4-0 Beattie well tank No 30587 and GNR Class 'C1' 4-4-2 No 251. The historic Soho railway workshop of the Stockton & Darlington Railway can also be visited nearby – it was finally closed by British Rail as a major wagon building and repair centre, which employed over 2,000 people, on 30 June 1984.

VINTAGE CARRIAGE TRUST MUSEUM OF RAIL TRAVEL

Ingrow Railway Centre, South Street, Ingrow, Keighley, West Yorkshire BN22 5AX
01535 680425
www.vintagecarriagestrust.org

Open: Daily, except 25 December

A purpose-built museum opened in 1990 which currently houses approximately half of the Trust's collection; sound and video presentations bring the collection to life. Formed in 1965, the Trust has won several awards and its exhibits have often been used in films and television programmes. The Trust owns 9 historic railway carriages built between 1876 and 1950, many of which have appeared on screen, including *The Secret Agent* (1995 cinema), *Tomorrow's World* (1995 BBC TV), *Cruel Train* (1994 BBC TV), *The Feast of July* (1994 cinema), *The Secret Agent* (1992 BBC TV), *Portrait of a Marriage* (1989 BBC TV) and *Sherlock Holmes* (1988 Granada TV). Included are examples from the Manchester, Sheffield & Lincolnshire Railway, Midland Railway, East Coast Joint Stock, Great Northern Railway and the Metropolitan Railway. Locomotives owned by the Trust include 0-6-0WT *Bellerophon*, built in 1874 by Haydock Foundry, 0-6-0ST *Sir Berkeley*, built in 1891 by Manning Wardle and 0-4-0ST *Lord Mayor*, built in 1893 by Hudswell, Clarke. Introduced by the Eastern Region of British Railways in 1958, Waggon und Maschinenbau Railbus No 79962 is currently being restored to operational condition. The museum's locomotives and coaches can also be seen operating on special events days on the neighbouring Keighley & Worth Valley Railway (see pages 158–60).

MUSEUM OF SCOTTISH RAILWAYS

Bo'ness Station, Union Street, Bo'ness,
West Lothian EH51 9AQ
01506 825855
www.srps.org.uk

Open: Daily, April to September & during Bo'ness & Kinneil Railway operating days in October

Opened in 1995, this large railway museum is located in a purpose-built 34,000-sq-ft exhibition hall adjacent to the Bo'ness & Kinneil Railway station at Bo'ness (see pages 192–3). By using the Scottish Railway Preservation Society's large collection of rolling stock, the exhibition traces both the practical and social aspects of the development of railways in Scotland. The wagon collection dates from 1862 up to 1963 and passenger coaches include Scotland's only Royal Saloon, which was built in 1897 by the Great North of Scotland Railway. Steam locomotives are represented by no fewer than 26 mainly industrial types, ranging from 1876-built 0-4-0ST *Kelton Fell* to 1955-built NCB 0-6-0ST No 20. The collection of 22 diesel locos includes many industrial examples as well as members of BR Classes 08, 20, 25, 26, 27, 37 and 47. Some of the SRPS steam locos are displayed at the Riverside Museum in Glasgow (see below) while others can be seen at work on the neighbouring Bo'ness & Kinneil Railway. Visitors to the museum can also see conservation work in progress.

RIVERSIDE MUSEUM

100 Pointhouse Place, Glasgow G3 8RS
0141 287 2720
www.glasgowlife.org.uk/museums/venues/riverside-museum

Open: Daily, except 24–26 December & 31 December–2 January

Opened on 20 June 2011, this modern purpose-built museum was designed by internationally renowned architect Zaha Hadid and engineer Buro Happold. The museum is located on the north bank of the River Clyde on the site of a former shipyard and replaced the previous home for the city's transport collection at Kelvin Hall.

Railway exhibits of locomotives built in Glasgow include 1886-built unique Caledonian Railway 4-2-2 No 123, 1894-built Highland Railway 'Jones Goods' 4-6-0 No 103 (the first 4-6-0 to be built in Britain), 1920-built Great North of Scotland 4-4-0 No 49 *Gordon Highlander*, and 1913-built NBR Class 'D34' 4-4-0 No 256 *Glen Douglas*. Built by the North British Locomotive Company of Glasgow in 1945, a massive Class '15F' 4-8-2 South African steam locomotive that once pulled the 'Blue Train' from Cape Town to Johannesburg is the star of the ground floor exhibits. Other exhibits include examples of Glasgow trams and trolleybuses and a full-size replica of a Glasgow 'Subway' station.

PHOTO CREDITS

t = top; b = bottom

Hugh Ballantyne: 94, 122, 165

Keith Barrow: 11

Henry Casserley: 74, 188, 193t

S. Chapman: 191

Colour-Rail: 10 (T. B. Owen), 14 (C. Trethewey), 15 (Bernard Miles), 16 (L. Rowe), 17 (Max Birchenough), 18 (G. Parry Collection), 21t, 23 (Paul Chancellor), 24 (T. B. Owen), 26t (T. B. Owen), 32, 33 (Paul Chancellor), 34 (J. Spencer Gilks Collection), 35 (Paul Chancellor), 36t, 36b (Craig Tiley), 43t (J. B. Hall), 45t (P. Moffat), 45b (Paul Chancellor), 47 (Paul Chancellor), 48, 49 (Paul Chancellor), 56 (N. Sprinks), 57, 58 (G. H. Hunt), 62 (F. Hornby), 64t (T. B. Owen), 64b (S. Chapman), 72 (R. Patterson), 79 (Martin Creese), 80, 82 (P. Moffat), 85t (F. Hornby), 88 (I. Davidson), 97t (F. Hornby), 97b (Martin Creese), 99 (Paul Chancellor), 100 (T. B. Owen), 102 (Bob Sweet), 103 (K. C. H. Fairey), 118 (G. H. Hunt), 123 (D. R. Barber), 125t, 127t, 129t (T. B. Owen), 130 (T. B. Owen), 134 (T. B. Owen), 137t, 137b, 141, 152t, 157t (J. Spencer Gilks Collection), 159, 163 (David Lawrence), 171t (L. Rowe), 185 (H. Winskill), 190 (T. B. Owen), 195t, 199t (K. C. H. Fairey), 199b, 200, 203t

Gordon Edgar: front cover, 7, 26b, 30, 39, 40–41, 50–51, 53, 63, 66–67, 69, 70–71, 75, 90–91, 93, 98, 107b, 109, 111, 113, 114, 115, 116, 120–121, 127b, 140, 142, 144–145, 147t, 150–151, 153b, 155, 158, 160, 161, 162, 164, 166, 167, 169, 171b, 173, 174, 179, 180, 181, 182, 189, 193b

Mike Esau: 107t

B. Fitzpatrick: 59

David Fletcher: 55

John Goss: 13, 21b, 25, 52, 61, 68, 149, 184

John Gray: 186–187

Julian Holland Collection: 6, 22, 29, 105, 196, 197

Michael Mensing: 175

Gavin Morrison: 38, 77b, 117, 129, 132, 133, 154, 168, 178, 195b

Les Platt: 89

Science Museum Group: 143, 148, 172

Brian Sharpe: 85b

Shutterstock.com: 8–9 (Victoria Ashman), 19 (Chris Jenner), 28 (Bewickswan), 31 (Ceri Breeze), 43b (Kev Gregory), 54 (Kev Gregory), 78 (Nicola Pulham), 81 (Martin Charles Hatch), 83 (Kev Gregory), 87 (Peter R Foster IDMA), 95 (Electric Egg), 101 (PJ photography), 108 (Electric Egg), 119 (david muscroft), 125b (Ajit Wick), 131 (tipwam), 135 (Wozzie), 139 (Darren Hedges), 147b (Kyaw Thiha), 157b (coxy58), 176 (ATGImages), 177 (Dave Head), 201 (Sandy Harvey)

Stephenson Railway Museum, Tyne & Wear Archives & Museums: 183

Bob Sweet: 203b

Mark Wisbey: 73

Unknown: 77t, 138

PHOTO CAPTIONS

Front cover
Designed by Henry Greenly and built by Davey Paxman in 1927, the visiting Romney, Hythe & Dymchurch Railway's 4-8-2 'Mountain' Class *Hercules* heads a passenger train on the Ravenglass & Eskdale Railway (see pages 172–3) on 23 July 2014.

Southwest England (p8–9)
Ex-London & South Western Railway Class 'M7' 0-4-4T No 30053 hauls a train on the Swanage Railway (see pages 38–9) near Corfe Castle. This loco was built at Nine Elms in London in 1905 and was withdrawn from Bournemouth shed in May 1964. Saved for preservation, it was shipped to the USA in 1967 for exhibition at Steamtown in Pennsylvania where it remained for 20 years. Repatriated in 1987 it then underwent major restoration before returning to steam at Swanage in 1992.

Southern England (p40–41)
Ex-LSWR Class 'O2' 0-4-4T No 24 *Calbourne* heads into the sunset near Ashey on the Isle of Wight Steam Railway (see pages 68–9).

Eastern England (p70–71)
The Mid-Suffolk 'Middy' Light Railway locomotive servicing facilities at Brockford station on 1 September 2012, with Hudswell Clarke 0-4-0ST *Wissington* built in 1938 taking on water. The 5-plank 'Moy' coal wagon is of local interest. Thomas Moy Ltd was set up in 1891 and apart from coal, it traded in coke, builder's materials, lime, salt and bricks (see pages 74–5).

Central England (p90–91)
A line-up of 3 historic preserved ex-LMS locos at Barrow Hill Roundhouse (see page 116) on 23 September 2015. From left to right 'Coronation' Class 4-6-2 No 46233 *Duchess of Sutherland*, 'Black Five' 4-6-0 No 45305 and Class '4' 2-6-0 No 43106.

Wales (p120–121)
The passengers' view of Snowdon Mountain Railway 0-4-2RT loco No 3 *Wyddfa* as their train approaches Clogwyn station, 28 June 2016. Built by the Swiss Locomotive & Machine Works in 1895 this is one of the 5 original rack locos built for the opening of the railway in 1896 (see pages 148–9).

Northern England (p150–151)
The issues faced by volunteers running trains along the heritage Bowes Railway demonstration line (see pages 180–1), where public access alongside the railway is considered by locals of any generation to be a matter of 'grandfather rights', is exemplified in this photograph. Two youths, making their way home from net fishing, try to keep up with a train on the Pelaw Curve on 18 October 2015. The loco is the 'W6 Special' Class Peckett 0-4-0ST *Merlin* built in 1939.

Scotland (p186–187)
Preserved Stanier 'Black Five' 4-6-0 No 45231 crosses 'Concrete Bob' McAlpines's viaduct at Loch nan Uahm with 'The Jacobite' train from Fort William to Mallaig (see pages 198–9). This loco was built by Armstrong Whitworth in 1936 and withdrawn in August 1968 when standard-gauge steam haulage ended on British Railways.

With thanks for research assistance and advice to:
Gordon Edgar